D1414549

THE CHALLENGE OF INFORMATION TECHNOLOGY FOR THE SECURITIES MARKETS

LIQUIDITY, VOLATILITY, AND GLOBAL TRADING

THE CHALLENGE OF INFORMATION TECHNOLOGY FOR THE SECURITIES MARKETS
LIQUIDITY, VOLATILITY, AND GLOBAL TRADING

by
The Center for Research on Information Systems
and
The Salomon Brothers Center for the Study
of Financial Institutions

Editors, Henry C. Lucas, Jr. and Robert A. Schwartz

STERN
Leonard N. Stern School of Business

NEW YORK UNIVERSITY

DOW JONES-IRWIN
Homewood, Illinois 60430

© RICHARD D. IRWIN, INC., 1989

Dow Jones-Irwin is a trademark of Dow Jones & Company, Inc.

This publication is designed to provide accurate and authoritative information in regard to the subject matter covered. It is sold with the understanding that the publisher is not engaged in rendering legal, accounting, or other professional service. If legal advice or other expert assistance is required, the services of a competent professional person should be sought.

From a Declaration of Principles jointly adopted by a Committee of the American Bar Association and a Committee of Publishers.

Project editor: Joan Hopkins
Production manager: Bette Ittersagen
Designer: Sam Concialdi
Compositor: Publication Services, Inc.
Typeface: 11/13 Times Roman
Printer: Arcata Graphics/Kingsport

Library of Congress Cataloging-in-Publication Data

The Challenge of information technology for the securities markets :
    liquidity, volatility, and global trading / by the Center for
    Research on Information Systems and the Salomon Brothers Center for
    the Study of Financial Institutions, eds., Henry C. Lucas, Jr. and
    Robert A. Schwartz. New York University Leonard N. Stern School
    of Business.
        p.   cm.
    Papers originally presented at a symposium held in May 1988.
    ISBN 1-55623-160-1
    1. Stock-exchange—Data processing—Congress. 2. Securities
industry—Data processing—Congresses. 3. Information technology—
Congresses. 4. Program trading (Securities)—Congresses. 5. Stock
Market Crash, 1987—Congresses. I. New York University.
Leonard N. Stern School of Business. Center for Research on
Information Systems. II. Salomon Brothers Center for the Study of
Financial Institutions.
HG4515.5.C46   1989
332.64'028'5—dc19   88-27336
                                                                         CIP

Printed in the United States of America

1 2 3 4 5 6 7 8 9 0 K 6 5 4 3 2 1 0 9

MESSAGE FROM THE
CENTER DIRECTORS

Information technology has become an integral part of financial markets. It has enabled the exchanges and other financial institutions to process large volumes of transactions. The financial community has also employed technology for analysis and to implement trading strategies. And the regulatory authorities are paralleling these developments with automated surveillance.

In May of 1988 the Center for Research on Information Systems and the Salomon Center for the Study of Financial Institutions at the Graduate School of Business Administration, New York University, sponsored a symposium on the impact of information technology on the securities markets. This book is a result of the symposium.

In the chapters that follow, leading academics and members of the financial community present an in-depth examination of information technology and the securities markets. The text contains papers from the presidents or chairmen of five major exchanges: The New York Stock Exchange, The American Stock Exchange, The Chicago Mercantile Exchange, the National Association of Securities Dealers, and the Toronto Stock Exchange. Also represented in the chapters are contributions from present and past regulators, including those from the Commodities Futures Trading Commission and the Securities and Exchange Commission.

The first section of the book addresses technology and the performance of the financial markets. Several of the chapters focus on the events surrounding October 19, 1987, and the stock market crash. The second section of the book is concerned with the impact of electronic systems on trading. Reactions to October may also be found in several chapters in this section.

The last part of the book looks at linkages among markets. Clearly the technology makes possible global financial markets. Are such linkages desirable? Are they inevitable? And if so, what is their likely impact?

This interdisciplinary book makes a major contribution to evaluating the impact of technology on securities markets. Managers and policymakers need to understand the role of technology and how to manage it in order to maximize the positive outcomes of the automation of securities markets.

Margrethe H. Olson

*Associate Professor
and Director of
Center for Research on
Information Systems*

Arnold Sametz

*Professor of Finance
Director of
Salomon Brothers Center for
the Study of Financial Institutions*

FOREWORD

If one were asked to identify the two or three most significant influences on the structure and behavior of securities markets in the post–World War II period, he or she would undoubtedly include developments in information technology. Along with increasingly institutionalized flows of investment capital and the globalization of investing, which itself has been stimulated by changes in computers and communications, technology has yielded consequences that were impossible to foresee only a few decades ago.

Who, for example, might have anticipated that the establishment of the New York Stock Exchange's DOT System, which was developed primarily to get relatively small orders to the floor in a more efficient manner, would become a key element in the emergence of portfolio and program trading strategies by major institutional investors? Certainly, the NYSE did not envision that the DOT system would be used in this way. With relatively little effort, of course, anyone familiar with the changes of the past quarter century could describe other developments—some anticipated and some unanticipated—that simply would not have been possible without advances in information technology.

Whatever has been witnessed to date almost certainly represents little more than the first ripples of the tide that is now running. As certain politicians are wont to say of late, "You ain't seen nothing yet."

In view of what has already taken place and what is likely to follow, it is heartening for me, as Dean of New York University's Leonard N. Stern School of Business, to see our Center for Research on Information Systems and our Salomon Brothers Center for the Study of Financial Institutions working together. In concert they are able to bring to bear the resources of two of our School's strongest areas for research and scholarship on problems of common interest.

The conference recently cosponsored by the Centers, "Information Technology and Securities Markets Under Stress," will, I predict, be but the first in a series of combined efforts. I attended the conference and can attest that it was a resounding success. The papers in this volume, based on that conference, provide the opportunity to gain new insight and a better understanding of the role of technology in the securities markets.

Dean Richard R. West

CONTENTS

Market Trends. Market Efficiency. Information Technology. The Second-Order Effect of Information Technology. Overview of the Book. Summary.

Kalman J. Cohen
Distinguished Bank Research Professor
The Fuqua School of Business
Duke University

Robert A. Schwartz
Professor of Economics and Finance
Graduate School of Business Administration
New York University

I. Problems in Market Performance. II. Call Markets and Electronic Trading. III. PSCAN: The Electronic Call Market. IV. Discussion. V. Conclusion. Appendix A: Rules and Procedures for PSCAN, the Electronic Call. Appendix B: Electronic Trading Systems. Appendix C: Acronyms and Abbreviations. Notes. References.

Yakov Amihud
Associate Professor
Tel-Aviv University
Visiting Professor of Finance
Graduate School of Business Administration
New York University

Haim Mendelson
Professor of Computers, Information Systems
and Business Administration
William E. Simon Graduate School of
Business Administration
University of Rochester

On the Desirability of Reduced Volatility. The Value of Liquidity. An Integrated Computerized Trading System (ICTS). The Clearing House. Concluding Remarks. Notes. References.

Studies of the Crash. Were Futures Markets Responsible? Policy Recommendations. Margins and Trading Halts: The Debate. Conclusion. Notes.

Junius W. Peake
Chairman
Peake/Ryerson Consulting Group
*   Incorporated*

Morris Mendelson
Professor of Finance
Wharton School of the University
*   of Pennsylvania*
Member of International Faculty
*   for Corporate and Capital*
*   Market Law*

R.T. Williams, Jr.
President
R. Shriver Associates

The Deficiences of the Present Markets. A Proposed Solution.
Conclusion. Steps Required to Implement PMW. Appendix A:
Present Systems and Their Defects. Exchange Markets. OTC Markets.
Derivative Markets. Appendix B: Comments About Systems Problems
in an Automated Market. Adequate Capacity. Appropriate Uses of
Automation. Appendix C. Appendix D: Glossary. Notes.

J. Pearce Bunting
President
The Toronto Stock Exchange

Anne E. Allen
Vice President, Floor Operations
New York Stock Exchange

Lois Zarembo
Managing Director, Capital Market Systems
New York Stock Exchange

History. SuperDot. The Specialist Book. Automation of the Specialist's Book. AT&T Divestiture. Expansion and Enhancement Efforts. Impact of SuperDot and Display Books. Future Plans.

Robert N. Riess
Vice President, Systems Planning
& Review
National Association of
Securities Dealers, Inc.

Background. Services. Enhancements to NASDAQ. An International System. Future Initiatives.

Michael F. Newman
Director, Markets Technology
International Stock Exchange

History. Quality of Markets. Impact of New Technologies on Market Systems. Conclusion.

Eric K. Clemons
Associate Professor of
Decision Sciences
Wharton School of the University
of Pennsylvania

Jennifer T. Adams
Wharton School of the University
of Pennsylvania

Increasing Importance of Global Capital Markets. Current Status
of Global Securities Trading. Competition among Trading Firms:
Necessary Strengths. Competition among Exchanges. Future of Global
Trading: Form of the Global Securities Markets. Conclusions. Notes.
Acknowledgments.

THE CHALLENGE OF INFORMATION TECHNOLOGY FOR THE SECURITIES MARKETS

LIQUIDITY, VOLATILITY, AND GLOBAL TRADING

CHAPTER 1

INTRODUCTION

Henry C. Lucas, Jr.
Robert A. Schwartz

During the past decade, technological change, deregulation, and the introduction of new financial instruments have transformed the securities industry. On and about October 19, 1987, unprecedented volatility altered our perceptions of technology's impact and raised serious questions about the structural soundness of our markets. A symposium was held at New York University's Graduate School of Business Administration on May 16 and May 17, 1988, to assess the challenge and promise of information technology for the securities markets. This book comprises the papers presented at that conference.

MARKET TRENDS

The impact of the new technology is best understood in the context of other trends that have occurred in recent years. These include institutionalization of the market, a sharp rise in global trading, and an increasing concern by investment managers with risk management and the control of execution costs. Leading brokerage houses are more cautious about

We would like to express our appreciation to Carole Larson and Anne Seaton for their efforts in arranging the conference and preparing this book. We also acknowledge the contribution of Professors Margrethe Olson, Rob Kauffman, and Arnold Sametz, and Dean Richard West, in organizing the conference.

taking capital positions to facilitate the negotiation of block trades in the upstairs market. Asset management is increasingly passive as institutional investors and large brokerage houses trade baskets of stocks to rebalance portfolios or to realize arbitrage profits between the cash markets in New York and the futures markets in Chicago.

These developments have had a profound impact on the relationships between brokerage firms, institutional investors, and the market centers. An ever-growing share of the order flow is from institutional traders. However, the reluctance of upstairs trading desks to commit capital to market-making has resulted in more orders being sent directly to specialist posts on the trading floor. This rechanneling of the order flow has been reinforced by the growth of basket trading. Rather than a single block being negotiated upstairs, a large number of different securities is being traded, each in relatively small amounts at the specialist posts, typically by market order.

These changes have had important consequences for the markets. Following the extraordinary turbulence of October 1987, much attention has turned to two interrelated developments: the apparent increase in price volatility, and the withdrawal of small investors from the market. Many believe that institutionalization of the market—in conjunction with the use by large traders of sophisticated trading strategies that span cash, futures, and options markets—has destabilized the market. This instability, in conjunction with a belief that small investors are unfairly positioned, has caused small traders to withdraw from the market. Their withdrawal is itself destabilizing. In addition, the foreboding size of large pension and mutual funds hangs over the market; what might happen if once again the elephants were to head for the exit door at the same time?

MARKET EFFICIENCY

These trends have added to a growing impression that the financial markets have in some ways failed. Market failure is a well-established concept in economics. It means that traders are not trading efficiently in a marketplace, and that a free, unimpeded meeting of sellers and buyers does not produce a desirable equilibrium price or an optimal redistribution of resources across market participants.

In the past, observers have by and large felt that our premier financial markets are reasonably efficient. Costless trading in competitive and stable markets, in the absence of externalities, should give a theoretically desired result and, hence, imply no market failure. Consequently, only relatively scant attention has so far been given to the possibility that market failure is a problem for the industry.

But securities markets are not stable, their competitiveness has been questioned, and trading is not a frictionless process. Rather, commissions, taxes, execution costs, trading restrictions, and other blockages impede the flow of orders to the market. In addition, the distribution of information is not equal across investors. Consequently, the interaction of orders in the market need not give perfect-world results. Rather, market failure may be manifested in investors trading non-optimal amounts at disequilibrium prices, and in disequilibrium process being excessively volatile.

Recognition of the possibility of market failure calls attention to the importance of a market's architecture, those procedures, rules, regulations, and protocols that determine how orders are handled and trades made. Neither orders nor trades are independent of market architecture. Recognition of this reality is of fundamental importance; it suggests that market performance can indeed be improved by market design.

INFORMATION TECHNOLOGY

An important aspect of market design is the information technology used to disseminate floor information (transaction process, quotes, and trading volume), to support decision making, to handle orders, and to translate orders into trades. The introduction of information technology in the last decade has had a profound impact on the securities industry:

1. Computer programs make it possible to create and manage extremely large portfolios. With computers and derivative products, it is feasible to regard the portfolio, not individual securities, as the object of interest.
2. Systems in place on the exchanges facilitate trading baskets of stocks.
3. Computer-based systems provide price information and the ability to discover price discrepancies between markets, thus making possible a wider range of arbitrage operations.
4. Technology makes it possible to clear and settle extremely large volumes of trades.

As the volume of trading has grown, the securities markets have become ever-more dependent on information technology. Certain parts of what is now a complex person-computer system can fail without closing the markets, but the failure of any component can create severe stress elsewhere. In particular, the inability of systems to keep up on October 19 was very costly. As trades entered growing queues, price information became outdated and at times unavailable. There were not enough market-makers or telephones to respond to investors. Crossed and locked markets interrupted trading in the NASD's electronic execution systems.

THE SECOND-ORDER EFFECT
OF INFORMATION TECHNOLOGY

One can think of the entire industry as a single system consisting of exchanges, institutions, investors, brokers, and so on. Within these various components are many subsystems that employ information technology. Actors have created these systems to meet immediate and well-defined demands; but when the subsystems interact, unintended effects appear. After a careful review of opposing arguments, it appears to us that technology can and does have a major impact on markets, and that it contributes to some of today's problems in these markets.

The information technology itself is neutral. The exchanges have developed the display book and SuperDot systems, for example, to cope with large volumes of transactions, not to destabilize the markets. Individual investors, institutions, and traders use computers to develop and implement investment strategies for their own use; they do not perceive the cumulative impact the systems together may have on the market.

The cumulative impact of information technology itself is a second-order effect of individual systems that are developed to meet specific needs. The second-order effects may entail an increased demand for liquidity and more volatile markets. As an example, consider the interaction of portfolio insurance and program trading.

Taken by itself, program trading and arbitrage in general should make markets more efficient and act as a negative feedback loop. However, it has been suggested that on October 19 portfolio insurance acted as a separate, conflicting system that combined with program trading to create a highly unstable, positive feedback system. The data to test this hypothesis exist, and it is unfortunate that the various studies of October 19 have not tried to do so in detail.

In the absence of portfolio insurance, can program trading contribute to volatility? Widespread program trading is a portfolio trading strategy, which means that a potentially large volume of stocks is traded at one time. Since program trades are usually based on extremely small price discrepancies that exist only for a short period of time, it is likely that even though program traders are acting independently, they all will send potentially large orders to the market at the same time. This high volume of orders may increase volatility.

How does one prevent the unintended impacts of technology? Given the complexity of the securities markets when viewed as a single system, it is unlikely that we will ever have agreement on the cause and effect relationships that operate within it, or on how the undesirable effects may be controlled.

What is needed is a mechanism for analyzing the overall *operation* of the securities system. For this purpose, it might be helpful to establish a standing committee on market operations. We recommend that the committee be staffed by representatives of the various market centers (self-regulatory organizations). The first task of the committee would be to build causal models of technology's impact on the markets and to test these models with data. This exercise should lead to a better understanding of the second-order impacts of information and to knowledge of what data should be collected and maintained. An extension of this first task would be to develop indicators that could be monitored for signs of technology-induced market stress.

OVERVIEW OF THE BOOK

The papers in this book focus primarily on the use to which electronic technology might be put in order to improve market performance. As is clear from the discussions, however, technological change cannot be properly assessed without considering other structural arrangements and regulatory issues. Structural issues discussed in this book include: the institution of electronic trading versus direct person-to-person interaction; the use of call market versus continuous trading; the design of intermarket and international linkages; and the development of post-trade clearance systems. Regulatory issues discussed include: the institution of circuit breakers; the imposition of uniform margin requirements; the introduction of stabilization procedures; and the allocation of supervisory responsibilities among the market centers and government regulatory agencies such as the Securities and Exchange Commission and the Commodities Futures Trading Commission.

The book is divided into three sections. The first deals with the relationship between technology and market performance, the second with operational features of electronic trading, and the third with intermarket linkages.

Technology and Market Performance

With regard to technology and market performance, the first two chapters by Cohen and Schwartz and by Amihud and Mendelson consider basic issues concerning system design and the quality of markets. Cohen and Schwartz propose that a market such as the New York Stock Exchange use an electronic call to open the market, suggest that the call market be integrated with continuous trading at other times during the trading day, and set forth rules and procedures that give their proposal concrete form. The central feature of their system is a price scan procedure that allows all participants, including those away from the trading floor, to have equal access to the floor while the market is being formed.

Amihud and Mendelson further consider the interaction between trading technology, liquidity, volatility, and market design. After suggesting that an alternative system may mitigate undesirable volatility and increase liquidity, these authors propose an Integrated Computerized Trading System. They also consider how their system would have coped with problems encountered during the week of October 19, 1987.

The importance of many issues concerning market performance was highlighted by the wild price movements experienced in October 1987, and many of the papers in this book refer to that period. In the third chapter in the section, Edwards focuses directly on the market crash. In so doing, he reviews the major governmental and industry studies of the crash, putting extensive detailed analysis into better perspective. Edwards' discussion covers issues concerning technology, fundamental economic causal factors, the derivative product markets, and policy recommendations.

The next three chapters are by leaders of three major U.S. exchanges—Grasso from the New York Stock Exchange, Levitt from the American Stock Exchange, and Brodsky from the Chicago Mercantile Exchange. All three pay particular attention to the stressful conditions experienced during the market break, and to recent policy recommendations. Grasso, after reviewing the enormous surge of order flow during the week of October 19 and the NYSE's subsequent expansion of its order handling capability, turns our attention to three issues: the serious decay in investor confidence in the markets; the need for large institutions to recognize that instantaneous liquidity cannot be obtained in the amounts they thought possible before October 19; and the interlinking of, and need for coordination between, equity markets and derivative product markets.

Levitt next provides a historical overview of the introduction of technology at the American Stock Exchange, and reaffirms that the fundamental purpose of securities markets is to provide capital for business. Like Grasso, Levitt expresses concern about the public having withdrawn from the market because of the unfairness perceived by individual investors. He also proposes that a commission be established to study the market from a longer-term perspective than did the groups appointed to investigate the events of October 19.

Brodsky calls our attention to three issues raised in the reports on the crash. First, he reiterates that the precipitous market decline was not the result of market structure and technology alone, but also of fundamental economic forces. Second, he considers the interlinkage between markets and the advisability of instituting circuit breakers. Third, Brodsky addresses the clearance and settlement systems, cross-margining, and the level of margin requirements in futures markets.

The next two chapters by Ketchum and Phillips discuss recent market trends, the regulatory actions the trends call for, and the increased use of technology that they have *induced*. Ketchum pays particular attention to the institutionalization of the equity markets and to the changing trading strategies of the institutions. Most important has been the development of the upstairs market, and then its partial eclipse, as institutions have recently started using both futures and cash markets to trade portfolios rather than individual stocks. Ketchum notes that these changes have put increasing pressure on the NYSE specialist as a major provider of liquidity. Regarding the regulatory response called for by the market crash, Ketchum discusses circuit breakers, the commitment of capital to market-making, margining and cross-margining requirements, clearance and settlement issues, and the broader objective of increasing the liquidity of the markets.

Phillips describes five developments that spurred the increasing computerization of the markets: (1) computerization of back-office operations, (2) increased use of the computer to handle orders and to display information on the trading floors, (3) development of institutional block trading activities, (4) introduction of financial futures and options, and (5) institution by brokerage firms and trading houses of sophisticated trading and arbitrage techniques that use computers. These developments called attention to market volatility and brought us to the October market crash. We also see from Phillips' discussion that the important issues today in technology concern not only technical matters such as screen display or the ability of a black box to accommodate trading, but control issues such as who should have access to a system, the advisability of imposing circuit breakers, and the regulation and monitoring of investor risk positions.

The next chapter by Wood takes a closer look at two current changes taking place in capital markets: a sharp rise in liquidity demand by market participants, and an increase in market volatility. Wood also discusses the use of circuit breakers and the impact of the futures and options in Chicago on the equity markets in New York. Black argues, on the other hand, that the technology has had little impact on the markets.

In the final chapter in this section, Kubarych raises a fundamental question: Is all the new technology really desirable? That is, should so much emphasis be placed on increasing the speed with which orders can be transmitted to the marketplace and translated into trades? In answering this question, Kubarych calls our attention to the importance of being able to modulate the pace of market events.

Electronic Trading

The second section of the book is concerned with electronic trading. Peake, Mendelson, and Williams, the first to advance a proposal for a large-scale electronic market, present a fresh view of their system. In so doing, they discuss major structural and operational defects in current trading systems for equity securities and their derivatives that were exposed by the October 1987 market crisis. Peake, Mendelson, and Williams emphasize the lack of real-time market information to all participants, a lack of equal and immediate market access and the opportunity for participation by all investors, restrictions on the eligibility of market participants to provide market making functions, and synchronous trading among underlying equities and derivative markets.

The next four chapters deal with the introduction of electronic technology in four market centers: Bunting discusses the experience at the Toronto Stock Exchange; Allen and Zarembo focus on the New York Stock Exchange; Riess, the NASD; and Newman, the London Stock Exchange. The Toronto Stock Exchange was the first exchange to introduce an electronic order execution facility, and its computer assisted trading system (CATS) has more recently been adopted by the Tokyo and Paris stock exchanges. Bunting discusses the Toronto Stock Exchange's development and implementation of CATS and describes how it is being modified. He also sets forth the objective of his exchange: to provide the best possible trading rules for its customers.

Allen and Zarembo then offer a perceptive view of the specialist's display book system on the exchange. The display book relies on the DOT and SuperDot systems that route orders automatically to the specialist. The display book is an electronic specialist's book that automates the older, manual book maintained for years by the specialist. They describe the development of the system through prototype and testing phases. The impact of the system has been positive and it is partially responsible for maintaining level clerical employment during a period of rising volume.

Reiss describes the basic structure of the NASD's on-line trading system for NASDAQ Securities. He presents the trends in volume that led NASDAQ to add computer capacity prior to the October crash. The U.S. system can logically be extended abroad to form a truly global trading environment.

Newman comments on the quality of markets after the automation of the exchange in London. The "Big Bang" did not go smoothly, for there were computer problems during the conversion. However, the systems performed well during the October crash. Newman describes different tests of the market's quality, all of them favorable. The London market did not close, and trading did not stop in major stocks.

The next five chapters focus on electronic trading. French, representing institutional investors, indicates the extent to which his firm depends on the technology; however, problems in October forced the firms to revert to contact with floor brokers. The future, however, lies in automation.

Madoff writes about the extensive systems his specialist firm has in place. The hardware performed well, but software problems occurred in October. Many of the difficulties came from edits designed to protect the user; conditions were so extreme that programs rejected legitimate transactions because they looked like errors. Coyle describes actions taken at NASDAQ to prepare for heavy volume. From an operation standpoint, the week of October 19 was not a major event. Next, Van Kirk provides a comprehensive review of the SIAC systems that support both exchanges and the clearing function for the markets. While there were problems, the systems in general processed twice the load for which they had originally been designed. Finally, Stevens discusses new technology planned for the Amex. From a structural standpoint, he is opposed to stock halts and price limits. He views the October crash as a sign of liquidity problems, and he wants to be sure that any actions taken do not exacerbate known problems.

Market Linkages

The final section of the book contains three papers dealing with market linkages. Wall provides a description of the NASDAQ system, focusing on the development of its worldwide network. He raises important issues of coordination, regulation across international boundaries, and confidentiality.

Hamilton considers the effect of electronic market linkages on the distribution of the order flow among market centers. His analysis is particularly important in light of the interlinking of national securities markets in an increasingly global market system. To provide a basis for predicting future developments, Hamilton turns to an empirical assessment of a historic event—the interlinking of national and regional stock exchanges in the United States by the Intermarket Trading System. While Hamilton finds that ITS did not have a major impact on order flow within the United States, it might have if certain key aspects of the system had been structured differently.

Clemons and Adams discuss the competitive aspects of global markets, present the current status of global securities trading, and look at the factors that affect the importance of global securities trading. What type of competition will exist among stock exchanges? Clemons and Adams conclude with thoughts on the ultimate structure of a global securities market.

SUMMARY

This book raises policy issues that need to be addressed as we move to global markets. How will new technology be employed? Will firms and countries recognize the overall impact of individual automation decisions? How will global markets be coordinated? Who will look for the second-order impacts of the technology?

Information technology and the securities markets are intertwined. The markets cannot function without the technology, and electronic technology offers much promise for further enhancing market performance; but new technology also causes apprehension. Program trading, for instance, would not be possible without the computer; but program trading has been blamed for destabilizing the market. The globalization of trading would not be possible without electronic linkages; but global markets can cause a rapid flight of funds across national boundaries, and so can be destabilizing. The computer speeds up the rate at which individuals can make decisions and implement them in the marketplace; but the computer also speeds up the pace with which market events occur, and so can be destabilizing.

Nevertheless, if properly structured, the undesirable consequences of computerization may be contained, if not entirely eliminated. Accordingly, an objective of this book is to show how the introduction of electronic technology has increased the efficiency of market operations in the recent past, and to suggest ways further improvements may be made in the future.

SECTION 1

TECHNOLOGY AND MARKET PERFORMANCE

CHAPTER 2

AN ELECTRONIC CALL MARKET: ITS DESIGN AND DESIRABILITY[1]

Kalman J. Cohen
Robert A. Schwartz

This paper is motivated by the events of October 1987, the weaknesses in market structure that these events have underscored, and the following question: Has the potential of electronic trading been sufficiently exploited or even adequately recognized?

We believe that, if properly structured, an electronic based trading system should result in far better market performance.[2] This can best be accomplished by developing an electronic call market that should be integrated with the present mode of continuous trading. We propose that the electronic call be used to open the market at the start of each trading day and to reopen the market after any trading halt. If proven successful at the opening, the electronic call could also be reactivated at regular, prespecified times during the trading day and/or at the market close.

Call market trading has various desirable properties; most importantly, it is cost effective, and it facilitates price determination, price stabilization, and post-trade clearance and settlement.[3] The current opening procedure on the New York and American Stock Exchanges resembles a call market system,[4] but it has several important shortcomings compared to our proposed electronic call: it is not as well-structured or as fully automated, and it does not allow participants off the trading floor to revise their orders as the opening price is being established. In contrast, our proposed electronic call is structured so that traders away from the exchange can respond to floor information as the market forms. Our system also induces these traders to reveal their orders to the market, and facilitates the entry of large orders.

Only recently has it been suggested that call market trading be more widely used. Wunsch (1987) sets forth some of the features of what he calls a single price auction, but he does not attempt to give the market concrete form. Schwartz (1988a, Chapter 13) outlines an electronic call market whose structure provides the foundation for the current paper. Our objective here is to delineate an implementable system that is based on computer technology and call market principles.

Section I discusses some of the critical issues in market performance that have recently attracted considerable attention. In Section II we structure the underlying problems of trading and price determination in securities markets, discuss the relative advantages and disadvantages of trading in a call market rather than in a continuous market, and identify the major problems of electronic trading. The economic rationale for, and the key features of, the electronic call are presented in Section III, where we also discuss its implementation. In Section IV we examine various issues concerning the electronic call such as the role of specialists, the implementation of circuit breakers, and the structuring of an environment in which appreciable capital can be used (if desired) to stabilize price. Our concluding remarks are contained in Section V. Detailed rules and procedures for the call are set forth in Appendix A, and descriptions of noteworthy proposed and existing electronic systems are provided in Appendix B.

I. PROBLEMS IN MARKET PERFORMANCE

Several weaknesses in the structure of the equity markets that have long existed were highlighted during the period of particular stress on and about October 19, 1987. Our discussion in this section focuses on four problems concerning market performance: price instability, the imperfect integration of submarkets, errors in price discovery, and a perceived unfairness to small investors. In varying degrees, these problems are manifestations of one factor—the illiquidity of the markets. Although the term is widely used, *illiquidity* is not subject to precise definition. It generally means a lack of depth, breadth, and resiliency. Alternatively stated, illiquid markets are thin, are characterized by inaccurate price determination, and generate execution costs for traders.[5]

Price Instability

A widely held perception is that securities markets are excessively volatile in the short run, and a common belief is that the instability is largely attributable to the markets for derivative products. Both perceptions may be accurate, but attributing the excess volatility to trading in the financial futures and options markets unfortunately obscures a more fundamental problem: instability is a natural feature of an asset market.

Investors do not seek to trade unless they are sufficiently dissatisfied with their portfolio holdings to incur the transaction costs of trading, and transaction costs are not inconsequential. As a result, there simply are not many orders on the trading floor or on the specialists' limit order books. Therefore, a relatively small transaction volume (vis-à-vis the number of shares outstanding) can have a sizable impact on a security's price. This was demonstrated dramatically on October 19, 1987: according to the Brady Commission Report (*Report of the Presidential Task Force on Market Mechanisms*, 1988, p. 3), "Only 3 percent of the total shares of publicly traded stock in the U.S. changed hands during this period, but it resulted in the loss in stock value of $1 trillion."

Price signalling further contributes to instability in the markets. For many of the more standard goods and services, a falling price, for instance, simply means that a product is less expensive. With price signalling, however, a falling price can also suggest that a product is less desirable. With respect to a company's common stock, a price decrease might signal to relatively uninformed investors that something has lowered the company's earnings potential. Grossman and Stiglitz (1976) have modeled price determination in a securities market where price changes signal information to uninformed investors. Schwartz (1988a, Chapter 13) has used the model to show that under conditions of particular stress, price decreases can cause investors to seek to hold *fewer shares* (i.e., the slope of the demand curve can change sign). When this happens, prices may adjust explosively in an asset market (i.e., price increases can lead to further increases, and price decreases can lead to further decreases). An explosive downward adjustment—which has been referred to as *free fall*—may in fact have occurred on October 19, 1987.

Relatively little is currently known about the strength of price signalling and the possibility of investors overreacting in the short run. Unfortunately, the efficient market hypothesis and the generally reported findings in the random walk literature have diverted attention from the issue. The intellectual heritage of most economists further dissuades researchers from looking for evidence that asset shares might be mispriced in reasonably competitive markets. Yet real world markets can make mistakes, transaction prices can deviate from desired equilibrium values,[6] and transaction prices can be far more volatile than equilibrium values. Increasingly, financial economists are finding that this is indeed the case.[7]

Our own study of the market has led us to expect that errors in price discovery and excessive short period price volatility will cause price movements that have more runs followed by reversals than is consistent with a random walk process. That is, for relatively short periods of time, upticks will tend to be followed by further upticks, and downticks by further downticks. These continuations, however, cause prices to move too far, and eventually result in a reversal (an uptick followed by a downtick, or a downtick followed by an uptick). After any reversal, a sequence of price movements in a direction opposite to that which led to the reversal may again ensue.[8]

We believe that short-term trending in the market and excessive price instability may be contained by committing appreciable capital to market-making when the market is in the call mode. A specific proposal for stabilizing the market, which entails the formalization of corporate share issuance and repurchase, has been set forth by Schwartz (1988b). Implementation of this proposal in the electronic call market is discussed further below.

Imperfect Integration of Diverse Markets

The Brady Report stressed the one market concept; in so doing, it considered the split between the markets for stocks and derivative products. We here focus on a different aspect of the one market concept, the split within the market for stocks between upstairs trading, crowd trading, and entered orders.[9] Under current arrangements, an intricate set of rules and protocols determine the sequence in which orders entered on the book and held by floor traders execute. Additional rules pertain to the execution of block trades on the floor of an exchange. However, the upstairs market is imperfectly integrated with the trading floor. Many large trades are negotiated upstairs (albeit with reference to floor information) and then brought to the exchange to be executed as "put-throughs."

Institutional traders fear that directly revealing their orders to the market will result in adverse price effects (market impact). The adverse price effects are due to the size of the orders themselves, to price signalling, and to the fact that the public announcement of a large purchase (or sale) gives contra-side sellers (or buyers) an incentive to wait for a higher (or lower) transaction price.

We believe that upstairs trading could be better integrated with floor trading in an electronic system that gives the upstairs traders direct access to the trading floor. The way this would work is explained in relation to the electronic call market that we propose below.

Errors in Price Discovery

Price discovery refers to the process by which a securities market attempts to establish transaction prices that remain reasonably close to theoretically desirable equilibrium values that are themselves frequently changing. Although it is widely recognized that prices will deviate from equilibrium values in thin markets, issues concerning price discovery have been largely ignored in the academic literature and in the debates concerning market structure.

Ho, Schwartz, & Whitcomb (1985), however, have shown that clearing prices may generally fail to be equilibrium values. Their analysis assumes that (1) the market consists of an arbitrarily large number of competitive traders, (2) orders are cleared in a call market, (3) investors do not know before any call what the clearing price will be, and (4) transaction costs prevent traders from submitting complete order schedules to the market. Their analytical result (imperfect price discovery) would be reinforced by the sequencing risk inherent in continuous market trading. The demonstration highlights the importance of instituting market mechanisms to facilitate discovering prices that are reasonable given investors' underlying demand propensities, and it suggests that an additional factor contributed to the enormous price swings during the market break in October 1987: in light of the complex job it had to perform, the market made mistakes.

Securities markets can make mistakes in price discovery for three reasons. First, the underlying demand functions of investors to hold shares of various securities can shift rapidly in response to news, and these rapid shifts result in transaction prices that are volatile over brief periods. Second, because price determination and trading are simultaneous and interacting processes, and because prices are volatile, investors may write their orders on the basis of erroneous estimates of the prices at which they can or will transact. Third, frictions that are inevitably a part of actual markets, but that are conventionally ignored in much economic analysis, keep investors from transmitting their complete buy-sell order schedules to the marketplace.[10] Instead, investors must make strategic trading decisions in determining when to send orders to the market, as well as the prices, sizes, and other features of their orders.[11]

As a consequence of these three factors (rapid shifts in investor demand, the simultaneity of the trading and price determination processes, and frictions in the marketplace), the resulting orders of investors are incomplete and often biased representations of their underlying demand functions. Therefore, when the orders interact in the marketplace, the resulting transaction prices may differ appreciably from their theoretically desirable equilibrium values.[12] Hence, trading arrangements that are instituted to facilitate order submission and price determination are of critical importance. These processes involve information dissemination, order handling, organized market opening procedures, and specialist participation in trading. The electronic call that we propose is structured to facilitate the price discovery process.

Perceived Unfairness to Small Investors

Instability and imperfect price discovery are different facets of one underlying reality: the security markets operate imperfectly. A further property of an imperfect market is that it favors some participants at the expense of others. Inevitably, large, professional traders have an informational and positional advantage relative to small, nonprofessional ones. This advantage may be exploited in a legitimate fashion by, for instance, professional traders responding faster to public news announcements, or in an illegitimate fashion by, for instance, front running customer orders.[13]

In addition to being inequitable, unfairness may also result in inefficiency because investors who perceive that they suffer from a relative disadvantage in the marketplace may reduce the frequency with which they bring orders to the market.[14] As those investors with the least favored position reduce their order flow, some other traders may in turn become more subject to exploitation, and they too may seek to trade less frequently. The ultimate effect is thinner markets and the less desirable performance characteristics they imply: larger bid-ask spreads, more volatile prices, and delayed price adjustments to new information.

Fairness is desired, therefore, for both equity and efficiency. Our final reason for advocating that computerized trading be structured as a call market is the fairness implied by clearing many trades simultaneously, in a multilateral matching, and at a single price.

II. CALL MARKETS AND ELECTRONIC TRADING

Having identified major issues relating to market performance, we next establish the salient characteristics of a call market system and of electronic trading. This discussion provides the conceptual underpinnings for the electronic call market that we propose in the section that follows.

Some people equate "more advanced technology" with "better technology." Examples include the use of electronic computers rather than desk calculators, and the use of tractors rather than horses. However, what is better is not determinable in an absolute sense, but depends on the relative costs of capital, labor, and other factors of production, as well as the nature of the tasks to be performed. Many people consider continuous markets to be more advanced, and hence better, than call markets. Consequently, proposed and actual electronic trading systems have, by and large, mimicked continuous trading. We alternatively propose that electronic trading may be more effectively instituted in a call market mode, but that both trading modes (call and continuous) should be retained. This section considers the issues involved.

Call Market Trading

A trade can occur in a continuous market whenever a buy order and a sell order match or cross each other in price during the hours the market is open. For the most part, trades in a continuous market result from a bilateral matching of one buy order against another sell order.[15] In a call market on the other hand, orders are batched (stored) for execution only at predetermined times when the market is called. At the call, all buy orders are aggregated into a downward-sloping demand function, and all sell orders are aggregated into an upward-sloping supply function. If these functions intersect, the crossing determines the call price and quantity traded.[16] The orders that trade, and the price and quantity at which they trade, are set by the multilateral matching, rather than by the sequence of bilateral matchings used to determine trades in a continuous market.

Stock markets in the United States (including the NASDAQ OTC market and the New York and American Stock Exchanges), Montreal, Toronto, London, Hong Kong, and Tokyo operate as continuous markets. Foreign stock exchanges that operate as call markets for at least some securities include those in Amsterdam, Brussels, Frankfurt, Luxembourg, Paris, Tel Aviv, and Vienna. Some stock exchanges have mixtures of continuous and call trading, at different times of the day. For certain heavily traded issues, the French, German, and Austrian exchanges allow, after a stock is traded in the call market mode, for it to be traded in a continuous mode during a brief call back period; the bulk of the trading volume occurs, however, at the calls. Some continuous markets, such as the New York and American Stock Exchanges and the Toronto-Tokyo CATS, operate in a call mode when the market is opened at the start of a trading day or after a trading halt. The Tokyo Stock Exchange opens and closes both a morning and an afternoon session with a call for certain heavily traded issues.

The Ideal Economic Environment

The ideal economic environment is one where all interested traders simultaneously submit their complete demand-to-hold curves for each asset, and where an auctioneer finds the single price that clears all crossing orders.[17] Following the economist's standard way of analyzing trading and price determination, we assume that investors have downward-sloping demand curves to hold shares of a risky asset. We also assume, however, that because of transaction costs and other trading frictions, investors do not transmit their entire demand curves to the marketplace, but instead submit discrete orders. They do so with reference to their demand curves, the prices at which they expect to be able to trade, and their knowledge of how orders are handled and translated into trades in the marketplace.

For the ideal solution to be attained in this context, it is necessary for investors to monitor the market as it is being formed and to update their orders appropriately. Doing so requires an appreciable amount of floor information,[18] as well as the ability to specify, transmit, and update orders with great speed.[19] In addition, investors must be able to avoid transacting at disequilibrium prices; doing so is not easy, however, when equilibrium values are not known at the time the orders are placed.

An important aspect of the call market arrangement we here propose is that it provides a fast, broad, and equitable distribution of floor information, sets prices that are realistically based on this information, and clears all crossing orders at a single price (which facilitates avoiding trades at disequilibrium prices). Unfortunately, people in the past have found call market trading to be undesirable because it places those investors away from the trading floor at a disadvantage. This limitation can be overcome, however, with the proper use of electronic linkages. Yet many people have also been unwilling to use an electronic system because of the difficulty of working large orders within it. Fortunately, the benefits of each (electronic trading and call market trading) overcome many of the weaknesses of the other because of the complementarities involved. How and why this is so will be clarified in the ensuing discussion. First, we take a closer look at the advantages and disadvantages of a call market as the sole trading system.

Advantages and Disadvantages of Call Market Trading

Costs

It is considerably less expensive to execute any given volume of orders in a call than in a continuous trading mode. This is because less time is involved, since the call price for a stock can usually be found in a few minutes (at most), and traders can then turn their attention to the next security to be called.[20] In a continuous market, on the other hand, the trading apparatus must be available for each stock as long as the market is open. Further, operating costs increase far less rapidly with the size of the order flow in a call market than they do in a continuous market. Finally, clearance and settlement costs are less in a call market, where all trades execute at the same price and specific buyers are not matched with specific sellers.

Price Discovery

Price discovery errors might be reduced by the time batching of orders that is inherent in call market trading. The more constant the information set during the time between calls, the greater is the likelihood of call trading occurring close to the equilibrium price.[21] Call market trading also eliminates much of the sequencing risk inherent in the somewhat arbitrary pattern in which orders may arrive at a continuous market. Most importantly, for a given set of orders, there is only a single call price, and this price is unaffected by the sequence in which orders arrive at the market between calls. In a continuous market, on the other hand, the pattern of transaction prices and quantities will change if the order arrival sequence is rearranged.

Stability

If properly designed, the call market arrangement might facilitate the stabilization of share prices. Time batching orders for multilateral execution at a single price eliminates price fluctuations caused by transactions bouncing between the bid and ask quotes, and by randomness in the order arrival sequence. Furthermore, the commitment of substantial capital to stabilizing a market is more effective when the stabilizing orders are entered in a call rather than in a continuous trading mode (see Schwartz [1988b]). The major reason for this is that stabilization rules, such as price continuity, cannot be reasonably enforced when prices jump from one equilibrium level to a discretely different equilibrium level, because attempting to do so in continuous trading would force trades at disequilibrium prices.

Market Impact

Large traders must be wary of their size in relation to the other side of the market because they might have an adverse impact on prices (e.g., a large sell order might drive down the price at which the security is sold). This market impact problem is reduced by call market trading to the extent that any given size of order is smaller in relation to counterpart orders when the latter are batched over time. Thus institutional investors may be able to operate more effectively in a call than in a continuous market. Crossing networks such as those of Instinet and POSIT attempt to capitalize on this advantage of call market trading.

Fairness

Call markets may also be fairer, especially to small, nonprofessional investors because all trades at the call occur at the same price. Thus no investor need feel that he or she has been taken advantage of by smart traders who are able to sell at the high or to buy at the low price of the day. The simultaneity of trades in a call market also eliminates the possibility of front running customer orders in the same security.[22]

Accessibility

Call markets also have their limitations. The most apparent disadvantage is that investors can trade only at those times when the market is called (typically once or twice a day in existing call markets). In contrast, investors can attempt to trade in a continuous market at any time during the trading day. The more limited accessibility of the call market is disadvantageous in three situations: (1) when new information motivates the trade,[23] (2) when an arbitrage opportunity motivates the trade,[24] and (3) when one trade must be completed before another is attempted.[25] These disadvantages can be overcome, however, by retaining continuous trading along with call market trading.

Floor Information

A major difference among call markets is commonly stated in terms of whether they use a written order entry or an oral order entry mechanism. The substantive distinction does not relate to the technology of order entry, but rather to whether some or all traders are able to observe and react to the sequence of trial prices at the market call. In a call market that permits only written order entry (e.g., the Paris *par casiers* system of trading), only prespecified orders are accumulated between the times of market calls, and the system does not provide traders with any indicated price (the price at which the already accumulated orders would transact if the market were to be called at that moment). Hence, in the *par casiers* system, traders have no meaningful opportunity to modify their orders as the market is being formed.

In contrast, in a call market that permits verbal order entry (e.g., the Paris *à la criée* system of trading), an auctioneer calls out trial prices for a security, and traders present on the floor can enter or revise their order quantities. If there is excess demand at the trial price, the auctioneer calls out a higher price; if there is excess supply, the auctioneer calls out a lower price. When the total quantities bid and offered at a price are equal (or sufficiently close), the auctioneer declares that to be the call price, and the appropriate trades occur. Because traders in an *à la criée* system can adjust their orders throughout the price determination process, this system facilitates price discovery and, hence, is a more desirable arrangement than the written order entry system. Consequently, our electronic call market mimics the oral entry system.

Transaction Certainty

We note one further disadvantage of call market vis-à-vis continuous trading. The quotes posted in continuous markets by some traders (e.g., dealers and others who find it advantageous to submit limit orders) not only reveal information to other traders, but also provide them with an option that does not exist in call markets: orders (at least those that are small enough) can transact with virtual certainty at the market quotes. Those traders who find it desirable to utilize the option of trading with certainty at a known price would prefer a continuous market, since bid and ask quotes are not posted in a call market.[26]

To summarize, the advantages of call market trading include lower operating costs, the possibility for more accurate price discovery, the possibility for greater price stability, smaller market impact for large orders, and enhanced fairness in the sense that trades execute at the same price at any given call. Some of the disadvantages of existing call markets relate to restricted accessibility to the market and limited dissemination of floor information.

Electronic Trading

Despite initial and continuing resistance by many traders, electronic trade execution is gradually making its way in the marketplace. The development and success of systems such as the Toronto-Tokyo CATS and Instinet are discussed in Appendix B. In this subsection, we note three concerns about electronic trading that have retarded its acceptance in most market centers: (1) the difficulty of working a large order electronically, (2) the danger of accelerating the speed of the trading process, and (3) the informational loss caused by the elimination of direct human interaction.

Market Impact
Many people have been unwilling to use an electronic system when they believe their orders must be carefully worked, either via direct person-to-person contact on the trading floor, or via telephone contact in the upstairs market. Institutional traders in particular feel that simply entering their orders into an electronic system would not provide adequate privacy or control.[27] Accordingly, we have designed our electronic call market with particular regard for the special needs of the large trader.

The Rapidity of Events
One potential advantage of electronic trading—the rapidity with which it enables orders to be transmitted and trades to be executed—may also have undesirable consequences if it is not properly controlled. Each investor individually, of course, wants to be the first to trade on news; all investors collectively, however, may be better off if the pace of events is slowed down. The reason is that accelerating the speed with

which decisions can be implemented may result in the capabilities of some parts of the total system outrunning the capabilities of other parts of the system and of the decision makers.[28]

All said and done, and despite all the electronic aids available, the formulation of investment and trading decisions continues to require human judgment based on accurate information. However, relevant information may be unavailable and judgment may break down when the pace of market events is sped up unduly. Greater price instability may indeed be the consequence. This is a major reason for our proposing that electronic trading be instituted in the call market mode: the pause between market calls gives investors and traders an opportunity to assess their positions, while the call procedure itself enables decisions to be made and implemented in an orderly fashion in the marketplace. Consequently, the call market procedure may be a solution to the problem noted by Kubarych (1988) that technology can drive the pace of market events too fast.

Direct Human Interaction
Some people believe that elimination of the trading floor (which could occur as a consequence of computerization) will eliminate one important way in which information is conveyed—via direct person-to-person contact.[29] However, traders would still be free to communicate with each other, much as they currently do in the upstairs market or in the OTC market. Furthermore, electronic trading, linked to electronic information systems, may support a far greater flow of relevant information. The reason is that electronic systems allow the merging of large, diversified data sets (see Amihud & Mendelson [1985]). Currently, upstairs traders do in fact have an advantage vis-à-vis floor traders in the ease with which they can tap into large data sets, such as those provided by Bridge Data and Reuters. In addition, an electronic trading system increases the geographic scope of a market, and so enables those participants away from the trading floor to interact with the market during the price determination process.

III. PSCAN: THE ELECTRONIC CALL MARKET

The electronic call market is proposed as a system to expedite handling small orders, to cater to the needs of institutional traders, to overcome a number of the deficiencies of nonelectronic call market trading, and to facilitate the adoption of electronic technology for trade execution. Its specific objectives are fourfold: (1) enable geographically dispersed traders to respond to floor information as the market forms, (2) encourage traders to reveal their orders, (3) facilitate the entry of large orders, and (4) find clearing prices that comprehensively reflect traders' desires to buy and sell shares. Because it reveals information while clearing prices are being determined and allows time for traders to respond, the system is a *transparent box*, not a *black box*.[30]

Our electronic call is simple and straightforward. Essentially, it mimics the *à la criée* system where traders on the floor of the exchange can revise their orders as clearing prices are determined. The key structural feature is a price scan procedure; accordingly, we have named the system PSCAN. We describe the scan itself in this section; a full set of rules and procedures that give the proposal concrete definition are presented in Appendix A.

Our proposal retains many of the desirable features of continuous markets such as the Amex and NYSE. Continuous trading itself would be maintained, specialists would have a critical function to perform in the electronic call, and the variety of orders (market, limit, percentage, etc.) and order qualifications (good-till-canceled, day, at the opening only, etc.) would be retained. Certain key aspects of the market would be improved. Information dissemination, order handling, and trade execution would be facilitated; more effective stabilization procedures could be instituted; and post-trade clearance and settlement would be expedited. Equally importantly, PSCAN could be easily implemented, not as a replacement of the current system, but as a superior means of opening the market at the start of the trading day.

The Price Scan

The price scan is a sequential search for a market clearing price that works as follows. The specialist first sets a starting trial price and gives traders a brief period (e.g., 10 seconds at minimum) to submit their orders at that price. During this period, traders can enter their orders in piecemeal fashion if they so choose.[31] At the end of the period, the computer tabulates the total share volume of buy orders entered at the price and higher, and the total share volume of sell orders entered at the price and lower. If the total number of buys is sufficiently close to the total number of sells and/or if the specialist is willing to absorb any difference, that trial price is locked in as the clearing price. If not, the trial price is raised (if buys exceed sells) or lowered (if sells exceed buys), and traders are given additional time to enter their orders at the new price. The scan continues until a reasonable balance is found between buy and sell orders. When this balance is found, the trial price is locked in as the clearing price and the call is ended.

PSCAN can be further described and distinguished from the NYSE's current opening procedure by use of an example. At the opening, specialists currently assemble information on market orders submitted via OARS, limit orders on the book, and orders announced in the trading crowd. Assume that, on the basis of these orders, the best opening price for XYZ common appears to be 50. The share volume of market, limit, and crowd orders that would transact at this price are shown in Table 2–1. Based on this information alone, the specialist might open the market at 50, sell 10,000 shares to absorb the buy-sell imbalance, and report 100,000 shares as the opening volume.

With PSCAN, on the other hand, the specialist might select 50 as the trial price at which to start the scan, and then allow additional orders away from the floor to be submitted. The path PSCAN might follow and the total volume of buy-sell orders that may be revealed are illustrated in Table 2–2. The number of shares shown in the table at each trial price includes orders submitted before the scan. As the price scan progresses, additional orders can be entered or withdrawn piecemeal at each trial price, depending on the arrival or withdrawal of other orders. Following the rules set forth in Appendix A, sell orders cannot be withdrawn, and buy orders cannot be increased, as the trial price is raised from 50 to $50\frac{3}{8}$.

TABLE 2–1
Orders Submitted before the Opening That Would Clear at a Price of 50

| | number of shares (in thousands) | | |
	Buy	Sell	Buy-Sell Imbalance
Market	5	10	− 5
Limit	35	50	−15
Crowd	60	30	+30
Total	100	90	+ 10

TABLE 2–2
Orders Submitted before the Opening and during the Price Scan

Step Number	Trial Price	total number of shares (in thousands)		Buy-Sell Imbalance
		Buy	Sell	
1	50	300	100	+200
2	50 $\frac{1}{8}$	250	125	+125
3	50 $\frac{1}{4}$	210	200	+ 10
4	50 $\frac{3}{8}$	195	210	− 15

As shown in Table 2–2, as the trial price progresses from $50\frac{1}{4}$ to $50\frac{3}{8}$, the buy-sell imbalance changes from + 10,000 shares to −15,000 shares. This implies that in the absence of price-quantity discontinuities, the equilibrium price would be between $50\frac{1}{4}$ or $50\frac{3}{8}$. Because an intermediate price is not possible given the minimum tick size of $\frac{1}{8}$, the specialist would select either $50\frac{1}{4}$ or $50\frac{3}{8}$ as the call price, according to the rules set forth in Appendix A. The price would then be locked in as the clearing price for the call, and any buy-sell imbalance would either be absorbed by the specialist or rationed, for example, by a time priority rule.

Economic Rationale for the Price Scan

PSCAN is proposed for three reasons. First, it lets institutional traders enter large orders in a piecemeal fashion at the call. Suppose, for instance, that the scan calls for orders for shares of XYZ common at the price of $50\frac{1}{4}$, and that a trader wishes to sell 60,000 shares at this price. The block could be entered in parts (e.g., as four 15,000 share orders) that are electronically activated upon the arrival of other orders.

Second, PSCAN would counter the tendency of traders to hold back their orders because of the negative market impact that revealing a large order might have. Public traders, not knowing when the current trial price will in fact be locked in as the clearing price, must enter their orders or risk missing the opportunity to trade at the current market call.

Third, the scan properly structures the economic question the market should ask a trader. In an unstructured environment, the trader must consider both the size of an order and the price at which the order is to be placed. PSCAN, on the other hand, presents a price and asks the trader how many shares he or she would like to buy-sell if that were in fact to be the clearing price. This structure encourages the trader to state the precise number of shares that would indeed be optimal, given his or her demand to hold shares.[32]

Implementation

Hardware and software must, of course, be tested, and relevant system parameters calibrated. For instance, the speed with which the price scan progresses in the electronic call and the spread between trigger prices in the stabilization program must be set. After a prototype is developed, our proposed electronic call should initially be introduced as a more structured procedure for opening the market at the start of a trading day and for reopening the market after any trading halt. In implementing the system for a specific market center, for example, the NYSE or Amex, the procedure can be introduced for the listed issues seriatim, much as the electronic display book has been introduced by the NYSE. Allen (1988) discusses how initial resistance to the electronic display book was overcome at the NYSE by its successful introduction at a few trading posts.

Various electronic linkages are in place in the NYSE's current system. At this time, one possible approach for instituting PSCAN would be to use some of these existing linkages. For instance, during the price scan, orders might be entered or withdrawn through the DOT system by subscribers, while information about the aggregate volume of buy-sell orders at the trial price or better might be displayed to the broad market by a data vendor such as Quotron or Bridge Data.

The primary obstacle to establishing the system, however, may not be technological, but economic: it requires opening the limit order book to the public and thus disclosing information to which specialists alone are now privy. We urge, however, that the system be as open and transparent as possible.[33]

If proven successful as an opening procedure, the electronic call could be used at other times during the trading day. The call mode could be used to close the market, as it is in Japan for the largest issues. This would be most appropriate for heavily traded stocks and, in particular, for stocks commonly used in index arbitrage and on which options are written. The electronic call could also be activated at various predesignated times during the trading day. Presumably, the more active an issue, the more frequent should be the calls.[34]

The successful implementation of a new system requires that people be trained to function in the environment. This task is best carried out using an interactive simulation environment.[35] The structural changes we propose all involve the use of computer technology for order entry and trade execution; thus computer-based training should be particularly germane. A human-computer interactive simulation could also be used to assess further how participants might behave in the new environment. It is particularly important to determine under operational conditions whether the system is inherently equitable, to assess the ease with which traders can function within the changed environment, and to ensure that the system would not induce the development of unanticipated trading strategies that prove to be destabilizing.

Political and economic realities often determine whether or not any proposed institutional change will be adopted. Even though a new system may in aggregate generate greater benefits than costs, its adoption may be blocked if important people feel they will be harmed by it. For example, in order to gain railroad union approval of the introduction of diesel locomotives, American railroads had to agree to maintain firemen in the cabs of the locomotives, although there would no longer be any coal to be shoveled into the furnaces. This consideration may not unduly inhibit institution of the electronic call, however. As we have noted, specialists—the firemen in the current system—would continue to play an important role in our electronic-based trading system. But for the system's implementation to be complete, specialists would have to accept the broad market's having equal access, along with themselves, to all information concerning the size of buy and sell orders at the market opening, or whenever the market is called.

IV. DISCUSSION

An Opening Call and the First Half-Hour of Trading

Trading volume on the exchanges is considerably heavier during the first half-hour of trading after the 9:30 A.M. opening and in the last half-hour before the 4:00 P.M. close, than during the rest of the trading day.[36] Heavy trading in the first half-hour is probably not attributable to an acceleration of news releases or greater instability of investor expectations during this period. Rather, many traders may hold back their orders until a price has been established at the opening, and then use the opening prices and ensuing quotes as pricing guides as they negotiate their orders upstairs or work them on the trading floor. If this is the case, it would indicate that the current opening procedure does not give traders enough pricing information before and at the time the market is opened. Consequently, the institution of PSCAN may indeed draw order flow to the opening call. In so doing, it would reduce the extra heavy volume during the first half-hour in the continuous market.

An Intra-day Call: The Automatic Circuit Breaker

The use of circuit breakers to halt trading during periods of particular stress has been proposed by the Brady Commission. The objective is to stabilize the market, facilitate price discovery, limit credit risks, and counter the illusion that markets can provide unlimited liquidity. Schwartz (1988b) has noted another reason—halting trading enables the market to switch from a continuous to a call market trading mode, a mode that is better suited for price discovery and stabilization procedures.

The current thinking is for a circuit breaker to be activated by a sufficiently large price move. We alternatively propose that the breaker be activated by the time clock. For instance, trading could be halted each day at 11:55 A.M., and the market reopened at 12:00 noon. For maximum effectiveness, the halt should be coordinated between the equity and derivative product markets.

A five-minute pause should be long enough for the transition to be made from continuous to call market trading, and short enough not to restrict access to the market unduly. Thus the five-minute pause would be benign under normal market conditions. However, under stressful conditions, the break would enable the market to rediscover appropriate prices, to adjust quickly to these prices without triggering trades at stale prices, and to activate the corporate stabilization procedure.

Because the break would occur each day at the same time, traders could plan for it in advance, and direct their intraday orders to the noon reopening if they so choose. This arrangement would provide an efficient crossing network on the exchange floor, and thus should attract order flow. Instituting a 12:00 noon PSCAN could also enhance the public's perception of fairness.

A Closing Call and the Last Half-Hour of Trading

Relatively heavy volume during the last half-hour before the 4:00 P.M. close is also associated with a widening of the bid-ask spread near the close.[37] Both volume and spread effects may be attributed to the increased pressure felt by many market participants to consummate trades by the close. Day traders and market makers attempt to rebalance their inventory positions by the close to minimize risk exposure before the overnight period (the phrase "trading down to a sleeping position" reflects the motive). In addition, traders actively wanting to acquire or to sell shares who may have been seeking a better price during the day, might compromise on price before the close because of the possibility of an adverse price jump occurring at the next market opening.[38] Therefore, as a consequence of both inventory considerations and trading strategies, more trades are made in the final half-hour of trading, more limit and crowd orders are cleared from the market, and the spread widens.

The behavior of transaction volume and the spread during the final half-hour underscores the importance of the trading and price discovery processes at this time. Price discovery at the close also has particular importance because closing prices are used for various legal and financial purposes (mutual fund redemption, inventory valuation for margin accounts, estate valuation, etc.). The importance of these considerations suggests the desirability of also instituting PSCAN as a closing procedure.

Stabilization

The instability of the market has been widely discussed following the market break of October 19, 1987. In particular, the need to commit substantial capital to market-making has been stressed by certain regulators and in the financial press. One major source of such funding could be the listed companies themselves.[39] Regardless of the source of the capital, however, price stabilization should be implemented in a call rather than in a continuous trading mode, as noted above.

Schwartz's (1988b) stabilization proposal involves a listed firm submitting limit orders to buy or sell shares of its own stock in response to sufficiently large price changes. The size of these orders and their limit prices are determined by a formula, the parameters of which are public information. The stabilization orders are entered at certain trigger prices that are set at discrete intervals (for example, at $2.50 increments). Most importantly with regard to the subject of the present paper, the stabilization orders are entered for execution only when the market first opens or at any subsequent time during the day that the market trades in the call mode.

The electronic call provides an efficient environment within which to implement the corporate stabilization proposal. The decision rules for corporate stabilization and the specific stabilization parameters for participating companies should be programmed into the electronic call. Then, during the price scan procedure, the computer would automatically enter the appropriate orders from the companies' stabilization funds at the specified trigger prices. This procedure, which would be monitored by the exchange, would ensure that the result is price stabilization, not price manipulation.

Role of Specialists

Specialists will have an essential and flexible role in our proposed electronic call market. Their operations would include determination of (1) the initial trial price at the start of each scan, (2) the speed at which the scan progresses, (3) the call price when there is no exact cross, and (4) whether or not to influence price by their own purchases or sales. The specialists would also operate in the continuous market much as they do in the current system. However, they would also be able to activate call market trading (with the permission of a floor official) so that the corporate stabilization procedure may be used at times of insufficient liquidity.

Integration of Market Segments and Information Sets

As noted in Section II, a critical limitation of a nonelectronic call is that traders away from the floor cannot interact with the market during the price determination process. An advantage of an electronic system is that it increases the geographic scope of the market and enables diverse components to be integrated in a single system. Specifically, our computerized call market with its price scan procedure would better integrate the upstairs market with the auction market on the trading floor, would facilitate the merging of large, diversified data sets, and would allow various decision algorithms to be implemented electronically.[40]

Clearance and Settlement

A report of all trades in our proposed call market could be instantly fed into clearance and settlement procedures and appropriate written confirmations printed using electronic technology. Post-trade procedures would be further facilitated because, as indicated in Section II, a call market produces a single price at each market clearing, making it unnecessary to match specific buyers with specific sellers. Thus, from the standpoint of these post-trade processes, implementing the electronic call market should be straightforward and cost effective. It might, in fact, be possible to expedite settlement (i.e., have one-day settlement) and to reduce commission rates for PSCAN trades.

Simultaneous Trading of Multiple Assets

A disadvantage of call market trading is that it is difficult to make interdependent trades in multiple assets because the market for individual securities is typically called sequentially. For instance, if a trader wishes to sell his entire position in ZYX shares and use the proceeds to buy XYZ, he is not able to size his order for XYZ until he knows the price at which his ZYX have sold. Therefore, if the market is called in alphabetical order, he or she will be unable to complete the double transaction in one trading session. The major cost of having to wait for another trading session is the risk that XYZ shares may increase appreciably in the interim.

A further problem concerning interdependent trades is that it is difficult to establish an arbitrage position in a call market.[41] This is not only for the reason cited above, but also because prices at which arbitrage trades could take place are not known until the call is completed. In contrast, quotes established in continuous markets give traders an opportunity to buy a security at a relatively low price in one market and to sell it (or a comparable asset) at a higher price in another market. This limitation could be particularly disruptive with regard to arbitrage between stock index futures and the cash market.

It is theoretically possible to overcome this limitation by having the calls for all securities made simultaneously, while allowing traders to condition their orders for some securities on the prices set for others.[42] Actually developing a computerized system that could handle the volume of orders and complexity of relationships involved, however, is difficult to envision at this time.[43] In part for this reason, we suggest that continuous trading be maintained after the opening call, much as it is in our current system.

Application to Futures and Options Markets

In futures and options markets, the settlement price of each contract has special economic significance. The reason is that this price is used in the marking-to-market of margin accounts. Therefore, accurate price determination is of special importance at this time. Accordingly, consideration should be given to using the electronic call at the market close if initial experience with the system shows it to be as efficient as we anticipate. For two reasons, it would also be desirable to use the call market to close trading in the cash market. First, to facilitate the execution of market-on-close orders, which can be useful for unwinding arbitrage positions; and second, to provide closing prices for use in mutual fund share valuation, estate valuation, and other legal and tax-related purposes.[44]

V. CONCLUSION

Far-reaching technological and regulatory changes have transformed the securities industry since the Securities Acts Amendments of 1975. Without question, the markets have far greater capacity than before to handle enormous order flow, to transmit orders and trade information worldwide, and to support trading in a variety of interrelated assets. By any historical comparison, our current markets must be rated as highly sophisticated.

Nevertheless, the market break in October 1987 was sobering. Extensive efforts have subsequently been made to analyze it (see Edwards [1988]). The size of the drop itself was no doubt largely due to investor expectations suddenly turning pessimistic; it is the chaotic price gyrations observed that require further investigation.

Some students of the market have pointed to the destabilizing influence of the derivative product markets (futures and options trading) and the associated index arbitrage and dynamic portfolio insurance trading. Others have emphasized the shortage of capital available for market-making, and some have stressed that only a handful of institutional investors brought enormous selling pressure to the market in a brief period of time. Each of these factors was no doubt operative to some extent. However, none of them individually or perhaps even collectively provides an adequate explanation.

Furthermore, looking for specific causes such as these tends to obscure a more fundamental reality: there was no smoking gun. The market drop was accompanied by an extraordinary amount of volatility because the market could not handle the stressful conditions that suddenly came to a head. The basic problem resides not with the specific factors that caused stress, but rather with the structure of the market itself.

The extreme events of October 1987 have pointed up a weakness that has always characterized the markets: they are typically thin, illiquid, and unduly price volatile, even under relatively normal conditions. These attributes are not, per se, due to the operations of market participants or to the financial instruments that are traded; rather, they are due to the design of the trading system. With this perspective, the key question we have asked in this paper is whether the trading system can be improved through the proper application of electronic technology.

We believe the answer is yes. The approach we have developed involves use of the computer to facilitate call market trading. In the call market mode, an electronic system may provide an environment within which (1) institutional investors can efficiently negotiate their orders, (2) prices that more closely approximate desired equilibrium values can be set, and (3) appreciable capital can be used to stabilize share prices. We have sketched the broad configuration that such an electronic market might have. Despite the advantages of call market trading, we do not suggest that it replace continuous trading, but rather that the two modes be integrated. Our proposed electronic call would initially be used only to open the market in the morning and after any trading halt; if successful, it might also be used to close the market, and/or at other specific times during the trading day.

In today's dynamic environment, electronic technology and governmental deregulation are rapidly spurring a growth in global trading that will have far-reaching consequences for the competitive structure of the equity markets. Those market centers that will attract the lion's share of the order flow in the future need not be the ones with a geographic advantage or power based on traditional ties. Rather, they will be those centers that are structured to service best the needs of institutional investors, to supply fair and cost effective trade execution for all participants, and to provide a reasonably stable environment for the broad market. It is with these goals in mind that we have designed our electronic call market.

APPENDIX A: RULES AND PROCEDURES FOR PSCAN, THE ELECTRONIC CALL

1. Activating the Call Market
    1.1. The call market procedure is used to open the market for each security at the start of the trading day, and at certain prespecified times during the trading day.
    1.2. The call market procedure is used to reopen the market for a security whenever its trading has been halted.
2. Order Entry
    2.1. Orders can be entered directly by floor traders and other exchange members who subscribe to the electronic call and have a hardwire connection with the exchange. Other traders must route their orders through a subscribing firm.
    2.2. Floor traders may declare orders by open outcry; these orders are entered into the computer system by a clerk at the specialist's post. Orders originating away from the trading floor are entered directly via an exchange-brokerage house computer linkage.
    2.3. Prior to a market call: orders can be entered at any time.
    2.4. At a market call: orders are entered during the price scan procedure described in Rule 4.
    2.5. Orders can be changed or canceled at any time prior to the market call; during the price scan, orders can be changed only in accordance with Rule 5.1.
3. Order Types and Qualifications
    3.1. Market orders: standard definition.
    3.2. Limit orders: standard definition.
    3.3. Order size: can be specified in terms of either number of shares or total dollar value.
    3.4. Order disclosure: market and limit orders can be either revealed to the market (disclosed) or not revealed (undisclosed). Disclosed orders are time stamped; undisclosed orders are not.
    3.5. Percentage orders: The order size for a percentage buy (sell) order is specified as X number of shares or Y percent of total nonpercentage buy (sell) orders at the price, whichever is less. Percentage orders are not disclosed until they are converted into an executable order.
    3.6. Order duration: Good-till-canceled (GTC) or day only.
    3.7. Further order qualifications: execute only in call trading mode or execute only in continuous trading mode.[45]
4. The Price Scan for Each Security
    4.1. The price scan is a sequential search for a market clearing price. The

procedure is controlled by the specialist as described in Rules 4.3, 4.4, and 4.6.

4.2. When a trial price is announced, all previously existing and currently executable orders at that price or better are disclosed (i.e., all undisclosed executable orders are converted to disclosed orders); this includes all market orders, all limit buy orders at the price or higher, and all limit sell orders at the price or lower.

4.3. The specialist sets the starting trial price; reasonable candidates include the last call price, the last transaction price, or the current indicated clearing price.

4.4. At each trial price, traders are given a brief period (e.g., 10 seconds at minimum) to enter their orders at that price. The specialist should permit the scan to pause for a longer time at a trial price if he or she believes additional orders are forthcoming. Traders can enter or withdraw their orders at a trial price in piecemeal fashion, if they so choose.[46] At the end of the brief period, the computer tabulates the total share volume of buy orders entered at the price and higher, and the total share volume of sell orders entered at the price and lower.

4.5. When the specialist declares that no additional orders may be entered at a trial price: (a) If at the initial trial price total buy orders exceed total sell orders, the trial price is successively raised by the minimum tick size ($\$\frac{1}{8}$ for most issues). (b) If at the initial trial price total sell orders exceed total buy orders, the trial price is successively lowered by the minimum tick size. (c) If at any trial price, the total number of buy orders equals the total number of sell orders, the scan will stop, and that price is selected as the market clearing price; all crossing orders execute at this price. (d) If the trial price has been raised and if at the new trial price total sell orders exceeds total buy orders, the scan stops, and either the new trial price or the last preceding (lower) trial price is selected as the clearing price. (e) If the trial price has been lowered and if at the new trial price total buy orders exceeds total sell orders, the scan stops, and either the new trial price or the last preceding (higher) trial price is selected as the clearing price.[47]

4.6. When the scan has stopped and an exact cross has not been found, the specialist selects either the last trial price or the next-to-last trial price as the clearing price, and excess buy or sell orders are rationed according to the secondary priority rules specified in 6.4.

5. Order Restrictions

5.1. During the price scan: (a) If the new trial price is higher than the last trial price, sell orders can be increased but not decreased, and buy orders can be decreased but not increased. (b) If the new trial price is lower than the last trial price, buy orders can be increased but not decreased, and sell orders can be decreased but not increased.[48]

5.2. A trader can maintain simultaneous buy and sell orders for the same security only if all of his or her orders are limit orders with the highest buy limit price less than the lowest sell limit price.[49]

6. Primary and Secondary Rules of Order Execution

   6.1. The primary rule of order execution is price priority.

   6.2. When the price scan has stopped according to Rule 4.5(c), there is an exact market clearing, and price priority alone determines which orders trade at the call price.

   6.3. When the price scan has stopped according to Rules 4.5(d) or 4.5(e), there is not an exact market clearing, and the secondary priority rules in 6.4 determine which orders on the heavy side of the market trade at the call price.

   6.4. When further rationing is necessary, the following secondary priority rules are applied sequentially as needed: (a) Public orders have priority over the orders of floor traders. (b) Agency orders have priority over principal orders. (c) Disclosed orders have priority over undisclosed orders. (d) Nonpercentage orders have priority over percentage orders. (e) Time priority (the time stamp on an order identifies the time at which an order is disclosed to the market). (f) Random selection (or, alternatively, pro rata execution).

7. Publicly Displayed Information

   7.1. Preceding the price scan: The display screen shows information concerning all disclosed orders and the executable portions of percentage orders.[50] Shown for each price are the aggregate number of shares sought for purchase at the price or higher, the aggregate number of shares offered for sale at the price or lower, and aggregate excess demand (the difference between the aggregate buys and sells).

   7.2. During the price scan: As each trial price is announced, the display screen shows, for that price, the aggregate number of shares sought for purchase at the price or higher, the aggregate number of shares offered for sale at the price or lower, and aggregate excess demand which includes previously undisclosed orders in accordance with Rule 4.2. These aggregate numbers are updated at regular intervals (e.g., every two seconds) as orders are transmitted to the market.[51]

8. The Corporate Stabilization Procedure[52]

   8.1. A listed company can, if it so elects, establish a fund to stabilize its share price. The corporate stabilization orders are determined according to a formula, the parameters of which are set by the listed company and are publicly known. The stabilization procedure is implemented by the listed company submitting buy and sell limit orders in predetermined amounts at predesignated limit prices.

   8.2. During the price scan at any market call, the exchange computer automatically determines and enters the corporate stabilization orders as disclosed limit price orders qualified as "executable at the call only"; the corporate stabilization orders are included (according to Rule 7) in the aggregate buy-sell orders displayed on the precall screen and during the price scan at the call.

9. Specialist Operations

   9.1. The specialist can, after seeing excess demand or supply at any trial price, enter his or her own orders to exactly equate demand and supply at that price, which then becomes the market clearing price, and the price scan is stopped.

   9.2. If the price scan is stopped under Rules 4.5(d) or 4.5(e), there is not an exact market clearing, and the specialist can decide whether to establish the last trial price or the next to last trial price as the call price. The specialist is then permitted to enter his or her own orders to reduce or to eliminate the amount of excess demand or supply at the call price, before applying Rule 6.4.

   9.3. The specialist does not have an affirmative obligation to provide price continuity from any previous market close to the clearing price established at a market call; however, the specialist does have an affirmative obligation to provide price continuity during the continuous trading after a market call.

   9.4. When the market is in the continuous trading mode, the specialist may, with the permission of a floor official, halt trading to activate the call market mode so as to trigger transactions by the corporate stabilization fund.

10. Timing of Calls Across Securities for Market-Wide Openings-Reopenings

   10.1. The price scans for different securities should be conducted simultaneously to the extent possible.

   10.2. If the securities assigned to a single specialist unit cannot be opened simultaneously, the sequence in which the price scans occur is based on one of the following criteria (to be determined): alphabetical order, transaction volume, random selection, or some other appropriate criterion.

APPENDIX B: ELECTRONIC TRADING SYSTEMS

This appendix surveys several proposed and existing applications of electronic technology to trading systems in order to place our proposed electronic call market in a historical perspective. Our focus is on those electronic systems that are capable of handling limit orders and that result in trades whenever two counterpart limit orders match or cross in price. Thus we do not include those electronic systems that have been developed for dealer markets, since they do not handle public limit orders. The best-known electronic dealer systems are those used by the OTC markets in the United States and by London's International Stock Exchange.[53]

Peake, Mendelson, and Williams

The earliest comprehensive outline of an automated securities trading system is the National Book System proposed by Peake, Mendelson, and Williams (PMW).[54] This system was envisioned as a means of developing a consolidated limit order book (CLOB). Consolidating all limit orders for a security in a single (electronic) limit order book was intended to prevent trade-throughs from occurring and to enforce strict time priorities.[55]

Key features of the PMW proposal include: (1) the enforcement of price (as the primary) and time (as the secondary) priority rules; (2) an open limit order book;[56] (3) there would be no physical trading floor, but all trading would be done through the electronic system; (4) because of the capabilities of electronic communication systems, the scope of the market could be very wide (in principle, worldwide); (5) all crossing orders would be automatically executed; and (6) there would be complete integration of the order entry, trade execution, information reporting, monitoring-surveillance, and clearance-settlement systems. As might be expected when such a dramatically different system is proposed, there was considerable opposition to it, especially from people with a vested interest in maintaining the existing system.[57] While the PMW proposal was never implemented in its entirety, it has had considerable influence in the design of several automated trading systems that have been implemented: NSTS, CATS, INTEX, and Instinet.

Amihud and Mendelson

One advantage of electronic technology is that it enables the related components of a larger system to be merged operationally. This objective is a major focus of Amihud and Mendelson's (1985, 1988) proposed electronic trading system.

The system consists of three interrelated subsystems: (1) the order execution subsystem, (2) the clearing and settlement subsystem, and (3) the portfolio subsystem.

In their order execution subsystem, Amihud and Mendelson would include both an electronic continuous market (which they call an "open auction procedure") and an electronic call market (which they call an "automated clearinghouse"). They do not take a position as to which type of trading mechanism is optimal, but instead state that market forces should be allowed to determine the correct mixture between these two alternatives for each security. Our own proposal is to use electronic trading only for the call market mode of trading, and to permit continuous trading to proceed much as it now does. In the future, if the electronic call market becomes well-established, similar advantages might be gained by further automating the continuous trading with which it would then be integrated. However, we do not wish to prejudge or predict the rate or extent to which the conversion of continuous trading to electronic systems will occur.

Amihud and Mendelson state that orders submitted for execution in a call market can be considerably more complex than orders submitted to a continuous market. Limit orders submitted to the continuous market must remain completely specified (in terms of limit price and order quantity) on the book until they are executed or withdrawn. In contrast, orders submitted to a call market could depend upon such parameters as cash available, market indexes, and interest rates; when the market is called, the values of these parameters can be computed, and the orders completely specified. To the extent that we consider it currently feasible, we have included some of this flexibility in our proposed electronic call. For example, the way in which percentage orders are treated (see Rule 3.5 in Appendix A) is fully consistent with the Amihud and Mendelson proposal. Furthermore, although not explicitly part of the exchange computer program, the way in which the orders of institutional investors may be entered during the price scan provides much flexibility that is consistent with the order flexibility proposed by Amihud and Mendelson.

NSTS

The National Securities Trading System (NSTS), introduced in June 1978, was initially developed by Weeden and Co. (which was then a major third market dealer); it is now owned and operated by the Cincinnati Stock Exchange (and has come to be known as "the Cincinnati experiment").[58] Brokers and dealers participating in NSTS enter market and limit orders via computer terminals. A central exchange computer automatically matches crossing orders and executes trades, in much the manner proposed by PMW. NSTS is linked electronically with the Intermarket Trading System (ITS), through which about 40 percent of its order flow is routed.

A major advantage of NSTS is that an NYSE member firm can function as a market maker in stocks on NSTS in a manner that NYSE Rule 390 prohibits on the NYSE; Merrill Lynch did this for several years, in effect becoming the major source of order flow for NSTS. But when Merrill Lynch stopped using NSTS for this purpose in April 1983, NSTS's share of consolidated volume for the stocks it handled fell from 2 percent to 0.6 percent.

There are two major reasons for NSTS's relative lack of success. First, it never was the sole (or even the major) trading arena for the issues it listed, and hence suffers from all of the disadvantages of a small market competing with a large market.[59] Second, NSTS never attempted to meet the unique needs of large upstairs traders, who are reluctant to expose their orders in the open limit order book system used by NSTS.

CATS

The world's first fully automated electronic exchange is Toronto's computer assisted trading system (CATS), which became operational in 1977.[60] Currently, all of the Toronto Stock Exchange's trading in about 800 of the generally less-actively-traded issues takes place in CATS, without there being any simultaneous trading of these same issues on the trading floor of Toronto or any other exchange. As in the PMW proposal, CATS is an open-limit order book system[61] with strict enforcement of price and time priorities. Although the morning opening and any reopening following a trading halt take place in a call mode, during the rest of the day CATS operates in a continuous trading mode. During the warm up period prior to the market opening in the call mode, orders can be entered, an up-to-date indicated price[62] and the current limit order book are displayed, but no trading occurs until the predetermined call time. Due to price and quantity discreteness, there typically is some excess demand or excess supply at the call price; this is allocated proportionally across those orders that are on the heavy side of the market at the opening price. A major advantage of CATS is that it increases the geographic scope of the market, since orders can be entered by exchange members using terminals located anywhere in the world.

The Toronto CATS has been successful and well accepted by traders. A variant of this system was implemented in 1982 for all stocks on the Second Section of the Tokyo Stock Exchange. In 1985 CATS was extended to the trading of all except 250 of the typically most-heavily traded stocks on the First Section of the Tokyo Stock Exchange. CATS was instituted on a third continent, when in June 1986 the Paris Stock Exchange implemented a modified version of the Toronto CATS.[63] Although initially only five securities were traded in the Paris CATS, by the end of 1988 all of the equities and bonds listed in Paris are expected to be traded in the system. As is true for the Toronto and Tokyo systems, the Paris CATS combines call trading for opening the market with continuous trading during the rest of the day that the market remains open.

There has been greater acceptance of fully automated trading in Japan than in the United States or Canada, for two reasons. Most importantly, in Japan CATS has not altered anybody's fundamental position in the trading arena, largely because there already had been an open limit order book system for trading on the Tokyo Stock Exchange floor. Furthermore, the large securities firms in Japan favor automated trading in CATS because they can reduce costs by interfacing with it the sophisticated computer systems that they already have in place.

INTEX

The first fully automated futures exchange in the world opened in Bermuda in October 1984; this is the International Futures Exchange (INTEX). INTEX has no trading pit where traders shout their bids and offers; instead, it operates through Vax computers in Bermuda, London, and Virginia. In this computer network, orders sent from terminals in the offices of subscribers in the United States and elsewhere are sorted and matched. Crossing orders execute as trades. The current market bid and ask quotations, and unfilled limit orders within a range of the market quotes (which is $2 for the gold contract) are displayed on these terminals.

INTEX is located in Bermuda for two reasons: (1) there is relatively little governmental regulation there; and (2) Bermuda is situated between the United States and the United Kingdom, the two main centers of futures trading. Although the commission rate is higher on INTEX than on traditional futures exchanges, the total cost of a transaction compares favorably with that on traditional exchanges, and execution is very rapid when there is sufficient counterpart demand. The volume of trading on INTEX, which was initially very low, has been gradually increasing; however, INTEX still captures only a small share of total futures trading in the contracts that it trades.

Instinet

Instinet (an acronym for Institutional Networks, Inc.) was developed in 1969 as an electronic block-trading system for institutions such as mutual funds, pension funds, and bank trust departments. For almost 15 years, Instinet handled a small volume of block trades, and was neither a great success nor an utter failure. Starting in 1983, however, Instinet introduced a series of innovations that enabled it to gain appreciable order flow in both exchange-listed and

OTC securities. Of special importance was an innovation called the Instinet Designated Market Makers[64] who guarantee execution within thirty seconds at the best market quotes for orders up to 1,000 shares for approximately 5,000 exchange-listed and NASDAQ-quoted securities. This feature is particularly attractive to brokerage firms, since they can offer their customers guaranteed execution (with an immediately printed confirmation) on orders that are larger than those currently being accepted by the small-order execution systems of the exchanges and the NASD, and at prices that are never any worse, but sometimes can be better. This has enabled Instinet to attract a large volume of relatively small retail market and limit orders, to supplement its block trading.

Another major feature of Instinet is an open limit order book (for Instinet limit orders) and the extensive amount of information provided on its terminals concerning the securities traded in the system. In particular, for any security in its system that the user selects, the Instinet screen provides the inside quotes (and depth at the quotes) for the eight U.S. markets on which a stock might be traded, and the time that each quote was last updated. The Instinet limit order book gives information concerning the price, size, and time entered (but not the identity of the placer) of each limit order entered into Instinet; these are arrayed in decreasing price order.

The introduction of the small-order execution service has transformed Instinet so that it no longer functions solely as an alternative market for institutional trades. It now functions as a broker's broker, routing orders efficiently to the best market and strengthening competitive forces among markets. It also provides a limit order book for OTC securities where none existed before. When it is used to facilitate the negotiation of block trades between institutional investors, Instinet allows two counterpart traders to conceal their negotiations from the market while they are being conducted electronically; the trades that result from these negotiations, however, become public information when they execute.

An interesting aspect of Instinet (as well as INTEX) is that it was formed as a profit-seeking corporation (unlike most securities markets, which are not-for-profit organizations). Instinet was acquired in 1987 by Reuters, the British general news and financial information products firm.

SOFFEX

The latest entry in electronic trading systems is SOFFEX, an acronym for the Swiss Options and Financial Futures Exchange. SOFFEX started trading options on individual Swiss stocks in May 1988. Futures contracts on a Swiss stock market index will be introduced in the near future.

SOFFEX was planned as an electronic trading system in part to take advantage of some features that electronic systems provide, and in part to eliminate the need for a physical trading floor.[65] It is a continuous market system, with some type of a call to open the market, but no special procedure to close the market. We suggest that an organized electronic call system, as we have proposed in this paper, be incorporated in SOFFEX both for a formal market opening and a formal market closing. The closing is particularly important in view of the importance of the settlement price for the marking-to-market of margin accounts.[66] SOFFEX enforces strict price and time priorities, gives public orders priority over dealer orders, and has a closed limit order book.[67]

An Interactive Simulation Environment

We conclude by considering one very different use of electronic technology: for testing electronic trading systems and training people to use them. A human-computer interactive simulation that we are developing[68] could be applied in this manner. The simulation consists of five major components: (1) the generation of dealer quotes; (2) the generation of public (i.e., nondealer) orders; (3) the procedures by which orders are handled and trades executed; (4) the limit order book; and (5) an external information generator linking observed security prices to fundamental determinants of share value. This five-part structure is itself capable of being run as an all-computer (noninteractive) simulation of the stock trading process. However, it is helpful to include one or more human participants to serve as market makers and/or public traders. Doing so permits replication of the essential features of possible new trading systems (e.g., the proposed electronic call market, corporate stabilization fund, etc.). The resulting human-computer simulation is a totally interactive system: the computer simulation prods a reaction from the human participants, and the decisions (orders placed or canceled, quotes established or modified, etc.) of the human participants in turn impact on the progress of the simulation (the orders, trades, prices, etc.).

Such a human-computer interactive simulation of stock market trading could be used in several ways for testing the proposed electronic call market. Professionals who are experienced in the marketplace would be introduced as human participants in the simulation. We would be particularly interested in observing how such professionals might react to the new system. Their suggestions will be helpful in designing specific aspects of the information displays that are provided, in calibrating system parameters, and in suggesting additional types of orders that might be permitted. Finally, the human-computer interactive simulation could help train both experienced market professionals and newly hired employees to use the proposed electronic call market.

APPENDIX C: ACRONYMS AND ABBREVIATIONS

Amex	American Stock Exchange
CAC	*Cotation Assistée en Continu* (the Paris Stock Exchange's computer assisted trading system)
CATS	Toronto Stock Exchange's computer assisted trading system
CLOB	Consolidated limit order book
CQS	Consolidated quotations system
DOT	NYSE's automated small order handling system
Instinet	An electronic system that provides order routing and a fourth market trading facility
INTEX	Bermuda-based automated futures exchange
ITS	Intermarket Trading System
MAX	The Midwest Stock Exchange's automated execution system
NASD	National Association of Securities Dealers
NASDAQ	NASD's Automated Quotation System
NASDAQ-NMS	NASD's National Market System stocks
NSTS	Cincinnati Stock Exchange's National Securities Trading System
NYSE	New York Stock Exchange
OARS	NYSE's Opening Automated Report System
OTC	Over-the-counter
POSIT	A crossing network used by institutional traders
PSCAN	An electronic call market based on a price scan procedure
SCOREX	Pacific Stock Exchange's automated execution system
SEAQ	London's International Stock Exchange's automated quotation system
SOES	NASD's automated small order execution system
SOFFEX	Swiss Options and Financial Futures Exchange
SuperDot	NYSE's automated small order execution system (an improvement over DOT)
Tokyo CATS	Tokyo Stock Exchange's computer assisted trading system

NOTES

1. We thank Yair Aharoni, Corinne Bronfman, F. Douglas Foster, Frederick Lindahl, Christopher Petruzzi, Donald Stone, and Robert Wood for their helpful comments on an earlier draft of this chapter.
2. Others have thought comprehensively about the capabilities of computerized trading systems, most notably Mendelson, Peake, & Williams (1979), Peake, Mendelson, & Williams (1989), and Amihud & Mendelson (1985, 1989). Until recently, however, much of the existing electronic technology has been introduced piecemeal. This includes backoffice automation, order routing systems (e.g., DOT and OARS), information display systems (e.g., the NASDAQ screen, CQS, and ITS), post-trade clearance, market surveillance, and stock watch. Moreover, the major piece in an electronic system, electronic trade execution, is largely missing in most market centers. There are, however, exceptions: CATS, Instinet, INTEX, and SOFFEX are computerized trading systems. Automatic execution for small orders can also be obtained through systems such as SCOREX, SOES, and MAX, although prices in these systems are often established in other marketplaces. (Relevant acronyms are identified in Appendix C.)
3. Call markets have been described and some of their properties analyzed in the microstructure literature. See, for instance, Amihud & Mendelson (1987), Garbade & Silber (1979), Ho, Schwartz, & Whitcomb (1985), and Mendelson (1982).
4. Some observers consider crossing networks (which are increasingly being used by institutions), such as that of Instinet and POSIT, to be call markets. All trades for a time interval in a crossing network are made at the same price. This price, however, is set elsewhere (e.g., the closing price on the NYSE), rather than by the buy and sell orders within the network itself. Thus such a system is not truly a market.
5. Execution costs are the implicit costs of trading that are due to the bid-ask spread, market impact (large orders having adverse price effects), and errors in price discovery. For further discussion of illiquidity and the trading costs involved, see Bernstein (1987), Schwartz (1988a, Chapter 11), and Schwartz & Whitcomb (1988).
6. Equilibrium values would clear the markets for all securities and result in every investor holding an optimal number of shares of each security. Thus no investor would desire to do any further trading unless there is a change in his or her information, utility function, exogenous (nonportfolio related) funds flows, and/or the structure of other traders' demand curves which results in a change in the market's equilibrium price.
7. The major indication of inaccurate pricing is serial and cross-serial corre-

lation patterns in returns data. For further discussion and references, see Cohen, Maier, Schwartz, & Whitcomb (1986, Chapters 6–7), Hasbrouck & Schwartz (1988), and Schwartz (1988a, Chapters 10–11).

8. Identifying patterns of runs and reversals is not as straightforward as locating generally positive or negative serial correlation. The reason is that a pattern of runs interspersed with random price movements and/or followed by reversals can cause serial correlation coefficients to be weak, and may otherwise obscure the dependency patterns. We are currently investigating the issue with a colleague, F. Douglas Foster (see Cohen, Foster, & Schwartz [1988]).

9. The term *entered orders* refers to market and limit orders that are priced, sized, and otherwise qualified (e.g., at the opening only, day versus good-till-canceled) by the trader and exposed to the trading floor without negotiation.

10. The frictions include information costs, trading costs, discreteness in prices and quantities, trading halts and other blockages, and other trading restrictions.

11. See Schwartz (1988a, Chapter 8) for more explicit analyses of trading strategy in various types of markets.

12. For further discussion of why price discovery is a major problem in securities markets, see Schwartz (1988a, Chapter 15).

13. *Front running* refers to a trader buying or selling after learning that a large buy or sell order is about to be executed on the market. The front runner expects to benefit from the temporary market impact large orders commonly have.

14. See Wallace (1988) for a report that in the months following the October 1987 crash, small investors have withdrawn dramatically from the equity markets.

15. The major exception relates to a large incoming order; such an order may execute against several counterpart orders, rather than just one counterpart order, and a portion of a large incoming order that starts to execute might remain on the limit order book, setting a new market quote.

16. Since prices and quantities are usually discrete (e.g., in multiples of $\frac{1}{8}$ dollar and 100 shares) rather than continuous variables, special procedures are needed when these functions cross each other at a nonadmissible price and quantity combination; these are discussed in Rules 6.3 and 6.4 in Appendix A below.

17. Two further considerations should be noted: (1) Because of price and quantity discreteness, no exact equilibrium price may exist and thus there needs to be a rule for finding the best clearing price; (2) In principle, a general equilibrium solution, where the demand curve to hold each asset depends upon the prices of all other assets, would be superior to the partial equilibrium solution we have described.

18. Floor information includes knowledge of recent transaction prices and volume, current quotes, and any other indications of potential buying or selling interest.

19. The value of floor information in existing markets is evident in the attempts of investors to specify their orders optimally in relation to current market conditions, and to time their orders so as to avoid trading at inferior prices.

20. In a call market, all orders that have been submitted since (or carried over from) the last call interact with each other at the same instant: the predetermined call time. Hence, other than the call itself, no special mechanism is required to enable counterpart orders to meet in time. Continuous markets, on the other hand, require some more costly mechanism, such as the services of a dealer and/or the continuous maintenance of a limit order book.

21. For further analysis and assessment of the informational content of short period price changes, see Bronfman (1988).

22. A final advantage of call markets is that they permit investors to obtain some protection from transaction price uncertainty, since they can submit their reservation prices, rather than prices from their ordinary demand functions. For elaboration, see Schwartz (1988a, Chap. 8).

23. The new information might on the one hand be knowledge that a large order is about to be transmitted to the market; the exploitation of this information, which is called front running, is largely eliminated in call market trading. On the other hand, information might include more fundamental determinants of share value. While those who receive news early are disadvantaged by call market trading, their greater profits under continuous trading arise at the expense of those who have not yet received the information. Hence, a call market may be more equitable across investors. This is one reason why trading is typically halted during the trading day on U.S. exchanges when there is substantial informational change.

24. While arbitrageurs may profit from exploiting (and hence reducing) price discrepancies, these profits arise from inefficiencies of continuous trading, and come at the expense of those who have traded at inferior prices. To the extent that call trading would lessen such short-run price discrepancies, it could be more desirable from an overall social welfare viewpoint.

25. For example, one might wish to sell an entire position in one security and to reinvest all of the proceeds in a second security. This is a major disadvantage of call trading when the market for the second security is called before the call for the first security. At present we know of no easy solution to this disadvantage of call trading, and our proposal for an electronic call market does not overcome it. However, further research might lead to improvement in this regard.

26. Another disadvantage of call markets relates to "the reservation price ef-

fect." Since this requires a rather technical analysis, the interested reader should consult Schwartz (1988a, Chap. 13).

27. One electronic, continuous trading system (Instinet) does allow two traders to gain privacy on the screen and to negotiate their trade electronically. However, for the most part, the electronic continuous market has not catered to the unique needs of large traders.

28. For example, during the October 1987 market break, many participants were unable to obtain up-to-date information concerning current quotes, recent trades, and even their own portfolio positions. Consequently, many were forced to fly blind. Orders entered under these circumstances undoubtedly were not those that would have been submitted had more current and complete information been available.

29. Relevant information may, of course, be transmitted by oral statements, body language, one's tone of voice, etc. More importantly, the meeting of brokers on the trading floor may allow them to infer who are the traders behind large orders. In order to retain this type of information, Toronto CATS includes trader identification numbers on its publicly displayed electronic order book.

30. The term *black box* is used for electronic systems that do not allow traders to observe and respond to the process that translates their orders into trades. One of the first proposals for a national market system, the consolidated limit order book (CLOB), was referred to as a *black box*; see Sametz (1979).

31. The specialist should allow additional time for orders to be entered at a trial price if he or she believes that the piecemeal entry of orders is not complete.

32. As shown by Ho, Schwartz, & Whitcomb (1985) and further explained by Schwartz (1988a, Chapter 8), the optimal response of a competitive trader in a call market environment with transaction price uncertainty is to pick an order from a reservation demand curve rather than an ordinary demand curve. The price scan obviates this effect, and results in competitive traders picking orders from their ordinary demand curves. This result is desirable; Ho, Schwartz, & Whitcomb have shown that the submission of reservation prices at a call can unduly destabilize share prices.

33. At its inception, an intermediate solution may be advisable. Traders could be encouraged to submit multiple orders and/or percentage orders at the opening, and the exchange could develop the computer capability to integrate the percentage orders with OARS market orders, display book limit orders, and crowd orders at the market's opening.

34. See Garbade & Silber (1979).

35. The simulation being developed by Cohen, Gultekin, & Schwartz that is described briefly in Appendix B is one example of this type of system.

36. This pattern of the order flow is well known to traders. See Wood, McInish,

& Ord (1985) for empirical evidence and Admati & Pfleiderer (1988) for theoretical analysis.

37. For empirical evidence, see Foster & Viswanathan (1988) and McInish & Wood (1988).

38. This willingness to compromise on price near the close would be consistent with the gravitational pull effect identified by Cohen, Maier, Schwartz, & Whitcomb (1981): the attractiveness of trading at a counterpart quote by market order is greater, ceteris paribus, the greater the probability that the counterpart quote will move in an adverse direction; therefore, because an adverse price jump is more likely to occur at the next market opening than during a short period of time within a trading day, counterpart offers exert a stronger gravitational pull near the market close than they do earlier in the trading day.

39. Schwartz (1988b) has proposed a corporate stabilization procedure that operates in a call market trading mode. The paper sets forth reasons for allowing corporations to stabilize the prices of their own shares, establishes rules and procedures for operating corporate stabilization funds, and discusses various key features of the proposal.

40. For further discussion, see Amihud & Mendelson (1985, 1989).

41. On the other hand, we note below that closing the market with a call can facilitate the unwinding of arbitrage positions by entering market-on-close orders.

42. In effect, this would give a Walrasian general equilibrium solution. For further discussion see Cohen & Cyert (1975, Chapter 9).

43. Amihud & Mendelson (1985, p.229 and n.2) have previously recognized this problem. Even in their elaborate proposed electronic system, they restrict their call markets to generating partial equilibrium solutions. However, Amihud & Mendelson (1989) state that they would like to have all markets called simultaneously, and to permit orders for any security to be a function of the clearing prices of other securities. While we agree with the ultimate desirability of doing so, we believe that it would be impractical to try to implement a simultaneous general equilibrium call market involving all (or even a subset of several) securities until after the partial equilibrium PSCAN-type of call market has been successfully implemented for all (or at least most) exchange-traded securities.

44. As discussed in Section II above, the call market price is likely to be closer to an equilibrium price than the closing price in a continuous market. It is interesting to note that SOFFEX, since it does not incorporate any formal system for closing the market, does not simply use the last transaction price, but also gives weight to the closing market bid-ask quotes and a theoretical price based on an option pricing model, to determine the settlement price of its option contracts.

45. Other types of qualifications, such as those currently in use, could be added.

46. The ability to enter or withdraw orders in a piecemeal fashion may be of value to an institutional investor who is concerned that the size of his or her order may impact the market adversely. The order entry procedure could itself be preprogrammed so that, for instance, the size of the order entered for the large investor is increased appropriately and automatically in response to the arrival of counterpart orders.

47. Theoretically, a more efficient search procedure could be suggested for the price scan than to have the trial price move in only one direction and always by the minimum tick size. For example, the number of trial prices examined might be reduced by permitting the specialist to change the price in larger increments, and to permit it to move in both directions during a scan. We have not proposed this, however, because we think that the market participants could be confused by uneven and nonmonotone movements in the trial prices. If the system has been successfully used for some time, however, more efficient search procedures could be explored and, if found suitable, adopted.

48. Rule 5.1 is intended to simplify the price scan procedure by ensuring that unidirectional movements in the trial price generate unidirectional movements in the buy-sell order imbalance. Experience with the system might subsequently show this rule to be unnecessary.

49. The rationale is to permit traders to reflect downward-sloping demand curves, but to prohibit manipulation (playing trading games) by inflating trading volume.

50. Orders designated "continuous market only" are excluded.

51. Updating the aggregates at fixed intervals rather than continuously with the arrival of orders helps to preserve the anonymity of individual orders.

52. For further discussion see Schwartz (1988b).

53. The various electronic systems associated with NASDAQ, the U. S. OTC system, are discussed in Coyle (1989), Riess (1989), and Wall (1989); those associated with SEAQ, London's International Stock Exchange system, are discussed in Newman (1989).

54. See Mendelson, Peake, & Williams (1979) for an early discussion of the PMW system. For a more recent discussion of the PMW system, especially in relation to the chaotic stock market conditions in October 1987, see Peake, Mendelson, & Williams (1989).

55. A trade-through is a trade that is made in one market segment that is inferior to a competitive bid or offer posted in another market segment that, according to price priority, should have executed first.

56. Individual buy-sell orders would not be disclosed, but the aggregate quantities bid and offered at each price would be public information to all traders.

57. For discussion and further references, see Bloch & Schwartz (1979).

58. See Davis (1985) for more information concerning NSTS.

59. The old Wall Street adage, "Order flow attracts order flow!", implies that

orders are more likely to be routed to a larger, rather than to a smaller, market.

60. Bunting (1989) discusses the development and implementation of CATS at the Toronto Stock Exchange, and also presents information concerning possible future modifications of this system.

61. The price and size of each individual order, as well as the broker number of the member firm that submitted it, are public information. Any trader may elect to conceal any portion of his order beyond 100 shares, but the cost of doing so is that the undisclosed portion of that order loses time priority.

62. This is the price that would prevail if the market were called at that very moment.

63. This is officially named CAC (*Cotation Assistée en Continu*). The Paris Stock Exchange appears to have instituted CATS in part in response to the threat of greater competition after deregulation of the London equity market. Versions of CATS have also been implemented more recently at the stock exchanges in Brussels and Barcelona.

64. There are specialists on the Pacific and Boston Stock Exchanges and OTC market makers.

65. The three main Swiss exchanges (Zurich, Geneva, and Basel) could not agree on a single location for a trading floor.

66. The settlement price on SOFFEX (which will be determined and approved by the Exchange Supervisors) is based on three types of inputs: (1) last transaction price, (2) closing bid and ask quotes, and (3) the calculated price from an option pricing model.

67. However, the market bid and ask quotes, and the depth of market at these quotes, are publicly disseminated.

68. This simulation is being developed jointly with Professor Mustafa N. Gultekin of the School of Business Administration at the University of North Carolina.

REFERENCES

Admati, A., & P. Pfleiderer. "A Theory of Intraday Patterns: Volume and Price Variability." *The Review of Financial Studies*, Spring 1988.

Allen, A., & L. Zarembo. "The Displaybook: The NYSE Specialist's Electronic Workstation," Chapter 15, this volume, 1989.

Amihud, Y., T. Ho, & R. Schwartz, eds. *Market Making and the Changing Structure of the Securities Industry*. Lexington, Mass.: Lexington Books, 1985.

Amihud, Y., & H. Mendelson. "An Integrated Computerized Trading System." In Amihud, Ho, & Schwartz (1985).

———. "Trading Mechanisms and Stock Returns: An Empirical Investigation." *Journal of Finance*, July 1987.

———. "The Effects of Computer Based Trading on Volatility and Liquidity." Chapter 3, this volume, 1989.

Bernstein, P. "Liquidity, Stock Markets and Market Makers." *Financial Management*, Summer 1987.

Bloch, E., & R. Schwartz, eds. *Impending Changes for Securities Markets: What Role for the Exchange?* Greenwich, Conn.: JAI Press, 1979.

Bronfman, C. "The Informational Content of Frequently Changing Prices: Implications for the Structural Organization of a Securities Market." Doctoral Dissertation (in process), Graduate School of Business Administration, New York University, 1988.

Bunting, J. "Moving from Today's to Tomorrow's Trading System." Chapter 14, this volume, 1989.

Cohen, K., & R. Cyert. *Theory of the Firm*, second edition. Englewood Cliffs, N.J.: Prentice-Hall, 1975.

Cohen, K., F. D. Foster, & R. Schwartz. "Instability and Price Discovery in Equity Markets." Paper delivered at meeting of the American Finance Association, New York, December 1988.

Cohen, K., S. Maier, R. Schwartz, & D. Whitcomb. "Transaction Costs, Order Placement Strategy, and Existence of the Bid-Ask Spread." *Journal of Political Economy*, April 1981.

———. *The Microstructure of Securities Markets*. Englewood Cliffs, N.J.: Prentice-Hall, 1986.

Coyle, F. "The NASDAQ Experience." Chapter 20, this volume, 1989.

Davis, J. "The Intermarket Trading System and the Cincinnati Experiment." In Amihud, Ho, & Schwartz (1985).

Edwards, F. "The Crash: A Report on the Reports." Chapter 4, this volume, 1989.

Foster, F. D., & S. Viswanathan, "Interday Variations in Volumes, Spreads and Variances: II. The Evidence." Presented at the 23rd Annual Conference of the Western Finance Association, Napa, California, June 1988.

Garbade, K., & W. Silber. "Structural Organization of Secondary Markets: Clearing Frequency, Dealer Activity and Liquidity Risk." *The Journal of Finance*, June 1979.

Grossman, S., & J. Stiglitz. "Information and Competitive Price Systems." *American Economic Review*, May 1976.

Hasbrouck, J., & R. Schwartz. "Liquidity and Execution Costs in Equity Markets." *The Journal of Portfolio Management*, Spring 1988.

Ho, T., R. Schwartz, & D. Whitcomb. "The Trading Decision and Market

Clearing Under Transaction Price Uncertainty." *The Journal of Finance,* March 1985.

Kubarych, R. "Is Technology Driving Us Too Fast?" Chapter 12, this volume, 1989.

McInish, T., & R. Wood. "An Analysis of Intraday Patterns in Bid/Ask Spreads for NYSE Stocks." Working paper, University of Texas at Arlington, 1988.

Mendelson, H. "Market Behavior in a Clearing House." *Econometrica,* November 1982.

Mendelson, M., J. Peake, & R. Williams. "Toward a Modern Exchange: The Peake-Mendelson-Williams Proposal for an Electronically Assisted Auction Market." In Bloch & Schwartz (1979).

Newman, M. "Quality of Markets: The London Experience." Chapter 17, this volume, 1989.

Peake, J., M. Mendelson, & R. Williams. "Black Monday: Market Structure and Market-Making." Chapter 13, this volume, 1989.

Riess, R. "NASDAQ: Experience with Pioneering an Electronic Market." Chapter 16, this volume, 1989.

Report of the Presidential Task Force on Market Mechanisms. U.S. Government Printing Office, January 1988.

Sametz, A. "A Modest Proposal Toward a National Market System—From CLUB to CLOB." In Bloch & Schwartz (1979).

Schwartz, R. *Equity Markets: Structure, Trading, and Performance.* New York: Harper & Row, 1988a.

———. "A Proposal to Stabilize Stock Market Prices." *The Journal of Portfolio Management,* forthcoming, 1988b.

Schwartz, R., & D. Whitcomb. *Transaction Costs and Institutional Investor Trading Strategies.* Monograph Series in Finance and Economics, Salomon Brothers Center for the Study of Financial Institutions, New York University Graduate School of Business Administration, forthcoming, 1988.

Wall, J. "Formal Links Among Exchanges." Chapter 23, this volume, 1989.

Wallace, A. "The Death of Investor Confidence." *The New York Times,* Business Section, pp. 1 and 17, May 15, 1988.

Wood, R., T. McInish, & J. Ord. "An Investigation of Transaction Data for NYSE Stocks." *Journal of Finance,* July 1985.

Wunsch, R. S. "Market Innovations." Paper delivered at meeting of the Institute for Quantitative Research in Finance, Colorado Springs, October 1987.

CHAPTER 3

THE EFFECTS OF COMPUTER BASED TRADING ON VOLATILITY AND LIQUIDITY

Yakov Amihud
Haim Mendelson

Assets can be traded even in the absence of organized capital markets, and, indeed, trading had taken place long before organized exchanges were first established. Even today, securities are privately placed and are subsequently traded in negotiated transactions between interested parties. Blocks of securities are also often traded in the upstairs market where brokers solicit orders on the other side of the transaction they have to carry out (for example, if they are selling, they will solicit buy orders). The question is then, Why markets?

The function of markets is to provide liquidity, that is, to ease the exchange of assets. Illiquidity can be assessed in two ways: either by the *cost* of effecting a transaction in a *given* period of time, or by the *time* it takes to transact (sell or buy) at a desirable price.[1] The former measure relates to traders who demand immediacy. Consider, for example, a trader who wishes to sell an asset immediately and exchange it into cash. The seller will then be willing to pay a price to someone who provides the immediacy service. Such immediacy services are usually provided in securities markets by dealers (or market-makers) who stand ready to buy and sell for their own account at the prices they quote. Sellers (or buyers) can execute their orders immediately by selling (or buying) to (or from) the dealer at the quoted bid (or ask) price.

Thus, dealers save traders the costs and delays of searching for trading partners with compatible interests. Dealers provide liquidity services and charge the spread between the quoted bid and ask prices as their compensation for these services. Therefore, in the case of immediate execution by a market-maker, our seller gains from the certainty of time and price at which the transaction is executed. Illiquidity is measured in this setting by the bid-ask spread, which is the sum of the price concession required for an immediate sale and the premium required for an immediate purchase.

Alternatively, the seller can establish a price at which he or she is willing to sell the asset, and wait for the arrival of a compatible buy order. In this case, the time to complete the transaction is uncertain, and unless the seller revises the price from time to time while waiting for a buyer to arrive, he or she may have to wait some arbitrarily-long time until the desired sale is consummated (for example, after having established the selling price, some bad news may arrive about the asset, and its value may then drop sharply). In this setting, illiquidity is measured by the time required to execute an order (Lippman and McCall, 1986).

The role of securities markets is to provide liquidity, that is, to enable traders to obtain immediacy at a lower *cost*, to reduce the expected *time* to execution at a desirable price, or to increase the *probability* of execution within a given time at a desirable price. As such, securities markets increase economic efficiency. The objective of this paper is to demonstrate how the efficiency of securities markets could be enhanced by applying an Integrated Computerized Trading System (ICTS) that we have proposed (Amihud and Mendelson, 1985). We will examine how trading technology—the mechanism that transforms orders into trades in the marketplace—affects liquidity and volatility. In addition, we will show how the generation of orders is affected by the available trading system. We present evidence on the value of increased liquidity and distinguish between the concepts of volatility and illiquidity, which are often confounded. Then, we demonstrate how exchange automation, when properly implemented, will increase the liquidity of traded assets (or, equivalently, reduce the costs of illiquidity), and we discuss the integration of continuous trading with a clearing house, a simultaneous trading procedure (Mendelson, 1982, 1987). Throughout our analysis, we will discuss the roles of liquidity, volatility, and automation in the context of the events of the October 1987 crash and show how a properly designed system could alleviate some of the problems encountered then.

Our approach to the automation of the trading system differs from the unplanned route followed by the exchanges so far, which, unfortunately, is so typical of many implementations of information technology. Instead of developing a system whose components are integrated, the exchanges have automated individual functions, especially those where pressure has built up or those which seemed more amenable to automation. As a result, the system's components may be uncoordinated, each capable of handling a different level of input and each delivering a different level of output. While the slack built into the system can normally make up for these shortcomings, this slack is used up under pressure, and the system may malfunction.

Another problem is that the existing computer-based systems apply the very same trading methods and procedures that were applied before automation. Rather than redesign the system to take full advantage of information technology, the exchanges chose to replicate the old system, with automated components replacing manual ones. While the old trading system was quite adequate for the past levels of information and trading intensity, it fails to be optimal for today's markets, where the relevant tradeoffs are quite different from those that prevailed years ago.

While many systems in the exchanges apply state-of-the-art computer technology, much of the trading activity is manual. In the NYSE, reporters mark cards and feed them into card readers, and sometimes they have to chase floor brokers to complete the details of a transaction. We observe floor clerks running between the telephone and the specialists' booths; and to execute a contingent swap between two stocks they have to maneuver between the two specialists' posts. Limit orders are sometimes recorded manually in an actual book, and changing them requires an elaborate procedure (for example, a telephone conversation with a broker who calls a floor trader, who then walks to the specialist's post and announces the change in the limit order). Some trades are recorded on paper by the specialists and then passed on to floor reporters, and some of the settlements of the executed orders follow a manual process. In the related futures markets, traders crowd in a pit and announce quotes and executions by open outcry and hand signals, and the level of automation is different from that of the stock exchange. Since these markets are not using compatible trading systems, the ability to execute an integrated trade is limited.

The way exchange automation has evolved—the piecemeal development of automated systems and the lack of a comprehensive and well-integrated Information Systems Plan—imposes high costs on institutions and individuals that try to develop their own trading systems to interface with those of the exchange. The exchange keeps adding systems and changing them in reaction to a variety of pressures and demands, rather than follow a well thought-out vision of the future. It is impossible to foresee the future configuration of the exchange's trading systems because—in the absence of a comprehensive strategic plan—the exchange itself does not know which course these trading systems will follow. The operating protocols can be changed, as was recently done with the SuperDot (the automated execution system of the NYSE), and even the whole system can be changed. This can render obsolete software, hardware, and trading operations that were developed at high cost. As a result, the development of systems that would interface with those of the exchange is discouraged, and there are barriers to entry that enable only a few large trading institutions to participate in automated trading. Rather than facilitate free entry and competition on the exchange, this mode of development of information technology achieves the opposite result because individuals or smaller institutions cannot take full advantage of the sophisticated systems that the exchange has developed.

In what follows, we will present our proposal for an Integrated Computerized Trading System and assess its expected implications in terms of market volatility and liquidity. We precede this assessment with a discussion of the desirability of reduced volatility and the value of increased liquidity.

ON THE DESIRABILITY OF REDUCED VOLATILITY

It is often argued that properly functioning markets should bring about lower price volatility. We have already pointed out that the fundamental role of markets is to reduce the costs of illiquidity. In this section we will show that, although the concepts of volatility and liquidity are related, they are not the same. Moreover, we will show that well-functioning markets can bring about higher, rather than lower, volatility, and that this increase in volatility will, in fact, be consistent with market efficiency.

To illustrate the difference between liquidity and volatility, consider two assets: a long term "on the run" government bond and a house. The liquidity of the bond is certainly higher: an investor can quickly buy or sell large quantities of these bonds at any time, and the cost of a round trip transaction—the bid-ask spread—is $1/32$ of $100, or 0.03 percent of the transaction value. The difference between the effective buying and selling price of a house is of a far larger order of magnitude, perhaps 5 percent or more. Using our second measure of illiquidity—the time to effect a transaction—it can take weeks to sell a house, whereas the sale of $500 million of government bonds can take minutes or less. In short, government bonds are by far more liquid than houses. Yet, housing prices are less volatile than those of long-term bonds. We thus observe that higher liquidity is not always consistent with lower volatility. At the same time, low liquidity can be conducive to higher volatility: the price reaction of a thinly-traded asset to a temporary imbalance between buying and selling pressures will be greater than the price reaction of a liquid asset to a similar imbalance. Thus, policy makers and market designers should carefully evaluate the volatility and liquidity implications of alternative exchange procedures.

A public policy intended to improve the operation of markets should certainly aim at increasing liquidity in order to reduce the friction in the marketplace, which is always costly and undesirable. On the other hand, reducing price volatility is not necessarily desirable. To illustrate, setting a daily price limit on stock prices (or a circuit breaker, as it now has come to be called) can reduce daily price volatility, but this will reduce liquidity because a trading halt that will take place whenever the rule is binding will make it impossible to trade, even if buyers and sellers both wish to do so at a mutually agreeable price. This is equivalent to setting an arbitrarily high bid-ask spread by the regulatory authority, implying that liquidity has been reduced. (Using our alternative measures of illiquidity, the probability of execution within a given time interval is reduced, and the expected time to execution is increased, again indicating lower liquidity). In addition, information about the asset will not be fully incorporated in the market price. The lower volatility is thus attained at the cost of reducing market efficiency[2] (a market is informationally efficient if value changes are immediately reflected in asset prices). We contend that the trading mechanism that prevails in the market determines both the liquidity and the volatility of the market, and that there is a tradeoff between the two.

The tradeoff between volatility and liquidity can be analyzed using Amihud and Mendelson's (1987) price-adjustment model. In this model, the observed price of an asset is the sum of a gradual price-adjustment process and random noise due to the trading mechanism. The behavior of the asset value over time is assumed to follow a random walk with drift, which represents permanent value changes (with the drift corresponding to the expected return). On the other hand, the price changes that are attributable to the noise are transitory in nature, and do not persist beyond the period when they occur. Such noise occurs, for example, due to price fluctuations between the bid and the ask, the temporary arrival of a sequence of orders on one side of the market, or changes in the market-maker's inventory position (Amihud and Mendelson, 1980, 1982).

Traders and market-makers are unable to discern fully between permanent and transitory price changes, hence they will set prices in an adaptive manner.[3] The change in the market price will equal the difference between the previously observed price and the assessment of the asset's intrinsic value, multiplied by an adjustment coefficient g, plus a random noise term. If $g = 1$, prices fully react to value changes; that is, a given change in value will be translated into an equal price change (the observed price will still be different from the asset's intrinsic value due to the noise disturbance). If g is smaller, prices adjust to value changes only gradually. The lower the value of g ($0 < g < 1$), the more gradual is the adjustment of market prices to changes in the underlying asset value. That is, $0 < g < 1$ implies price smoothing in the market, and the lower the value of g, the greater the price smoothing that takes place. Naturally, price smoothing brings about lower return volatility. Indeed, Amihud and Mendelson (1987) demonstrated that the return variance is an increasing function of the adjustment coefficient g. The question is whether a capital market should be designed to achieve more price smoothing in order to reduce volatility. We address this issue by simulating the development of the price of a stock for alternative values of g.

Figure 3–1 demonstrates the consequences of the partial adjustment process on the price of a stock over a 100-day period. Assuming that both the permanent value changes and the transitory noise have a daily standard deviation of 1 percent, the figure considers three alternative values of the adjustment coefficient g for a given realization of the value returns and the noise: $g = 1$, $g = 0.3$ and $g = 0.01$. Even with $g = 1$ (that is, complete price adjustment to changes in the intrinsic stock value), observed prices hover around the stock value because of the noise. When g is lower, the deviations of price from value increase (in absolute value), while the price path is less variable than the path

FIGURE 3–1
Stock value and price over 100 trading days for three alternative values of the adjustment coefficient g: $g=1$, $g=0.3$, and $g=0.01$. The standard deviation of daily value is 1 percent, and that of the noise is also 1 percent.

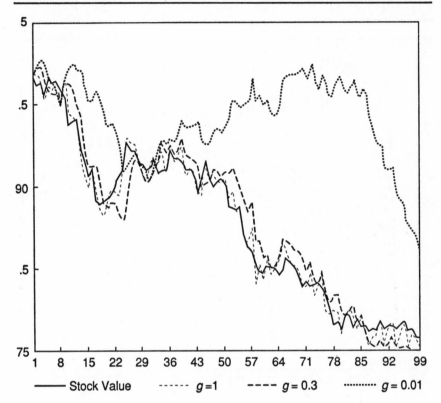

that characterizes the stock's intrinsic value. The figure demonstrates that with lower g, price volatility is lower, but the deviations of price from value are greater.

A market is considered to be (informationally) efficient when new information is immediately reflected in asset prices. Figure 3–2 demonstrates the diffusion of new information for alternative values of the adjustment coefficient g. The new information implies that the value of the stock in trading day 101 should increase to $100. When $g = 1$, we observe a quick (though imperfect) adjustment of the asset price to this (upward) value change. When $g = 0.3$, we obtain sluggish price adjustment to the new level (the adjustment takes

FIGURE 3–2

The effect of an unexpected value change to $100 for three alternative values of the adjustment coefficient *g*: *g*=1, *g*=0.3, and *g*=0.01. The standard deviation of daily value changes is 1 percent, and that of the noise is also 1 percent.

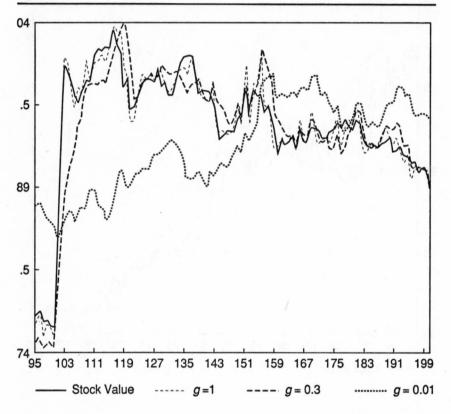

——— Stock Value   ------ *g* =1   ----- *g* = 0.3   ·········· *g* = 0.01

more than a full week); whereas with $g = 0.01$, prices seem to adjust to their new level in about 50 trading days. Thus, we observe a trade-off between volatility and price efficiency. With slow adjustment of prices to value changes (corresponding to lower values of g), price volatility goes down, but at the same time prices are less informative about the value of the asset. As g increases towards unity, both effi-ciency and volatility are increased.[4] This is shown in Figure 3–3, which demonstrates the *differences* between prices and values for the three alternative values of g. The absolute values of these differences clearly

FIGURE 3–3
The difference between prices and values for three alternative values of the adjustment coefficient g: g=1, g=0.3, and g=0.01. The standard deviation of daily value changes is 1 percent, and that of the noise is also 1 percent.

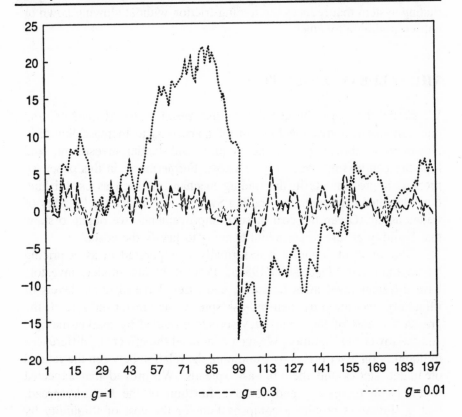

decline with g for $0 < g < 1$, showing that the less-volatile price series are the ones whose deviations are the highest.

It is thus questionable whether reducing volatility per se is a proper policy objective, and whether the design of a market trading system should opt for a trading mechanism that reduces volatility at the cost of reducing liquidity or hampering the informativeness of observed market prices. On the other hand, if volatility (return variance) is reduced by reducing the variance of the noise, which reflects friction in the market, the lower volatility is consistent with both higher liquidity and greater price informativeness. Thus, in order to reduce volatility while increasing liquidity and keeping asset prices informative, the trading mechanism should be conducive to the adjustment coefficient g being close to unity and the variance of the noise being low. This can be achieved by a trading system that reduces the trading friction without slowing down or halting trading altogether.

THE VALUE OF LIQUIDITY

We started this paper by questioning the *raison d'être* of markets, and our response was that the function of markets is to increase liquidity. However, establishing a market requires substantial investment, and liquidity can be improved only at a cost. Furthermore, in this paper we propose improvements in the trading mechanism, such as establishing our Integrated Computerized Trading System, to enhance the liquidity of traded assets. Given the cost of such improvements, we ought to show that liquidity generates sufficient benefits to justify the costs.

The value of liquidity was formally incorporated in asset pricing by Amihud and Mendelson (1986a, 1986b). In our model, investors have different investment horizons, and assets have different levels of illiquidity, measured by their bid-ask spread: the greater the spread, the greater the cost of the immediacy service provided by market-makers, and the lower the liquidity. We then examined the effects of differences in liquidity on asset prices by examining the relation between the returns on traded stocks and their bid-ask spreads. We proved that expected return is an increasing and concave function of the bid-ask spread; that is, investors require a compensation for the cost of illiquidity by paying a lower price for low-liquidity assets. Testing this hypothesis on stocks traded on the New York Stock Exchange, we found that for the period 1961 to 1980, an increase of 1 percent in the bid-ask spread (within the sampled range) was associated (on average) with an additional monthly return of 0.21 percent, after adjusting for differences in the systematic risk. We also found (Amihud and Mendelson, 1988a) that the unsystematic risk and the market value, or size, of the stock issue did not have a significant effect on stock returns, controlling for systematic risk and the bid-ask spread.

It is instructive to translate these findings into value effects that will allow us to assess the value of increasing asset liquidity. For example, consider a security generating a perpetuity of $1 per month whose monthly required return is 1.5 percent and whose bid-ask spread is 1 percent. Its value is then $1/0.015 = 66.67. If its spread is reduced to 0.5 percent, our findings show that its value will rise to $71.68.[5] This increase in value reflects the savings in the cumulative cost of illiquidity: the total cost of illiquidity reflects the fact that trading costs are incurred *repeatedly* throughout the lifetime of the security, which could be infinite. The value increase thus reflects the present value of the reduction in all trading costs paid throughout the lifetime of the security.

Another demonstration of the value of increased liquidity is provided by the observed discounts on letter stocks, whose trading on the public exchanges is restricted and the transfer of whose ownership involves some legal requirements.[6] Many companies issue letter stocks together with publicly traded stocks. The letter stocks are not registered with the Securities and Exchange Commission (SEC) for public trading, but are otherwise identical to their publicly traded counterparts. The *Institutional Investor Study Report* (1971) of the SEC documented the differences between the prices of letter stocks traded in private transactions and the market prices of the publicly-traded versions of the same stocks traded at the same time. The results are demonstrated in Table 3–1. The median discount in the prices of the restricted stocks, in a sample of 398 transactions, was between 20 and 30 percent. This suggests that the value of the greater liquidity afforded by trading in the securities market constitutes about a quarter of the value of those traded stocks. In another study, Solberg (1979) analyzed the discounts assessed by the

TABLE 3–1
Discounts on Letter-Stock Trades

% Discount	Number of Trades	% of Trades
−15 % − 0%[7]	26	6.6
0.1% − 10%	67	16.8
10.1% − 20%	78	19.6
20.1% − 30%	77	19.3
30.1% − 40%	67	16.8
40.1% − 50%	35	8.8
50.1% − 80%	48	12.1
TOTAL	398	100

Source: Institutional Investor Study, 1971

courts for the lower marketability of restricted securities. The median discount on letter stocks in his sample of 15 cases was 38.9 percent.

We can thus conclude that the value of liquidity is substantial. It could therefore be worthwhile to invest significant resources in improving the exchange's trading systems, since the securities traded in the market will then enjoy greater liquidity and their values will correspondingly increase. Amihud and Mendelson (1988b) showed that, given the value of liquidity, firms have incentives to invest resources in increasing the liquidity of their claims, thus increasing their value. We presented a detailed analysis of corporate financial policies that firms can apply to increase the liquidity of their financial claims, and we examined the costs and benefits of each such policy. However, the outcomes of efforts by firms to increase the liquidity of their claims are constrained by the market's trading mechanism. And, while greater liquidity is beneficial, it is probably not worthwhile for a single firm to invest resources to improve the trading mechanism of the exchange where its stocks and bonds are traded. This is because the firm alone will bear the cost, while the resulting benefits are a public good, which will benefit all firms whose claims are traded in the same exchange. This positive externality effect implies that the investment in increased liquidity should be carried out by an entity that can internalize much of the externalities generated by increased liquidity, such as a central exchange authority. Alternatively, a new exchange can be established and attract firms to list in it by providing superior liquidity.

In what follows, we describe our proposal for a trading system that we believe will increase the liquidity of securities traded in the U.S. capital markets.

AN INTEGRATED COMPUTERIZED TRADING SYSTEM (ICTS)

We have proposed (Amihud and Mendelson, 1985) an Integrated Computerized Trading System, which is based on three fundamental principles:

1. *Integration* of three subsystems: information and portfolio management, execution, and settlement.
2. *Competition* between alternative exchange mechanisms.
3. *Flexibility and accessibility* in operation.

We briefly discuss each of these principles below.

1. *Integration.* The Integrated Computerized Trading System will fully integrate the activities associated with trading (see Figure 3–4). These activities are naturally separable into three interfacing subsystems:

- The information and portfolio management subsystem.
- The order execution subsystem.
- The clearing and settlement subsystem.

FIGURE 3–4
The Integrated Computerized Trading System

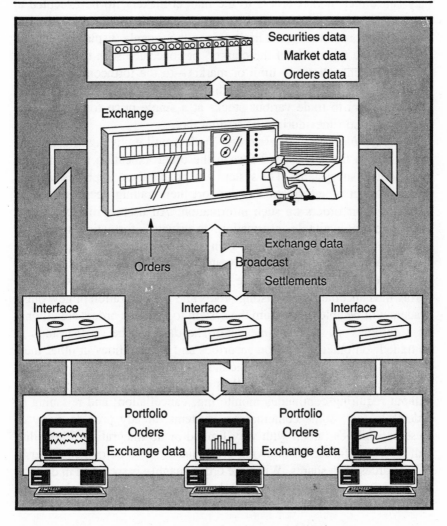

The integration of these three subsystems will eliminate bottlenecks and incompatibilities that are likely to arise in a system whose components are not integrated.

2. *Competition.* The ICTS will enable traders to choose between competing trading mechanisms, enabling them to trade off price, volatility, and probability of execution. The result will be a system that increases traders' welfare and enables the market to adjust better to changing conditions: sometimes one mechanism may be more heavily used, whereas in different situations a competing mechanism may be superior. Investors will be able to choose between alternative ways of executing an order: they can direct market orders to the market-makers, to be executed at the quoted bid or ask prices; they can enter limit orders on the book, with the option of having the limit order either openly displayed to invite traders on the other side of the market[8] or concealed with the specialist; or they can enter orders—limit or market—to the forthcoming clearing in the clearing house. The latter trading mechanism will simultaneously execute orders to trade various stocks at a single price for each stock, all at specified times during the trading day.

3. *Flexibility and Accessibility.* Traders will enjoy significant flexibility due to the interfaces between the order execution and portfolio management subsystems. The system will enable them to process a comprehensive set of information to support their trading decisions and to condition their orders on such information. All users will have access to all publicly available information, to private information sources to which they subscribe, and to their own order and portfolio data, all being supplied in real time. When an investor's order is executed, the system will immediately update the state of his or her portfolio, possibly triggering the cancellation of existing orders and the generation of new ones. Traders will be able to program the system to generate orders conditional on a complex set of real time data. The data can be on the stock to be traded, on other stocks, on securities and commodities in other markets, or on various macroeconomic indices. This will enable investors to keep abreast of the market as well as of changes in their own portfolios without requiring continuous monitoring, cancellation, and reissuing of orders. In fact, some contemporary systems already provide many of these capabilities, albeit with very limited or no integration. Flexibility will also be afforded by allowing order quantities to be quoted either in dollar values or in shares. When the order quantity is specified in dollars, the number of shares executed will depend on the execution price; when

it is specified in shares, the quantity traded will be fixed, while the cash settlement will depend on the execution price. Price quotations will be in dollars and cents rather than in the archaic $\frac{1}{8}$ ticks, possibly reducing the bid-ask spread in some stocks. This not only will contribute to lower-cost transactions and greater liquidity, but will reduce noise volatility, which is created by the bouncing transaction prices between the bid and the ask (Amihud and Mendelson, 1987).

The ICTS is particularly valuable in market environments that are highly volatile, since in them it may be humanly impossible to process the information generated in the market in order to make rational trading decisions, as was the case during the week of October 19, 1987. When conditions are not amenable to rational trading, traders may choose to withdraw from the market altogether. This reduces market depth and liquidity, which is certainly undesirable.

The handling of limit orders under the ICTS exemplifies its contribution to greater liquidity and lower volatility. Limit orders constitute an important part of the trading process, since by absorbing much (in active stock, most) of the incoming market orders they provide depth and liquidity. Usually, more limit orders in a stock are consistent with a narrower bid-ask spread.[9]

The current trading and information systems make it infeasible or too costly for most traders to place limit orders on a timely basis when they wish to do so.[10] In the recent past, and in the present for some market segments, the specialist's limit order book was literally a book, with limit orders recorded in pencil. The recent automation of the book merely replicated the original manual function without integrating it with the rest of the system. Entering and removing a limit order on the book is still often done through the intermediation of the specialist, and the structure of the orders is exactly the same as before the system was automated. As a result, traders are reluctant to place limit orders, or they place them with limit prices that are far from their true reservation price.[11]

The problem associated with limit orders is what we call the sitting duck problem: a limit order (including the specialist's) is executed against a market order at the very price quoted in the limit order. The trader who placed the limit order may find his order hit by another trader who knows that the quoted limit price is out of line. For example, a trader who places a limit buy order at a price of $50, which he considers to be the stock's true value, can be sold the stock by an informed trader who knows that the value of the stock is, in fact, less than $50. This problem exists not only when the buyer has inside information, but when he possesses superior technology that enables him to access the limit order book faster. In a volatile market, when prices fluctuate widely and quickly, the seller in our example can reach the limit order book before the trader who had placed the limit order can remove or modify his limit order. Being aware that he may be disadvantaged, the trader who considers placing a limit order sets a price that is, in the first place, lower than the value he assesses for the stock. In our example, he will set a limit buy price of, say, 49\frac{3}{4}$ instead of $50. In the aggregate, buy order limits will be quoted at lower prices and sell orders will have higher limit prices than the traders' assessment of the asset values (given the available information). As a result, the bid-ask spread will be wider, implying lower liquidity.

The ICTS enables a trader to make a limit order conditional on a comprehensive set of information, such as the prices of other stocks in the same and in related industries, changes in a market index, trading volume, or external announcements (earnings, money supply, interest rate changes, etc.). This reduces the need to monitor the market and to be continuously ready to change the limit order. Under today's system, the fact that a fast change in market conditions can render a limit order's price out of line necessitates continuous monitoring and voluminous communication with the exchange. If the limit order is not changed fast enough, it will be hit by another trader who can react more quickly. The problem is augmented by the unequal access of traders to the technology with the shortest reaction time. As pointed out above, some are disadvantaged not only in the information they have, but in the technology they can apply in placing and removing limit orders. Under the ICTS, the limit order will automatically track the relevant market conditions, and the limit price will be automatically recomputed as necessary. This will reduce traders' reluctance to place limit orders because it will reduce the need to monitor them and the associated costs (and risks). It follows that there is a tradeoff between the ability to monitor and change limit orders on time. The tradeoff is determined by the market's technology and the liquidity of the market, reflected by an increase in the quantity bid or offered at the narrowest bid and ask prices and by narrower bid-ask spreads. In short, our trading system can help increase market liquidity.

THE CLEARING HOUSE[12]

The execution system of our proposed ICTS includes two major competing trading mechanisms. One is the continuous trading system, similar to the current ones, where traders can place limit or market orders and trading is carried out continuously through an open auction. The other is the *clearing house* mechanism analyzed by Mendelson (1982, 1985, 1987). In this section, we briefly outline the mode of operation of the clearing house and analyze its consequences.

The clearing house will clear participating orders periodically, at specified points of time during the trading day—for example, at the opening, at 1:00 P.M., and at 3:30 P.M. Orders designated for the clearing house will accumulate prior to these clearing times. While clearing-house orders accumulate, the continuous auction market will keep operating up to the clearing epoch (for mid-day clearings) and immediately afterwards without any interruption. Thus, the clearing house will not cause any trading halt and will not interfere with the ordinary continuous trading. At clearing time, all qualifying orders will be executed *simultaneously* at a *single* price.

Two types of orders will be submitted to the clearing:

1. Conditional orders, i.e., orders whose execution depends on a set of specified conditions, such as the price of the security for which the order is entered (which is the equivalent of limit orders entered today) or on other conditions, such as the clearing prices of other securities that participate in the clearing at the same time.
2. Unconditional, or market, orders.

All orders will remain sealed until clearing time, but traders will be allowed to reveal (advertise) them if they wish to solicit matching orders for the clearing. At clearing time, a computer system will solve the set of equations and inequalities implied by the existing orders to determine for each security the quantity traded and the market-clearing price. This will be done by interpreting each order as a multicommodity excess-demand function and finding a competitive-equilibrium solution corresponding to these functions.[13] All qualifying orders for all participating securities will be executed simultaneously.

Trading in the opening transaction in actively traded stocks on the NYSE is similar, in some respects, to our proposed clearing house (Amihud and Mendelson, 1987), but it is certainly not identical. Also, some European stock exchanges apply clearing procedures that are similar to the opening for each single stock (Whitcomb, 1985). In all these trading systems, however, orders for each security are cleared *separately*. The only conditional orders allowed are simple limit orders, and the unconditional ones are market orders, specified only in number of shares. Thus, these systems do not support simultaneous execution across securities, and certainly cannot allow conditioning an order in one security on the conjectural clearing prices of other securities. Cohen and Schwartz (1988) propose a trading arrangement that is similar to the NYSE opening, named "electronic call market," which allows more interaction between traders using a price scan procedure. In each stock, there will be an iterative process where traders enter orders in response to the advertised excess demand or supply, with each stock possibly opening at a different time (as is now the case in the NYSE opening). The Cohen-Schwartz proposal shares a number of the advantages of our clearing house.

The clearing house may seem to have a major shortcoming: it does not provide immediacy of execution. The market is cleared periodically rather than continuously, and some traders may be unwilling to wait until their orders are executed. If the inter-clearing time intervals are shortened, the number of orders per clearing will go down and the market will become thinner, which is undesirable.[14] However, since under our ICTS the clearing house is not the *only* trading procedure available to traders in the marketplace, its introduction does not impose a constraint because traders can choose the mechanism that best suits their specific preferences. When immediacy of execution is important and traders are willing to pay its price, they will choose the specialist's services or the open auction. When immediacy is not as important—e.g., when traders enter limit orders for delayed execution—they may prefer to use the clearing house.

An important advantage of the clearing house over the continuous trading mechanism is that in the clearing house, the sitting duck problem is substantially eliminated. Since all qualifying orders for each security are executed at a single price, traders are provided the benefit of their order being executed at a price better than their quote. This is because the execution price is determined by the intersection of the demand and supply schedules constructed by batching orders with different limit prices.

Consider, for example, the case of a single security with simple limit prices. At a market clearing price of $25 there may also be executions of buy orders with quotations at 25\frac{1}{8}$, 25\frac{1}{4}$, and so on, as well as sell orders quoted at 24\frac{7}{8}$, 24\frac{3}{4}$, and so on. This generates a *surplus* to traders whose orders are executed, equal to the difference between their limit price and the execution price. This important advantage is also shared by the system proposed by Cohen and Schwartz (1988).

Traders who place limit orders at the clearing house can also benefit from the fact that their limit price and the size of their order are not disclosed to the rest of the market, nor to a specialist (unless they choose to disclose them). This is particularly useful for block trading, where the disclosure may have an adverse effect on price.

The important feature that distinguishes our proposed clearing house from other single-security procedures is the simultaneous execution of all securities, which enables orders for one security to be conditional on conjectural market conditions, and—particularly—on the market-clearing prices of other securities. This enables traders to construct portfolios according to their specifications, a task that is problematic under the continuous trading mechanism where orders can be conditional only on *past* information. In the current systems, when an order is generated by satisfying some condition, that condition may have changed by the time of execution and the executed order may not satisfy the condition any more. For example, consider the order "If the price of the IBM stock rises above $110 *and* the price of Digital Equipment Corporation falls below $105 *and* the price of Apple Computers is above $45, sell 40,000 shares of IBM and use the proceeds to buy DEC." In the current system, it is possible to guarantee only one of these conditions, but not all three. And, although the available automated systems shorten the time lag between observation and execution, the fast changing prices make a response time of even a fraction of a second insufficient to guarantee the desired execution. In addition, the market impact of the very order that is executed can change the market-clearing price. Even if the observed price of DEC falls below $105, the impact of the buy order itself may be to drive the execution price above $105, and this would be particularly so if many traders apply the same trading rules at the same time. Only in the clearing house can an order of the type described above, contingent on conditions current at the execution epoch, be executed.

This feature of the clearing house becomes more valuable in highly volatile markets. When prices are stable, one can first observe the quotes on the desired set of securities and then execute the order at prices the same as, or very close to, those previously observed. The loss in this case due to a deviation from the desired condition is an increasing function of the size of the order, but it may well be negligible. However, if prices change quickly and in large magnitude, this problem becomes serious. During the week of October 19, 1987, there were apparent arbitrage opportunities, e.g., between the cash market and the futures or options markets. These opportunities, however, could hardly be exploited because it was impossible to construct an exact arbitrage portfolio. If observed price differences triggered simultaneous orders to two assets, there was no guarantee that the orders could be executed at the prices observed when they were generated. Thus, an apparent profitable transaction might have ended in a loss.

The simultaneous execution capability across different securities of the clearing house, which enables the exploitation of profitable price differences, is valuable not only to traders and arbitrageurs but to the market as a whole, since it may help reduce undesirable noise in asset prices. Nowadays, a number of trading institutions track the market and enter orders automatically through the SuperDot system when a profitable price gap between securities is observed. Rather than close the gap, this activity can sometimes cause price oscillations and keep triggering orders that attempt to exploit the observed price gap. The probability that the price gap will exactly close is practically zero under the current trading system. Under the clearing house, however, orders can be designed to bring about the exact closing of the price gap, and the prices of related securities will be kept more in line.

The clearing house operation should also bring about lower transaction costs. Under the clearing house, investors save the bid-ask spread; and the associated brokerage fees should also be lower than in the current system because of the simplicity of order placement and execution. By using the simultaneous execution features of the clearing house, traders will be able to construct and effectively trade portfolios, or baskets, of securities, which are now traded as separate assets (e.g., stock index futures). While the existence of derivative assets is also motivated in part by other factors, an important reason for their existence is the increasing demand for portfolio transactions (Figlewski, 1987). While futures will still play a useful role given the clearing house alternative (for example, they will enable continuous trading in predefined asset portfolios), we expect that the ability to construct custom-made portfolios at low cost using clearing house orders will be valuable to traders.[15]

Some of the tradeoffs associated with the clearing house can be inferred from the findings of Amihud and Mendelson (1987), who compared the opening and closing transactions in the thirty stocks on the Dow Jones Industrial list during the period February 8, 1982, through February 18, 1983. While the opening transaction in active stocks is not identical to our proposed clearing house, it simulates it in some respects. They found that the volatility of the open-to-open price changes was, on average, 20 percent higher than the volatility of close-to-close price changes. If we take the open-to-open returns as a proxy for the price behavior in a clearing house, while the closing prices represent the results under the usual specialist-based trading procedure, these findings suggest a disadvantage to trading at the opening, since the prices generated by this trading mechanism are more volatile. Yet, there was significant demand for trading in the opening despite this shortcoming: the trading volume of the single opening transaction constituted between 2.1 percent and 8.4 percent of the daily trading volume in these stocks, with the median being 5.85 percent. This suggests that traders find this method of trading of considerable value despite its higher volatility.[16]

CONCLUDING REMARKS

We opened this paper with the question, "Why markets?" We responded that markets exist to provide liquidity. During the week of October 19, markets failed to carry out their role because liquidity had dried up. This was reflected in the unusually high market impact of buy and sell orders, the inability of traders to execute their orders promptly, the atmosphere of panic selling, the unavailability of information on market conditions, and the sharp increase in price volatility.

Our proposed ICTS is expected to improve market liquidity and reduce noise-related volatility by combining the application of superior technology with trading mechanisms that take full advantage of it. We can illustrate some of the potential advantages of our proposed ICTS by comparing the functioning of the current systems during the week of October 19, 1987, to that expected had the ICTS been in place. At the outset, we emphasize that while electronic (or program) trading is often blamed for the extreme volatility observed in the market during that period, we believe that electronic trading is not the culprit. On the contrary, we suggest that with a better electronic trading system—specifically, with our ICTS—some of the problems observed in October 1987 would have been eliminated, or at least mitigated.

We consider first the role of limit orders in the October crash. The swift changes in market prices and the lack of on-line information made the placement of limit orders particularly risky. Traders realized that their limit orders might be hit before they could adjust them to the changing conditions, which meant that a limit order could be executed at an unacceptable price given the state of the market at the time of execution.[17] This made traders more reluctant to place limit orders; or, if they did, they set limit prices that were further away from the observed transaction prices. Thus, the bid-ask spreads became much wider, and market depth was substantially reduced. This further exacerbated the problems, since the price impact of arriving orders was much greater than before.

In addition, information was incomplete and unreliable. The manual reporting of many transactions could not cope with the pace of trading, it was often impossible to know whether or not an order had been executed, and there was no real-time information on quotes. This made the placement of limit orders even more risky because of the asymmetry of information between traders on the exchange floor and those who were not there.

Further, even if traders had the information and could process it, they could not physically place their orders or change them fast enough because most did not have access to a system that enables order placement directly to the exchange floor. Only a handful of trading institutions have the technology required to place large orders directly into the SuperDot system, and even fewer traders have the capability of interacting with this system. As a result, there is a great deal of inequality in the ability of traders to access the market, and a basic ingredient of a competitive market—having many traders who are small relative to the market as a whole, with none having an appreciable impact on market prices—is missing. The effects of the dominance of a few big trading institutions on prices during October 1987 has been documented in the reports on these events. Unfortunately, the barriers to entry have not diminished because the technology that provides superiority in trading has not yet reached, and is generally unavailable to, many market participants.

An important problem observed in the October crash is that the malfunctioning of the market generates a process that feeds on itself, since thinness attracts thinness in the market. When the market becomes thinner, the market impact of orders increases, large price changes are more likely to occur, and this further discourages traders from entering orders, making the market even thinner. This is the down side of the positive externalities associated with liquidity.

We suggest that technology and its proper use provide the key to the solution of these problems. Our proposed ICTS could have helped resolve these problems by making information available on-line for all quotes and transactions, by processing it immediately following traders' specifications, and by generating orders that take into account current market conditions as well as traders' portfolio positions. The flexibility afforded in the specification of conditional orders exempts traders from continuously monitoring the market and, thus, eases the provision of liquidity. By providing flexibility, easing access to the market, and shortening traders' reaction time in a symmetric fashion, many of the problems discussed above would have been solved or mitigated.

Finally, using the ICTS, traders can take advantage of the clearing house, where a large volume can be transacted instantaneously. Being less adversely affected by trading with those who have superior information, the sitting duck problem is mitigated, and traders are more agreeable to entering limit orders, thereby increasing the liquidity of the market. In a chaotic market, traders could find more guidance in the prices generated in such clearing transactions, and the ability to place orders simultaneously for many securities would have kept their prices in line with each other.

Our solution to the malfunctioning of the market is to improve its operation by implementing a better trading system. We disagree with the proposed remedies of establishing circuit breakers, that is, instituting trading halts when prices move outside of a specified bound. Such trading halts are intended to enable traders to learn about the existence of order imbalances and to enter orders, giving the market greater depth and thus reducing price fluctuations. The implicit premise is that given the limited speed with which traders can react to changing market conditions, more time will enable more offsetting orders to be entered. However, in terms of the impact of trading halts on market liquidity, the remedy may be worse than the problem it intends to solve. As we have shown, by their very nature trading halts hamper the liquidity of the market. A better way to achieve the same benefits without ruining market liquidity is to improve access and reaction speed through the use of better technology than that available today. Our suggestion is that instead of allowing more time for new orders to arrive, the exchange should reduce the time it takes orders to reach it by establishing a better trading system. The number of orders available at clearing time should be increased through the use of modern data-communication and information technologies. By increasing the flexibility and sophistication of the orders themselves, our system will allow orders already on the book to react automatically to temporary imbalances without requiring the submission of new orders. This will enable the market to reach equilibrium instantaneously rathei than through noisy, and sometimes destabilizing, adjustments.

Liquidity has value and can be enhanced through the proper use of information technology. This paper has proposed a technology-based strategy for increasing the liquidity of securities markets as well as criteria for its evaluation. The next step is its implementation.[18]

NOTES

1. A related measure is the probability of execution at a desirable price within a given period of time.
2. See Schwartz (1988, Ch. 11) for a discussion of the relation between liquidity, execution costs, and volatility. See also Bernstein (1987) and Cohen, Maier, Schwartz, and Whitcomb (1986) for a discussion of the relation between liquidity and volatility.
3. For a discussion of adaptive price-adjustment models, see Garbade and Silber (1979).
4. Reduced volatility is consistent with increased efficiency only in the unusual case of overshooting, which corresponds to $g > 1$ (Amihud and Mendelson, 1987).
5. The required monthly return will decline (approximately) by 0.21×0.5 percent due to the 0.5 percent decline in the bid-ask spread; the magnitude of the decline is obtained from Amihud and Mendelson (1986a).
6. We benefited from a discussion with William Silber on this issue.
7. A premium of 0 to 15 percent.
8. This mechanism follows the National Book System approach pioneered by Mendelson, Peake, and Williams (1979) and adopted by a number of securities exchanges. See Chapter 13 in this book for an updated proposal for such a trading system.
9. Black (1971) proposed to change the role of the exchange specialist to process investors' limit orders at his discretion. Thus, investors who place

limit orders are, in effect, playing the role of market-makers. On the effects of competition among market makers, see Ho and Stoll (1983).
10. See also Black (1971, p. 25) on this point.
11. See also Harris and Raviv (1981) and Ho, Schwartz, and Whitcomb (1985).
12. Our clearing house is a trading mechanism and should not be confused with the institution where settlements take place after transactions are executed.
13. Standard theorems on the existence of competitive equilibrium provide sufficient conditions for finding such a solution.
14. The tradeoffs in determining the trading interval are studied in Mendelson (1982) and Garbade and Silber (1979).
15. Our suggestion that the clearing house will make it feasible to trade baskets of securities, such as the S & P 500 portfolio, is different from the recent proposal to establish a post at the exchange for trading in baskets of securities. In our system, traders will be able to buy or sell the actual stocks, and the composition of the portfolio is determined by the investor, possibly as a function of market conditions.
16. Note that, unlike the opening transaction in the NYSE, our clearing house will operate in parallel to the continuous market. We expect that this will eliminate, or at least mitigate, the higher volatility found in the opening.
17. This is possible in a technologically-deficient environment that is due to the lag between order placement and execution.
18. This paper is based on our research which has appeared in Amihud and Mendelson (1985, 1986a, 1986b, 1987, 1988a, 1988b). We benefitted from comments on an earlier version of this paper by Fischer Black, Kalman Cohen, Robert Schwartz, Adam Shimrat, and William Silber. Partial financial support by the IBM Program of Support for Education in the Management of Information Systems is gratefully acknowledged.

REFERENCES

Amihud, Yakov, and Haim Mendelson. "Dealership Market: Market Making with Inventory." *Journal of Financial Economics*, 1980, pp. 31–53.
_____. "Asset Price Behavior in a Dealership Market." *Financial Analysts Journal*, May–June 1982, pp. 50–59.
_____. "An Integrated Computerized Trading System." In Y. Amihud, T. Ho, and R. Schwartz, eds., *Market Making and the Changing Structure of the Securities Industry*. Lexington, MA: Lexington Books, 1985.
_____. "Asset Pricing and the Bid-Ask Spread." *Journal of Financial Economics*, December 1986a, pp. 223-246.
_____. "Liquidity and Stock Returns." *Financial Analysts Journal*, May–June 1986b, pp. 43–48.

————. "Trading Mechanisms and Stock Returns: An Empirical Investigation." *Journal of Finance*, July 1987, pp. 533–553.

————. "The Effect of Beta, Bid-Ask Spread, Residual Risk and Size on Stock Returns." Working Paper, William E. Simon Graduate School of Business Administration, University of Rochester, 1988a.

————. "Liquidity and Asset Prices: Financial Management Implications." *Financial Management* 17 (Spring 1988b), pp. 5–15.

————. "Liquidity, Volatility, and Exchange Automation." Working Paper, William E. Simon Graduate School of Business Administration, University of Rochester, 1988c.

Bernstein, Peter. "Liquidity, Stock Markets and Market-Making." *Financial Management* 16 (Summer 1987), pp. 54–62.

Black, Fischer. "Toward a Fully Automated Stock Exchange." *Financial Analysts Journal*, November–December 1971, pp. 24–28, 86–87.

————. "Noise." *Journal of Finance*, 1986, pp. 529–543.

Cohen, Kalman, Steven Maier, Robert Schwartz, and David Whitcomb. *The Microstructure of Securities Markets*. Englewood Cliffs, NJ: Prentice-Hall, 1986.

Cohen, Kalman, and Robert A. Schwartz. "Realizing the Potential of an Electronic Trading System." Chapter 2 in this volume, 1988.

Figlewski, Stephen. "The Interaction between Derivative Securities on Financial Instruments and the Underlying Cash Markets: An Overview." *Journal of Accounting, Auditing and Finance*, Summer 1987, pp. 299–318.

Garbade, Kenneth D., and William Silber. "Structural Organization of Secondary Markets: Clearing Frequency, Dealer Activity and Liquidity Risk," *Journal of Finance* 34 (June 1979), pp. 577–593.

Harris, Milton, and Arthur Raviv. "Allocation Mechanisms and the Design of Auctions." *Econometrica* 49 (1981), pp. 1477–1499.

Ho, Thomas, Robert Schwartz, and David Whitcomb. "The Trading Decision and Market Clearing under Transaction Price Uncertainty." *Journal of Finance*, March 1985, pp. 21–42.

Ho, Thomas, and Hans R. Stoll. "The Dynamics of the Dealer Markets under Competition." *Journal of Finance* 38 (September 1983), pp. 1053–1074.

Lippman, Steven A., and John J. McCall. "An Operational Measure of Liquidity." *American Economic Review*, March 1986, pp. 43–55.

Mendelson, Haim. "Market Behavior in a Clearing House." *Econometrica* 50 (November 1982), pp. 1505–1524.

————. "Random Competitive Exchange: Price Distribution and Gains from Trade." *Journal of Economic Theory* 37 (1985), pp. 254–280.

————. "Exchange with Random Quantities and Discrete Feasible Prices." Working Paper, William E. Simon Graduate School of Business Administration, University of Rochester, 1986.

————. "Consolidation, Fragmentation and Market Performance." *Journal of Financial and Quantitative Analysis* 22 (June 1987), pp. 189–207.

Mendelson, Morris, Junius W. Peake, and R. T. Williams. "Toward a Modern Exchange: The Peake-Mendelson-Williams Proposal for an Electronically Assisted Auction Market." In E. Bloch and R. Schwartz, eds., *Impending Changes for Securities Markets*. Greenwich, CN: JAI press, 1979, pp. 53–74.

Peake, Junius W., Morris Mendelson, and R. T. Williams. "Black Monday: Market Structure and Market Making." Chapter 13 in this volume, 1988.

Schwartz, Robert A. *Equity Markets: Structure, Trading and Performance*. New York: Harper & Row, Publishers, Inc., 1988.

Securities and Exchange Commission. *Institutional Investor Study Report*. U.S. Government Printing Office, 1971, 5: 2444–2456. (House Document No. 92–64, Part 5).

Solberg, Thomas A. "Valuing Restricted Securities: What Factors Do the Courts and the Service Look For." *Journal of Taxation*, September 1979, pp. 150–154.

Stoll, Hans R. *The Stock Exchange Specialist System: An Economic Analysis*. New York: Salomon Brothers Center for the Study of Financial Institutions, Graduate School of Business, New York University, 1985.

Whitcomb, David K. "An International Comparison of Stock Exchange Trading Structures." In Y. Amihud, T. Ho, and R. Schwartz, *Market Making and the Changing Structure of the Securities Industry*, Lexington, MA: Lexington Books, 1985, pp. 237–255.

CHAPTER 4

THE CRASH: A REPORT ON THE REPORTS

Franklin R. Edwards

From the close of trading on Friday, October 16, to its lowest point on Tuesday, October 20, a period of just 10 trading hours, the S & P 500 Index fell 22 percent. During the same 10 hours, the S & P 500 Futures Index fell 36 percent. This precipitous drop in prices on October 19 and 20, 1987, and the events that surrounded it, are now known as the Crash of 1987. The 1987 stock market plunge was the worst ever. Even in the infamous year 1929, no day was worse than October 19. (On October 18, 1929, the Dow Jones Index fell 12.82 percent.)

The crash was not without warning. In the three days prior, from Wednesday, October 14, through the close on Friday, October 16, the S & P 500 Index fell 10 percent. Over the intervening weekend, fear overwhelmed investors and produced massive sell orders in the early hours of October 19, even before any markets in the United States had opened. From its high point in August 1987, to its lowest point on Tuesday, October 20, 1987, the stock market fell by 40 percent, a remarkable episode even measured by the cataclysmic events of 1929. Indeed, there are striking similarities between the two crashes. In 1929, the Dow Jones Industrial fell by about 34 percent from its peak in September to the end of 1929. In 1987, the Dow fell by 31 percent from its peak in August to the end of 1987.

The 1987 crash was not restricted to U.S. markets: stock prices plunged throughout the world from their high points in 1987. The London stock market dropped 26 percent; in Tokyo it fell 20 percent; and in

Hong Kong the collapse far exceeded what happened anywhere else. It is little wonder that in just four months since the October crash we have had some six extensive studies of what happened. What went wrong? Are we heading toward another Great Depression? Do we need new— and immediate—regulations to prevent an impending disaster?

The studies by the Presidential Task Force (the Brady Commission), the Commodity Futures Trading Commission (CFTC), the Securities and Exchange Commission (SEC), the General Accounting Office (GAO), the New York Stock Exchange (NYSE), and the Chicago Mercantile Exchange (CME)[1] have already produced a large number of conclusions and recommendations, as well as almost 3,000 pages of analyses. Not surprisingly, the reports do not draw the same conclusions, nor do they arrive at the same policy solutions, and in some instances their recommendations stand in glaring conflict.

The purpose of this paper is to put these studies and their conclusions in perspective. It is not a line-by-line comparison and analysis. That itself would result in still another study of several hundred pages. Instead, my focus is on major conclusions and theses, and on determining what it all means. Each of the studies in its own way has held a magnifying glass to the events of last October and has discovered a wealth of rich detail. This paper adopts a more distant perspective, stepping back from this detail to see if a coherent picture can be constructed.

STUDIES OF THE CRASH

Each study of the crash addresses two obvious questions: What caused the crash? and Did the crash expose weaknesses in our institutional structure? Some studies point to the disorderly market conditions that existed on October 19 and 20 as clear evidence of weaknesses in our financial system.

What caused the crash? The SEC report puts it bluntly: "As a threshold matter, the Report does not answer the question of why in October of 1987 the value of common stocks was reduced by approximately 30 percent. We may never know what precise combination of investor psychology, economic developments and trading technologies caused the events of October" (p. xi).

The Brady Commission report says simply: "The precipitous market decline . . . was 'triggered' by specific events: an unexpectedly high merchandise trade deficit which pushed interest rates to new high levels, and proposed tax legislation which led to the collapse of the stocks of a number of takeover candidates" (p. x).

And, finally, in recent testimony before the Senate Banking Committee, Chairman Greenspan of the Federal Reserve summarized: "The bull market of 1987 had brought stock prices to levels which stretched to incredulity expectations of rising real earnings and falling discount factors. Something had to snap. If it didn't happen in October, it would have happened soon thereafter. The immediate cause of the break was incidental. The market plunge was an accident waiting to happen."

To generalize somewhat, and perhaps to go further than some of the studies would wish to, all of the reports conclude that a combination of speculative euphoria in world stock markets and serious underlying macroeconomic disequilibria set the stage for a crisis of confidence that inevitably would have, and finally did, precipitate a market break. The reports do not analyze these economic forces, and do not recommend what we might do to prevent the same factors from initiating still another crash. It is clear that the same fundamental economic problems that existed last October still exist today. Perhaps this is why Nicholas Brady said in recent testimony before the Senate Banking Committee, "We are looking down the barrel, and the gun is still loaded."

Disorderly markets. The studies devote most of their attention to the speed with which prices fell on October 19, to the market dislocations that resulted, and whether, according to the SEC report, "the trading systems for stock and its derivatives (i.e., options and futures) . . . contributed to the rapidity and depth of the market decline" (p. xi).

Two main concerns permeate the studies: (1) concern about the disorderly conditions that existed in the stock, futures, and options markets on October 19 and 20; and (2) concern about what could have happened but did not: a general economic collapse caused by the failure of futures and options clearing associations, and by the widespread bankruptcy of broker-dealers and market-makers.

Disorderly conditions in both the stock market and the derivative markets were common on October 19 and 20. Unprecedented trading volume caused breakdowns in computer systems, in the NYSE's designated order turnaround system (DOT), and in the ITS communication system linking the seven major stock exchanges and the NASD. For example, NYSE specialists failed to respond to 65.9 percent of the trade messages they received from regional specialists at the six other stock exchanges.

Large order imbalances swamped market-makers who either did nothing or changed prices in a haphazard and disorderly fashion, often refusing to take orders at all. Uncertainty was pervasive. Investors did not know whether they could (or did) execute trades. Quoted prices were fictitious, in the sense that substantial (or any) trades could not be done at these prices.

All markets were closed at one time or another. On October 20, the S & P 500 futures market was closed from 12:15 P.M. to 1:05 P.M. Even worse conditions prevailed on the NYSE. On the morning of October 19, 197 stocks failed to open for trading promptly; and by 11:30 A.M., 41 of these remained unopened. On October 20, 90 stocks failed to open; and by 11:30 A.M., 15 still remained unopened. During the course of the day, trading had to be halted in 175 stocks, including some of the most actively traded issues. The worst conditions existed at the CBOE. On October 19, free trading did not begin until 12:36 P.M.; and on October 20, not until 3:23 P.M.—allowing just 52 minutes of free trading. There was, therefore, almost a total breakdown of trading on the CBOE.

The financial community was shocked by the seeming frailty of these markets. Lost in the confusion was the striking fact that the markets ultimately succeeded in weathering an unprecedented rise in trading volume and the sharpest price drop in our history. That liquidity was not all that we had hoped it would be is not terribly surprising. How many other financial markets would have fared as well in the face of such a crisis of confidence? Still, the crash did expose weaknesses in our institutional structure, and it provides an unprecedented experience we can use to forge an even-better institutional structure.

Fear of an economic collapse. In some of the six studies there is a clear undercurrent of concern that a general financial collapse could have occurred because of the insolvency of a clearing association or the widespread bankruptcy of broker-dealers. When stock prices plummeted, enormous variation margin was demanded of customers with long futures and long put option positions. The speed with which prices fell prevented customers from liquidating their positions before incurring massive losses. On October 19 alone, the CME, BOTCC, and the OCC made intra-day variation margin calls of $3 billion. On October 20, the same clearing associations called for another $3 billion in margin during the day. Although almost all of these demands were met by customers on October 19 and 20, a concern permeates some of the studies that the outcome could have been much worse. If the market had continued to fall on Tuesday, October 20, instead of rising as it did, would customers and clearing firms have been able to meet the additional margin calls? And, if not, would clearing associations have collapsed, closing futures and options markets? Broker-dealers, too, might have suffered large defaults in margined stock accounts, throwing them into bankruptcy. Finally, if all this happened, banks could have experienced massive loan defaults, threatening their viability as well.

A number of institutional failures in the clearing process also caused unnecessary liquidity problems that could have undermined some firms. For example, in one case variation margin payments of about $1.5 billion, owed to two clearing firms, were paid five hours later than due, causing a severe liquidity problem for these firms because they had to make margin payments to other firms before receiving what was due them. There also was a lack of coordination among the different clearing associations regarding the margins imposed on traders and the collections and payments of variation margins, again causing an unnecessary liquidity squeeze. Problems such as these, it was feared, might have precipitated bankruptcies with potentially far-reaching effects.

How close this came to happening, we shall never know. None of the studies attempts to draw out a possible disaster scenario so that we might gain some appreciation of the potential gravity of the events of October.

The Brady Commission, in a little-known Appendix titled "A Comparison of 1929 and 1987," does examine the similarities between October 1987 and 1929. It concludes, among other things, that the 1929 crash was not caused by margin calls forcing stock sales to cover margin requirements, and that the 1929 crash was the result not of a simple crisis of confidence, but of a continuing deterioration in the real economy. The study goes on to say that today's economy "appears to be far more stable than it was in 1929," and that "the Great Depression appears to have been caused not by the stock market crash but by the interaction of a number of diverse circumstances (such as the declines in agriculture and housing) and misguided policies (such as the Smoot-Hawley Tariff, the tight monetary policy in late 1931 and the tax increase in the summer of 1932). . . . As long as a similar set of circumstances and policy initiatives are avoided, a comparable economic contraction should remain only a remote possibility" (pp. viii–10).

We are, therefore, left with the unanswered and unsettling question of whether the circumstances and economic policies that caused confidence to evaporate in October 1987—and that continue to exist today—might strike us once again in the future to initiate still another contraction. Are we not as vulnerable today to misguided policies as we were in 1929?

WERE FUTURES MARKETS RESPONSIBLE?

A striking feature of all of the studies is their focus on the role that derivative markets played in the crash. Some of the studies (such as those of the CFTC and CME) are defensive, explaining why futures and options markets could not have played a destructive role. Others (such as the NYSE and the SEC) are accusatory, attacking futures markets especially as having had a destabilizing effect. The SEC, for example, says "futures trading, and strategies involving the use of futures, were not the 'sole cause' of the so-called market break. Nevertheless, the existence of futures on stock indexes and the use of the various strategies involving 'program trading' (i.e., index arbitrage, index substitution and portfolio insurance) were a significant factor in accelerating and exacerbating the decline" (pp. 3–11). To understand the attention devoted to futures markets, it is necessary to recognize the market developments that preceded the October crash.

The first and perhaps most instructive development is that well prior to the crash stock index futures began playing a significant role in securities markets. In just five years from their introduction in 1982, the SEC report states stock index futures "became the market of choice for many institutions that trade actively" (pp. 3–17). Daily trading volume in S & P 500 index futures alone grew to more than twice the average daily dollar volume of trading on the New York Stock Exchange—the equivalent of about $16 billion a day. In addition, options on stock indexes became the fastest-growing segment of the options market. By October 1987, they accounted for more than 43 percent of total options contract volume.

Second, the institutionalization of equity markets has steadily increased in the United States, caused by the rapid growth of pension funds and mutual funds, along with more aggressive institutional investment strategies. Institutions now hold equity equal to about 40 percent of the value of all NYSE listed stocks, and may account for as much as 80 percent of total trading volume. Further, in recent years block transactions alone have accounted for 50 percent of volume on the NYSE.

Third, in the last few years the value of indexed assets under management has grown remarkably, to over $200 billion. This in turn has produced the rapid growth of program trading, through which institutions make large trades simultaneously in many different stocks (such as those that make up the S & P 500 index). This has become known as basket trading. Currently, as much as 25 percent of all institutional trading is accomplished by the use of program (or basket) trades.

Fourth, futures markets have become the markets of choice for such program trading because they provide a cheaper and more efficient transaction mechanism. Brokerage fees are much lower for futures transactions; and, because of greater market liquidity, execution costs in futures markets are substantially below what they are in the cash (or stock) market. In general, it costs seven to ten times more to execute the same trade on the floor of the NYSE than to do it with S & P 500 futures at the CME. Put simply, futures exchanges have provided a superior trading vehicle for large institutions.

Fifth, these developments were responsible for the advent and growth of portfolio insurance futures trading strategies. Used as a substitute for direct selling on the NYSE (through, for example, the placing of limit orders), portfolio insurance provided what appeared to be a significantly lower-cost strategy for protecting (or hedging) a portfolio. By 1987, as much as $100 billion of managed portfolio assets were covered by this strategy.

Sixth, because of temporary liquidity inadequacies, large institutional selling and buying of futures contracts frequently drove futures prices to levels above or below their fair value levels—the price level consistent with the underlying stock values adjusted for net carrying costs. The result was a sharp increase in stock index arbitrage and "yield-enhancing" program trading activities.

Finally, these trading strategies combined to produce excessive stock price volatility on certain days, such as at the expiration of S & P 500 futures contracts (known as the Triple-Witching Hour). As a consequence, there was widespread fear that futures markets had in general become a destabilizing force. Although there was no evidence to support this view, it nevertheless caused calls to curb stock index futures trading.[2]

With this background, it is easy to understand why a central preoccupation of the studies was the role that futures trading played in the October market break.

What is the evidence that futures-related activities either precipitated or deepened the price plunge? The Brady Commission and the SEC point to two pieces of evidence. The first is the direct impact of institutional selling in futures markets, and particularly of portfolio insurance sales. The Brady Commission report claims that on October 19 such sales amounted to 34,500 contracts (equivalent to $4 billion of stocks), which was 40 percent of total S & P futures volume that day, *exclusive* of locals' (or floor traders) transactions (p. 36).[3] The SEC report states that on October 19 arbitrage and substitution programs, together with portfolio insurance selling strategies, comprised 14.7 percent of total NYSE volume and 21.1 percent of S & P 500 stock volume, and that between 1:00 P.M. and 2:00 P.M. on that day "the combination of selling from portfolio insurance and index arbitrage totalled more than 40 percent of volume in the stocks comprising the S & P 500 index— and totalled more than 60 percent of S & P 500 stock volume in three different 10 minute intervals within that hour" (p. xiii).[4]

The second piece of evidence relates to the alleged indirect "negative market psychology" effects of futures markets. The Brady Commission says, "the large discount between futures and stocks acted as a 'billboard', worrying many investors that further [stock] declines were imminent" (p. 40). At its low on October 20, for example, the S & P 500 futures price implied a Dow level of about 1400. The SEC argues: "the knowledge by market participants of the existence of active portfolio insurance strategies created . . . a market 'overhang' effect in both futures and stock markets; this resulted in the maintenance of futures discounts that discouraged institutional traders from participating in the stock market on the buy side, specialists from committing capital to maintain fair and orderly markets, and block positioning firms from maintaining normal levels of activity" (p. xiii).

Neither piece of evidence is convincing. First, with respect to the effect of portfolio insurance sales, the fact that such sales were 20 percent of total futures sales on October 19—the largest volume day and the sharpest price drop ever—suggests that such sales were *not* a dominant feature of the sell-off. Eighty percent of the sales came from other sources! The fact simply shows that the sell-off was general, and not specific to portfolio insurers. Second, looking at particular short time segments, such as 10-minute intervals or even specific hour intervals (as the SEC does), is not a useful mode of analysis. Since trading is sequential, it is obvious that it is possible to pick an arbitrarily small time interval to show that a particular seller's proportion of total sales is whatever percentage we would like to make it—even 100 percent. What is a relevant time interval within which to analyze a particular trader's market impact? And for what purpose? Evidence drawn from discretionary short intervals of time is so arbitrary that its meaningfulness is open to serious question. Third, it is doubtful that looking at the proportion of total sales accounted for by a particular type of seller is meaningful. While it does show that these sellers were present in the market, it certainly does not show that their selling "caused" the price decline. Prices are determined by both sellers and buyers (and by their expectations). The buyers who were not there on October 19 were just as responsible for the price decline as the sellers who were there. The issue of price determination and causality is considerably more complicated than the studies seem to recognize.

With respect to the alleged negative psychology effect of futures, the studies misplace the emphasis. The large and unusual discounts that futures prices exhibited on October 19 and surrounding days were almost certainly due largely to the prevalence of fictitious price quotations on the NYSE. Specialists were unable to cope with the trading volume and order imbalances and, as a consequence, either did not open trading in stocks or quoted prices at which little trading could be done. Futures prices, on the other hand, continued to reflect market forces. Futures prices fell below *quoted* stock prices because futures prices reflected market forces whereas stock prices did not. If this discount had a negative market impact, it was for good reason: it reflected the current market outlook. Should markets that transmit investors' expectations and psychology accurately be condemned as "causing" a later fall in prices that were previously kept artificially high?

It might be argued that futures prices overreacted, falling to excessively low levels. Stock prices never fell to levels reached (or implied) by the lowest level reached by futures prices. On October 20, the S & P 500 futures reached a low of 216, implying a Dow level of about 1400. The lowest *recorded* (or quoted) level reached by the Dow was only 1738, on October 19.

Is this evidence of futures overshooting? Not necessarily. First, at that time stock prices were not reflective of market forces. Some stocks were not trading at all, and most had unrealistic price quotations. The NYSE was simply not functioning well. Stock prices were obviously being kept artificially high. Second, stock index arbitrage activity (or arbitrage between futures and cash markets) that would have provided buying support for futures was severely curtailed because DOT was no longer available to key market participants and because stock orders could not be executed at the prevailing fictitious stock price quotes. In addition, rules against selling stocks short on a downtick may have inhibited stock index arbitrage. Thus, if futures prices went too low, a large part of the blame must be placed at the doorstep of the NYSE, which inhibited arbitrageurs from buying futures. Whether futures markets should be held responsible for the resulting alleged negative psychological effect is questionable. Equally destructive psychologically was the malfunctioning of the NYSE and the breakdown of the market-making system in the over-the-counter stock market.

Finally, if the market plunge was caused by temporary futures trading activities, how can we explain the fact that the crash was worldwide? Stock markets in London, Tokyo, Hong Kong, Sydney, Singapore, Paris, Milan, Frankfurt, and elsewhere experienced massive sell-offs on October 19 and 20, despite the absence of significant (or any) futures trading in those markets.[5] (New York and London fell 23 percent, and Tokyo 17 percent.) It is ironic to note that a post-crash study by the London Stock Exchange concluded there is a need "to encourage techniques such as index arbitrage . . . [to] help minimize the difficulties experienced." Further, the U.S. stock market did not quickly recoup its losses, and has still not regained its pre–October 1987 levels. If short-term futures selling and temporary negative market psychology were the causal factors, we would have expected the market to regain its losses soon after the disappearance of these factors. That it has not suggests that fundamental economic conditions, and not futures-related activities, were the true causes.

In summary, at least from this reader's vantage point, neither the Brady Commission nor the SEC is able to construct a convincing case against futures markets, despite what appears to be an extensive effort to do so. I am doubtful a convincing case can be made.

POLICY RECOMMENDATIONS

Of the six reports, three make sweeping policy recommendations that may require significant new regulations: the Brady Commission, the NYSE, and the SEC reports. While the GAO, CFTC, and CME reports all recognize certain institutional and market failings, they do not envision that the correction of these will require significant regulatory intervention. For this reason, I single out for description and analyses the major recommendations made by the Brady Commission, the NYSE, and the SEC. .

The Brady Commission concludes that the major lesson of the crash is "the pressing need for coordination of intermarket issues" and that most of the problems "could be traced to intermarket failures." The Commission makes five specific recommendations.

1. There should be one super government agency with the authority to coordinate intermarket regulatory issues and to monitor and mediate intermarket concerns. The close intermarket relationships among stock, futures, and options markets are seen as necessitating a more unified regulatory approach. Further, since central banks have primary responsibility for the health of their financial systems, the Federal Reserve is the best choice to bear this responsibility in the United States.

2. Clearing and credit mechanisms need to be unified. Stocks, stock index futures, and stock options should all be cleared through a single mechanism. Unified clearing is seen as improving risk management and facilitating a more orderly flow of margin funds. The result is seen as enhancing the soundness of clearing organizations and the stability of the financial system.

3. Margin levels on stock index futures need to be raised to levels consistent with the margins imposed on professional market participants in the stock market. These are currently in the 20 to 25 percent range. This recommendation stems from the belief that leverage determines the volume of speculative activity. It is alleged that by controlling speculative behavior we can prevent the overvaluation of stocks and thereby reduce the potential for a precipitous price decline. The Federal Reserve would presumably establish margin levels in all markets.

4. There is a need to design and implement coherent, coordinated trading halts. All markets, it is contended, have a limited capacity, and there are limits to intermarket liquidity as well. When these are reached, as in turbulent and disorderly markets, breakdowns and trading halts are inevitable. Thus, the Brady Commission believes it is preferable to have trading halts occur in a predictable and coordinated fashion, rather than as *ad hoc* emergency actions. No specific plan or design for trading halts is advanced, although price limits are mentioned as one possible type of trading halt mechanism.

5. Intermarket monitoring and information systems need to be improved. A trading information system should incorporate the trade, time of the trade, and the name of the ultimate customer in every major market segment. This would permit the appropriate regulatory agency to indentify threats to the intermarket system in a timely fashion and to assess the nature and cause of a market crisis.

The report commissioned by the NYSE prior to the October crash (the Katzenbach study) focused on the role of futures markets. Its report makes the following recommendations:

1. The NYSE should consider trading one or two broad stock indices on its own floor, similar to those traded by futures exchanges.

2. Interrelationships among exchanges need to be dealt with either by regulatory agencies or by agreements between the exchanges that are approved by regulatory authorities.

3. The NYSE should use the DOT system to accommodate large block sales by making the sale simultaneously available for bid by all interested broker-dealers. This is an attempt to make trading more open than it is under the existing specialist system.

4. Settlement in index futures should be "in kind" and not on the basis of cash settlement, as is currently the case. The report believes that "cash settlement . . . leads to excessive leverage, speculation, and an impression of more liquidity than in fact exists" (p. 31).

5. Margin requirements on index futures and options should be raised to levels consistent with those on stock transactions. The report states, "We are convinced . . . that the present system encourages speculation by making it so inexpensive and so leveraged" (p. 31).

6. The exchanges, together with the Federal Reserve Board, should develop a coordinated contingency plan in the event of an emergency.

The report also draws two additional conclusions, which, while not policy recommendations, are nevertheless of interest:

- the institution of either position limits or price limits will not solve the problems that exist; and
- there is no serious risk that foreign exchanges will be able to trade futures and options on a cash settlement basis and thereby attract trading away from the United States. However, the reports that "serious negotiations with [foreign] regulating authorities take place in an effort to achieve some common policies with respect

to trading, manipulation, open information, security transactions, and so forth" (p. 31).

The SEC's study begins by adopting "the fundamental assumption that extreme price volatility is undesirable." Such volatility, the SEC maintains, reduces overall market liquidity, lessens market efficiency, and reduces investor confidence in the stock market. To curb market volatility the SEC suggests limiting certain computerized trading strategies that use stock index futures and altering a number of market regulations.

The SEC study makes the following recommendations:

1. Higher margins should be imposed on stock index futures.

2. A specialist post should be established on the floor of the NYSE to trade the cash (or spot) baskets of stocks represented by stock index futures, where the baskets of stocks would presumably be backed by some kind of index certificates.

3. Owners of stock index futures contracts should have the right to receive delivery of the underlying stock at the expiration of the contract. (In other words, the present cash delivery provision would be replaced by physical delivery.)

4. Trading in stock index futures and options should not begin until most of the individual stocks that make up the index are trading.

5. Program trading information should be publicly disseminated, and the NYSE's DOT system should be enhanced.

6. The uptick short sale restrictions now applicable to stock transactions should also be imposed on short selling of stock index futures.

7. Better market-surveillance systems, increased reporting requirements for large trades including program trading, and higher capital requirements for specialist and broker-dealers are needed. The Commission (as well as the CFTC) expressed concern over cross-market trading abuses, such as intermarket front-running. However, in contrast to the Brady Commission, the SEC does not call for the creation of a super-regulator (such as the Federal Reserve) to decide key issues involving the stock, options, and futures markets. (In later testimony, Chairman Ruder indicated that the SEC should be given final regulatory authority for all equity-related products where critical intermarket decisions are involved.)

8. Price limits should not be imposed on stock trading, although brief trading halts based on preset standards warrant further consideration.

9. Various improvements should be made to increase the efficiency of the automated settlement systems used by clearing associations; and clearing associations should improve their risk management systems to decrease the chances of default.

To summarize, all the studies call for better intermarket coordination, and better reporting and market-surveillance systems, although they differ about how these should be achieved. The Brady Commission, SEC, and NYSE recommend that margins be raised on stock index futures transactions to levels consistent with stock transactions. The Brady Commission recommends some form of circuit breakers or trading halts, while the SEC suggests that we study their usefulness. Since consistency across markets and exchanges would be desirable, recommendations for new margin and trading halt policies would presumably require new regulations.

The margin and trading halt recommendations are an effort to bolster the present market-making systems, which showed a significant frailty during the crash. Noticeably missing in the studies is a call for substantial reform of current market-making systems. It seems apparent that an important lesson of the crash is that we need to review our market-making systems, and especially the specialist system, to determine their ability to deal adequately with the emerging institutional trading. Proposals to establish a specialist post to trade stock indices and to increase the capital available to specialists are a recognition of this deficiency, but they implicitly accept the present market-making system as potentially adequate. We should explore other, quite different, market-making systems as well.

MARGINS AND TRADING HALTS: THE DEBATE

Of all the recommendations, two appear to have attracted considerable support, and, if adopted, would probably require additional government regulation. These are to raise margins on futures transactions (and presumably on stock index futures options) and to require exchanges to implement trading halts.[6] Many see them as measures that would stabilize markets without imposing appreciable costs on investors or traders.

The Securities and Exchange Act of 1934 gave the Federal Reserve Board authority to regulate initial and maintenance margins on all private securities purchased on credit. The Board has used this authority to set *initial* margins on stocks and stock options (including stock index options), leaving the responsibility for setting maintenance margins to self-regulatory organizations, subject to the SEC oversight. It has been argued that Congress should extend this authority to futures and options on futures indexes. In the remainder of this section, the consequences of imposing such regulations are considered.

Margins

The debate about whether higher margins should be imposed on stock index futures is *not* a debate about whether current margin levels in futures markets are sufficient to maintain market integrity. Futures margins are security deposits, whose purpose is to ensure that futures traders honor their contractual obligations. In the event of a trader default, futures commission merchants (FCMs) and futures clearing associations are protected because they hold customer margin deposits. Margins on futures do not involve extensions of credit, as they do in securities markets.

Futures margins are now established by FCMs and clearing associations, and not by government. Margin levels vary for different commodities and different types and sizes of transactions, and they can be changed at any time. Their levels are related to the risk associated with specific commodities and transactions. Customer positions are marked-to-market daily, and additional variation margin is called for daily (or even intra-day) if a customer incurs trading losses.

The events of October 1987 showed this system to be remarkably sound. Although substantial margin calls were issued ($3 billion by futures and options exchanges on both October 19 and 20), there were few defaults. Despite a historic market drop, futures markets came through almost unscathed. There were no major FCM defaults and no clearing association defaults. Whether this system might have cracked had prices continued to fall, and at what point, we do not know. That it did not break in October is testimony to its strength.

The recommendation to raise margins on futures contracts to levels consistent with those imposed on stock trading is based upon a belief that higher margins *reduce speculative activity* and, as a consequence, *increase market stability*. For example, the Brady Commission report declares: "Controlling speculative behavior is one approach to inhibiting overvaluation in stock and reducing the potential for a precipitous price decline fueled by involuntary selling that stems, for example, from margin calls" (p. 65). The SEC report similarly argues:

> Low derivative product margins may contribute to the increased velocity of institutional trading in two ways. First, . . . present margin requirements permit institutions to buy and sell larger futures positions without being required to substantially increase the amount of their assets maintained in cash equivalents. Second, low margins contribute to speculative trading that, under normal conditions, contributes to the illusion of almost unlimited liability in the futures markets. During a market break, however, that liquidity disappears at a rate geometrically larger than liquidity in the lower leveraged stock market. (pp. 3–22)

These recommendations do not appear to be based on the events of October 19 and 20. Higher margins on those days would have made no difference. The selling in futures markets that the reports point to as particularly harmful was by pension funds, trusts, and other large institutions. These institutions do not operate with leverage, and would not have been constrained by higher margin requirements. They could easily have borrowed against their stock positions to meet higher futures margins. In addition, futures exchanges permit such institutions to use letters of credit to meet initial margin requirements, and, in any case, require only hedger margins of these institutions, which are much lower than speculator margins.[7] Thus, at least with respect to October 19 and 20, higher futures margins would not have prevented the market plunge.[8]

More likely, the impact of higher futures margins would have fallen most heavily on speculators. On October 19 and 20, both large and small speculators were net buyers, offsetting rather than reinforcing the sell-order imbalance. If higher margins had been in place during the crash, the result could very well have been worse: speculators might have been deterred from playing the stabilizing role that they did.[9]

The argument for higher futures margins, therefore, rests not on a factual basis but on two propositions: first, that higher margins reduce speculative activity; and second, that by reducing speculative activity, prices can be made more stable and excessive price fluctuations eliminated. While it is possible that higher margins would reduce speculative activity (as well as other trading), it is not clear that less speculative trading would diminish the magnitude of price movements in either direction. Speculation is as likely to be stabilizing as destabilizing.[10]

Our experience, for example, with the dramatic increase in silver prices during 1979–80 is not reassuring. As silver prices rose, exchanges substantially increased margins. The effect, however, was not to deter the long speculators, but to make participation in the market by both short hedgers and short speculators more expensive. Many of the shorts exited the market, causing prices to rise even further. Therefore, there is little evidence that in this case higher margins succeeded either in controlling speculative activity or in dampening price fluctuations. In practice, the effects of different margin levels are more subtle and less obvious than intuition might suggest. The impact of higher margins can fall on either longs or shorts or both, with unpredictable results.

Stock and other asset prices may also be determined more by the expectations of asset holders than by marginal trading activity. Asset prices can change sharply with little trading. There need be no direct relationship between the volume of futures trading and the magnitude of a commodity's price change. The value of real estate, for example, often changes substantially with few transactions, or even with no transactions. Stock and futures markets are no different. Higher futures margins, which work by increasing trading costs and reducing trading activity, need have no predictable or appreciable impact on either price levels or price volatility.

Higher futures margins also are not without cost. They increase the costs to futures market participants and, in particular, to speculators. This will reduce both the volume of trading and open interest, and, therefore, market liquidity. The result will be higher transaction costs and possibly greater price volatility. In addition, hedgers' costs may rise because of increased basis risk and possible increased risk premium. Thus, the argument that higher margins on futures contracts will be beneficial because they curb speculative excesses without cost is questionable.

In a 1984 study of margins, "A Review and Evaluation of Federal Margin Regulations," the Federal Reserve Board reviewed evidence about whether low margins caused instability in stock prices or temporary speculative bubbles. It concluded:

> The evidence and arguments reviewed . . . do not indicate a need for margin regulation to curb short-term speculation. . . . The behavior of stock prices since the enactment of margin regulation also does not support the argument that controlled margin trading will tend to reduce stock volatility. Despite the relatively high federal margin levels and the very low levels of margin credit since the early 1930's . . . stock prices have continued to be about as volatile as they were in the 50 years preceding margin regulation. (pp. 152 and 167)

There is, therefore, no reason to believe that higher futures margins will reduce price instability in either the stock or futures markets. The only certainty is that they will impose higher costs on investors and traders.[11]

Trading Halts

Trading halts, or circuit breaker mechanisms as the Brady Commission has dubbed them, are perceived as cushioning the impact of market movements and protecting both markets and investors. They do this, the Brady Commission argues, by providing a time-out from trading, which gives market participants an opportunity to make credit arrangements, to assess market conditions, to consult with clients, and to locate additional orders that would enhance market liquidity. In addition, if there are computer or back-office problems, they allow time to resolve these.

Trading halts can take many forms and can be triggered by a variety of predetermined threshold variables. One of the most common types of trading halt is the daily price limit: when a price move of more than a prescribed amount occurs in either direction, the market is closed for the remainder of the day.[12] Such limits are common in futures markets, but until recently they were not imposed on stock index futures.[13] Trading halts can also be imposed, for example, if trading volume hits a certain level or a substantial order imbalance appears. Or such halts can take the form of regular time-outs (every hour, for example). There is no limit to how one can construct and institute a trading halt, but imposing a price limit is usually the one that first comes to mind.

The SEC, unlike the Brady Commission, is not convinced about the virtue of price limits, but nevertheless it leaves open the possibility of other types of trading halts. It says:

> We do not believe . . . that price limits should be imposed on stock trading, although brief trading halts based on pre-set standards may warrant further consideration. The automatic closure of stock trading for the remainder of the day . . . imposes unacceptable burdens on those market participants who wish to liquidate their positions and increases the potential that a volatile market situation can slide into panic. . . . The closure of the Hong Kong Stock Exchange provides a graphic example of the risks entailed in closing a stock market. (pp. 3–24)

Price limits. There are several arguments against using price limits. First, if new information requires a price change larger than the allowable price range, trading halts will delay the determination of equilibrium prices. This may cause trading to take place at disequilibrium prices, injuring some traders. It also interferes with the price discovery function of futures markets because quoted prices no longer reflect existing economic information.

Second, if futures markets are closed, traders are deprived of their use at the very time they would want to use them the most: when new information dictates a substantial change in prices. At such times, hedgers may want to put on new hedges or to lift prior hedges. Price limits can both lock them out and in. The inability to trade at these times could be a serious deterrent to the use of futures markets by potential hedgers. The prospect of being locked-in is anathema to speculators as well, for it prevents them from getting out when they need to most. Discouraging speculation can result in less market liquidity.

It is also possible that, if market participants know that trading will be halted when prices reach a certain level, price limits may become self-fulfilling: traders may buy or sell frantically to beat the closing of the market so that they are not locked-in.

The argument in favor of price limits rests upon the notion that large price movements may be the result of excessive (or irrational) speculation. In this case, there may be a reason to slow things down, since market prices are wrong to begin with. However, even in this case it is not clear that trading halts will hasten the return to correct prices. Preventing prices from changing may increase the response time of rational traders to disequilibrium prices, slowing the return to more rational prices. Further, at times price limits may have the opposite effect from what we expect: they may increase uncertainty and cause even greater irrational market activity.

The dramatic rise and fall of silver prices from September 1979 to March 1980 again demonstrates how trading halts due to daily price limits worked in a situation of substantial price instability. During this seven-month period, practically every day was a limit-price day—trading halted when prices moved the allowable daily range. It is questionable, however, whether these limits dampened the overall price movements in silver. Silver prices rose from about $8 to almost $55 an ounce, and then fell to almost $10. Trading halts did delay these price movements, but whether that was beneficial is not clear.

Another argument is that price limits are useful in slowing down large price movements that otherwise might inflict severe damage on the financial structure because of institutional rigidities. This argument raises two questions. First, would artificially slowing down price adjustments successfully insulate an institutional structure in the face of true changes in equilibrium prices? If everyone understands what the true prices are, will they not adapt their behavior accordingly? Second, if large price changes are due to infrequent speculative excesses, do the social benefits of curbing these infrequent episodes outweigh the social costs of interfering with markets on a regular basis? If speculative excesses are rare, which I believe to be the case, the costs of having price limits may outweigh their benefits.

Other types of trading halts. Another possible type of trading halt is to stop trading when large buy or sell order imbalances occur. Market-makers could, for example, delay changing prices for a predetermined length of time—say 5 or 10 minutes—to see if counterbalancing orders might arise during this time interval. Presumably, the existence and magnitude of the order imbalance would be disclosed to a broad range of traders, or even to the entire public. In this case, the market remains open for trading at the quoted (or last) price, in contrast to the usual procedure for daily price limits. If the order imbalance persists, market-makers might then change prices according to a predetermined schedule, waiting for a short time at each new price for new orders to surface. At all times, however, the market would remain open for counterbalancing orders.

The rationale for this procedure is that an information deficiency (or asymmetry) often exists. In the case of a sell-order imbalance, for example, sellers may misperceive the fundamentals, or potential buyers may lack complete information, part of which is the existence of the sell-order imbalance itself. Thus, short trading halts may prevent prices from moving to short-term disequilibrium levels because of a temporary absence of liquidity.

The reports, unfortunately, neither propose specific types of trading halts nor discuss the specifics of how such halts might work. It is difficult, therefore, to place much weight on their recommendation that we institute trading halts. The institutional details of how and when such halts would be used is critical to appraising their probable effects. In addition, various types of trading halts have been employed for years in foreign equity and futures markets. It would be useful to study how well these have worked those markets before experimenting with them at home. Such circuit breakers obviously did not succeed in keeping foreign markets from falling sharply on October 19 and 20. Nevertheless, it may be constructive to study in greater depth the usefulness of order imbalance types of trading halts.

One thing is clear, however. If trading halts such as price limits are imposed on futures markets, they should be imposed on stock trading as well. The arguments in favor of halts apply equally to the stock market. Further, if only one market is closed, the natural trading links between the two markets will result in trading pressures and order imbalances being transferred to the market that is still open.[14] This distortion will exacerbate market pressures, which is precisely what happened on October 19 when the NYSE effectively prevented arbitrage between the futures and cash markets.[15]

CONCLUSION

While the reports of the crash provide a large body of interesting and instructive information, we are left with two major impressions. First, we still do not understand what forces caused the October stock market plunge. As a consequence, we do not know whether the same economic forces still exist and, if so, whether they are likely to cause another crash in the future. Second, none of the reports makes a convincing case for new government regulations or initiatives. There is no reason to think, for example, that higher margins on futures contracts or trading halts would have prevented the precipitous drop in prices in October, or would prevent a similar market crash in the future.

The reports, however, do identify weaknesses in the present institutional mechanisms where improvements can be made—in intermarket coordination, clearing mechanisms, information collection and sharing, computer systems, and so forth. Any market or institutional structure subjected to the kind of severe shock we had in October is going to show unexpected weaknesses. Exchanges themselves are likely to be the first to recognize these and to take steps to remedy them.[16] The key is to identify weaknesses where improvements are needed, but where entrenched self-interest groups prevent actions to remedy these deficiencies. This is where government intervention could be productive. Where changes are likely to be made voluntarily because it is in the interests of exchanges to make them, additional government regulation may be counterproductive. The reports do not provide any guidance about which weaknesses are likely to be self-correcting and which may require government action.

There is, finally, a noticeable conservativeness in the recommendations related to the various market-making systems employed by the different exchanges. It seems clear, for example, that the growth of institutional trading of baskets of stock will continue unabated into the future, and that the specialist system as presently constituted at the NYSE is not adequate to cope with the potential order imbalances that such institutional trading can create. We should, therefore, be exploring totally different market-making systems, which have as a central feature larger and more competitive market-makers and a fuller disclosure of order imbalances when they occur.[17] It would have been helpful if the reports had devoted more thought and analysis to the central question of what kind of market-making systems are needed in the future, as well as to the related issue of which regulations are consistent with the desired market-making systems. Such an effort would have been especially useful because there are good reasons to believe that self-interest groups now in power at exchanges have a vested interest in preserving the *status quo*.

All the studies agree with the SEC report that futures and options markets "provide valuable hedging and market timing benefits to institutions" (pp. 3–17). In many ways, therefore, the reports confront us with a situation similar to that in 1910 had people then suddenly been given the use of the modern automobile. While modern automobiles would clearly have been faster, safer, more comfortable, and more efficient, in 1910 there would have been no highways and roads to exploit such advantages. Without adequate roads, automobiles travelling at high speed can be dangerous. Officials in 1910 would have had several alternative courses of action:

- ban the use of the modern automobile completely (similar to prohibiting portfolio insurance, program trading, and index arbitrage);
- restrict its use by raising the cost of obtaining the automobile (similar to raising margins and requiring physical delivery on index futures contracts);
- impose severe speed limits (similar to prohibiting the use of the DOT system by arbitrageurs and imposing the up-tick rule on futures markets);
- require short periods during which automobiles could not be used; for example, fifteen minutes every hour on the hour—in order to permit pedestrians safe passage (similar to requiring trading halts); or

- build a new road system that would permit them to reap the benefits of the modern automobile (similar to developing a better market-making system).

Mercifully, our forefathers chose the latter course of action—to build better roads. We too should develop a market-making system that can cope with the burgeoning institutional trading and that can take full advantage of the benefits that the derivative markets offer. In our search, nothing should be held sacrosanct; everything should be open to examination and improvement. An essential first step is to open a constructive dialogue between stock and futures exchanges on all aspects of trading and operations.

NOTES

1. See *Report of the Presidential Task Force on Market Mechanisms* (January 1988); U.S. Commodity Futures Trading Commission, Division of Economic Analysis and Division of Trading and Markets, *Final Report on Stock Index Futures and Cash Market Activity during October 1987* (January 1988); U.S. Securities and Exchange Commission, Division of Market Regulation, *The October 1987 Market Break* (February 1988); U.S. General Accounting Office, "Financial Markets: Preliminary Observations on the October 1987 Crash." Report to Congressional Requesters (January 1988); N. Katzenbach, "An Overview of Program Trading and Its Impact on Current Market Practices" (The New York Stock Exchange, December 21, 1987); and J. Hawke, B. Malkiel, M. Miller, and M. Scholes, "Preliminary Report of the Committee of Inquiry Appointed by the Chicago Mercantile Exchange to Examine the Events Surrounding October 19, 1987" (December 22, 1987).
2. For evidence on historical volatility, see F. R. Edwards, "Does Futures Trading Increase Stock Market Volatility?", *Financial Analysts Journal*, January–February 1988, pp. 63–69.
3. If locals' transactions of $10 billion are included, as they should be, the percentage falls to 20 percent.
4. There is a difference in the numbers reported in the Brady Commission and in both the SEC and CFTC reports. My impression is that the SEC and CFTC survey numbers are the more accurate. See CFTC Report pp. 80–107. In addition, a distinction should be made between stock index arbitrage trading and portfolio insurance (or hedge) trading. Stock index arbitrage

selling constituted only 6 percent of selling on the NYSE on October 19, and almost nothing on October 20. In contrast, it was more than 13 percent of the selling on October 14 (CFTC Report, p. 38).

5. It should also be noted that the institutional and market-making systems vary significantly in foreign countries, both in comparison to the United States and to each other. Yet, all markets experienced a sharp and rapid price decline.

6. Legislation introduced since October 19 would both authorize and require the Federal Reserve to set margin levels on futures transactions. (See H.R. 3597 and S. 1847). In addition, Senator Patrick Leahy is proposing a bill that would establish an Intermarket Monitoring Council to review, among other things, "the consistency and adequacy of margin requirements and settlement practices in various markets, and make recommendations to the appropriate regulatory agencies or exchanges . . . for appropriate margin levels for various instruments, as the Council deems appropriate" (p. 4).

7. In a recent speech echoing the SEC Report, SEC Chairman Ruder said that increased velocity and concentration of trading volume in the stock and futures markets and between those markets had increased stock price volatility and that this was partly due to the lower levels of margins in futures markets (*Investors Daily*, February 24, 1988, p. 5). An issue I do not discuss in this paper is the SEC's contention that the growing concentration of trading in the hands of a few institutions is causing greater price volatility. It is difficult to see the connection between this argument and the one that low margins cause greater price volatility. In addition, it is important to recognize that institutions such as portfolio insurers and mutual funds may be acting in response to decisions of individual investors and fund managers. The mutual fund sales that occurred on October 19, in particular, were the result of hundreds of independent decisions by investors to redeem their fund shares.

8. It also is a strained argument to contend that low futures margins was the cause of the 30 percent increase (from January to August of 1987) in stock prices leading up to the crash. On October 15 the open position in the S & P 500 futures contract was less than 1 percent of the value of stocks listed on the NYSE. How could this position be held responsible for a 30 percent increase in the value of stocks?

9. It is interesting to note that in Japan one response to the crash has been to lower margins, not raise them. Lower margins can be expected to generate greater market liquidity.

10. There has been a long and inconclusive academic debate about whether speculative activity is on net stabilizing or destabilizing. The results of theoretical models depend critically upon the underlying assumptions that are used. It also has proven difficult to test empirically the effects of

speculation. See, for example, M. Friedman, "The Case for Flexible Exchange Rates," in *Essays in Positive Economics* (Chicago: University of Chicago Press, 1953); A. Beja and B. Goldman, "On the Dynamic Behavior of Prices in Disequilibrium," *Journal of Finance*, May 1980, pp. 235–248; and O. Blanchard, "Bubbles, Rationale Expectations, and Financial Markets," in *Crises in the Economic and Financial Structure*, ed. P. Wachtel (Lexington: Lexington Books, 1982) pp. 295–315.

11. Many studies have attempted to determine the effects of higher margins on both price levels and price volatility in the stock market. In general, these studies find little or no effect. See, for example, R. Grube, O. Joy, and D. Panton, "Market Responses to Federal Reserve Changes in the Initial Margin Requirements," *Journal of Finance*, June 1979, pp. 759–775; T. Moore, "Stock Market Margin Requirements," *Journal of Political Economy*, April 1966, pp. 158–167; G. W. Douglas, "Risk in the Equity Markets: An Empirical Appraisal of Market Efficiency," *Yale Economic Essays*, Spring 1969, pp. 3–45; W. L. Eckards and D. L. Rogoff, "100 Percent Margins Revisited," *Journal of Finance*, June 1976, pp. 995–1000; J. A. Largay, "100 Percent Margins: Combatting Speculation in Individual Security Issues," *Journal of Finance*, September 1973, pp. 973–986; and J. A. Largay and R. R. West, "Margin Changes and Stock Price Behavior," *Journal of Political Economy*, March–April 1973, pp. 328–339.

12. The only exception to this in the United States that I am aware of is the price limit on orange juice futures. In that case, the market is closed for only 15 minutes. To my knowledge this limit has never been triggered, however; so we have no experience with how it works.

13. The CME and CBOT recently imposed daily price limits on stock index futures. On an S & P futures contract with a value of 275 or less, the price limit is 15 index points; on contracts valued from 275.05 to 325, the limit is 20 index points; and on contracts valued at more than 325, the limit is 25 index points. In addition, there is now an opening price limit of 5 index points applicable during the first 10 minutes of scheduled trading each day.

14. This possibility also exists internationally. For example, when the CBOT T-bond futures market hit its price limit on October 20 and was then closed, trading shifted to London, where the volume of trading in U.S. T-bond futures rose eightfold.

15. We are already in some danger of this happening. Subsequent to the crash, the CME and CBOT unilaterally imposed price limits on stock index futures, while the NYSE has unilaterally imposed an automatic restriction on the use of its DOT system by index arbitrageurs—if the Dow moves by more than 50 points, the system is closed to arbitrageurs. If there is another large market move, these restrictions will cause the futures and stock markets to unlink automatically, with potentially serious repercussions.

16. For example, the Chicago Board of Trade Clearing Corporation (BOTCC) is already negotiating with the clearing organizations of options and stock markets to develop a central system to share information. Five years ago, the BOTCC arranged a sharing of daily profit-and-loss information with the Chicago Mercantile Exchange. Last July the eight largest U.S. futures exchanges agreed to share daily profit-and-loss information. The BOTCC operates a computer system that nets clearing members' positions on the participating exchanges.

17. Exchanges could, for example, hold "single price auctions" one or more times a day, where participants would be advised of order imbalances and where all buy and sell orders would be filled at one time and one price. If order imbalances were known, new bids might be forthcoming that would balance the market. In this system, markets could clear without specialists or market-makers having to risk their own capital.

CHAPTER 5

THE VIEW FROM THE NEW YORK STOCK EXCHANGE

Richard A. Grasso

I have a different focus coming out of the October experience than most people. I think of some of my colleagues who were in the trenches during perhaps the most tumultuous week in the history of financial markets. From Friday to Friday, October 16 to October 23 (and the twenty-third was an abbreviated trading session), the NYSE received and processed a volume equivalent to all that we handled in 1967. In five and one-half trading sessions, we saw an entire year pass before our eyes.

It was a difficult time, a challenging time, and a time that many in the financial community have much to be proud of, especially in the planning ranks at the New York Stock Exchange.

Prior to the week of October 19, our stated maximum capacity both for ourselves and the broker-dealer community was between 420 and 450 million shares. Beginning on Friday the sixteenth, we saw successive tests of new levels of activity: 330 million shares on that Friday, 604 million on Monday, and 608 million on Tuesday. Then we had rather mundane days in the 400 million area, and finally we got back to the 300 million and 200 million area. That is an enormous compliment to the flexibility of our trading capabilities and to the imbedded capacity of the industry.

Not until 1982 was the first 100-million-share day experienced; not until 1984 was the first 200-million-share day experienced; and not until January 1987 did the industry experience a 300-million-share day. January the twenty-third became a very fortunate day for those who were involved in long-range planning—on a volume of 303 million shares, the Dow experienced its first triple-digit dislocation. We finished the day off 108 points. To us, that signaled the need to accelerate significantly our planning calendar.

I am happy to have been involved in the process that forecasted a 600-million-share day for the NYSE. I am not particularly pleased that that day was forecast for late in 1990. But our planning staffs built a capacity that withstood the most severe test the institution has ever seen. A snapshot of the order flow to the floor of the NYSE will show how severe that test was. In 1987 we had been experiencing a typical peak of about six orders per second; on Monday, Tuesday and Wednesday, that peak grew to about 25 orders per second. Volume velocity, whether measured in terms of share volume or order messages, was off the seismograph.

But that is all history. There is much to learn from that experience, and our institution has begun to do that in a number of different ways. On the planning and capabilities side, we have developed, together with the industry, a team approach because a team is needed. It is not sufficient for the NYSE to build a capability to handle a six-million-share day or a one-billion-share day if in fact our broker-dealer community cannot accommodate that level of trading activity.

Shortly after the October experience, we assembled a group of operating executives from across the financial community. We have been meeting as frequently as five times a week since October to deal with how the industry, as an integrated unit, can handle the next 600-million-share day and even the first one-billion-share day (which we forecast being able to do by the end of 1989).

Recently, however, volume has dropped off considerably. When you strip away the dividend-capturing on General Telephone, only 105 million shares changed hands on May 16, the slowest day to date in 1988. It would be very easy—in the traditional wisdom of the financial community—to begin throwing capacity over the side as the red ink begins to flow in the second quarter. But one must recognize that long-range planning in our business involves an enormous amount of lead time, both at the market center level and in the broker-dealer communities.

Thus, we have embarked on a specific timetable to handle a 600-

million-share day as it was in October, and to make it feel no different from a 200-million-share day by the mid-part of this year. By the end of next year, we plan to take our first one-billion-share day as a relatively routine exercise.

Will a one-billion-share day arrive in the foreseeable future? Perhaps not, but it will one day. Meanwhile, in terms of the loss of investor confidence, the current period probably is equaled only by the early 1970s. In the period 1973 to 75, ownership actually shrank for the first time since 1952, from some 30 million direct owners of stock and stock mutual funds to some 25 million. It was only when the market began to rebound in late 1976–77 that we again had the 30 million owners that we had experienced coming out of the 1960s.

Investor confidence is at a low for the 1980s. Confidence is affected by a number of issues. There is an enormous perception that the markets, through the use of innovative technology, have created an advantage for the sophisticated institution or individual over the typical retail participant. That perceived advantage goes much further than the 100- or 200- or 500-share purchaser. Active asset managers have an enormous institutional attitude that there has been a tilting of the scales in the equities arena. And we in the equities arena have an enormous responsibility to respond to that perception.

It is not a quick process. It is not subject to interim fixes, nor can it be done by a public relations campaign. Rather, a substantive effort by this industry is required to deal with both the realities and the perceptions of inequity.

This perception was underscored not so much by October 19, as by January 8. When the public saw the market decimated in the last hour of trading on Friday, January 8, feelings caused by the October decline were renewed. It was an important signal to those of us in the business that we need to insure that both perception and reality are at parity regarding how we treat the smallest as well as the largest user in the marketplace.

In the short term, there have been initiatives taken by various self-regulatory organizations. Whether it is limits on the futures side of the business or collars on the equity side of the business, each organization has tried in its own way to deal with the perceived inequality. But we are not there yet. A look at the enormous growth in money funds over the last three months shows that the public is piling up cash. Both individuals and institutions on the active side of the business are doing so, awaiting fundamental signals that they will be treated the same as any other participant in the securities markets.

But risk is inherent in any equity investment or speculation. The public must also understand that these initiatives are not intended to prevent a significant rise or fall in securities prices.

A second implication coming out of October is also clear: there has been an enormous shift in the way money is managed in this country on the so-called passive side. With the birth of the passive indexer, a new category of participant has entered the arena who has certain perceptions of liquidity. Those perceptions do not match the reality of liquidity. This failure to understand caused no harm from 1982 through 1987, a period during which the market grew enormously. The Dow increased threefold, volume quadrupled, and participation (as measured by indirect and institutional ownership) grew enormously.

But a so-called insurance policy was built into that growth factor, which only worked provided no one utilized it. It did not work when the elephants all headed for the door at the same time. It was equivalent to trying to buy fire insurance for a house that was already burning down. And so the institutions, those sophisticated high-end users, learned a lesson in October: there is no such thing as unlimited liquidity.

If one develops an asset base over a period of months or, in many cases, years, and then chooses to liquidate that asset base in a matter of minutes, clearly the last sale would not be an accurate reflection of the asset valuation. This reality must be better understood by a wider range of institutions as well as by the general participant in the marketplace. No matter how much capital one were to put in front of that speeding freight train on October 19, the result would have been the same. The markets simply were not meant to create instantaneous liquidity for hundreds of billions of dollars. Many of these asset managers were handling portfolios in excess of $10 billion; the thought that they could create instant cash from those positions at relatively close to the last sale is clearly a victory of perception over reality.

I believe that message has been painfully instilled into the community, but Wall Street has a way of repeating lessons it has learned. The more we reinforce, the more those institutions will understand the difference between their perceptions and reality, and the less likely is it that all the elephants will again head for the door at the same time.

October has a final message for the financial community. The interlinking of products and the need for cooperation and coordination across markets is essential. It may run the risk of complacency to say that we will cooperate, and that by coordination we will eliminate the prospect of another market crash. There is in fact enormous work to be done among the self-regulatory organizations, a clear responsibility on the part of the regulators, and perhaps a role for Congress. But having watched this process over the last 20-odd years, I am a great believer that some of the best change in this industry has come as a result of the initiatives of the industry itself. Some of the most innovative developments in product, applications of technology, and services that meet the needs of both large and small consumers have occurred not because the regulatory agencies or Congress have pointed a gun at the industry.

The regulatory agencies, however, have played a useful critical role. The reports of the SEC and the Brady task force in particular have set an agenda that the private sector can now deal with. It would be wrong for us to default simply because of the perception that there is little likelihood of congressional action in 1988. But the lack of action by Congress this year does give our industry time to deal substantively with the issues raised by October 1987.

I have watched the reshaping of the financial markets in the mid-1970s as a result of regulatory reform, and in the early 1980s as a result of technical upgrade and product innovation; and I believe there is now a clear agenda for the industry. I am confident that the industry—in partnership with the self-regulators, and with proper prodding from the SEC and the CFTC—will move ahead toward solving its problems.

CHAPTER 6

THE VIEW FROM
THE AMERICAN
STOCK EXCHANGE

Arthur Levitt

Wall Street's fascination with technology is, of course, not new. If you look at prints or engravings from the mid-1880s, you see the streets of the financial district criss-crossed with telegraph wires. Wall Street's use of new technologies inspired Thomas Edison to improve the original ticker tape. After he invented the electric light, it was not accidental that the first central power plant was built in New York City on Pearl Street. In 1876, Alexander Graham Bell patented the telephone, and among the first 271 subscribers in New York to that fledgling system were 45 brokers and bankers. Examples of eager application of technology in the financial community continue well into this century. Somewhere along the way, however, the industry grew complacent and lost the desire to implement the best technology had to offer. And I think, of course, that we paid the price.

Rising volume in the 1960s resulted in the paper crunch of that time, something that probably few people can remember. Investor confidence in firms was shaken, and those firms unable to cope with that horrendous period either went out of business or merged. But the survivors had a healthy new respect for technology. And now, throughout the financial services arena, you are seeing still more technological advances. In this age of global ties and competition, the edge will go to firms and markets that are best able to apply these contributions. I can assure you that by the end of the day on October 19, I was very pleased that the American Stock Exchange had pursued its own commitment to technology. Since that dramatic period, our board has voted unanimously for record new investments in automation, and I am absolutely confident that we are on the right course despite the tremendous challenges that we face as an industry.

Now, what does concern me is that many of the conditions that existed during the near market meltdown of October 19 and 20 are still present today, creating a kind of economic time bomb that threatens our system. Most thoughtful observers agree that there is no single cause for that precipitous decline. Macroeconomic conditions, highly speculative markets, and technological overloads contributed to the crash. Had there been no market rebound these past few months, we would be approaching these problems with a much greater sense of urgency.

Recently I spoke with Paul Kennedy, the author of the controversial best seller *The Rise and Fall of the Great Powers*. Our conversation reminded me that whether you are talking about nations or markets, complacency is an invitation for history to repeat itself. It is unrealistic to assume that the financial markets will remain immune from the economic problems growing in all sectors of our society. The budget deficit, the global industrial competition, and strains in the banking system are signs of our very precarious environment. Beyond that, we are suffering from self-inflicted wounds. One is the old case of looking so closely at the trees that we don't see the forest. For the last decade, we have seen new products and many new strategies in our industry. But each marketplace, each securities firm, was intently staring at its own innovation, while the system as a whole was not in focus. The Brady report and other studies performed a real service, for they reminded us that the various markets for stocks, stock index futures, and stock options are, in fact, one market.

In that respect, the Brady report, with whose findings I essentially agree, differed from the findings of the Katzenbach report by the New York Stock Exchange. The Brady report, as I understand it, called for an opening up of the roadway between markets; and I think that is a very important and valuable consideration.

It also seems prudent and reasonable to follow the various other recommendations of these reports. We should slow down the market process and dampen speculation during periods of turmoil. We should forge closer cooperation across the markets and implement the circuit breakers for use when needed or perhaps selectively rather than across markets. In my judgment, the most compelling and urgent recommendation of the Brady report is to put in place linkages between clearing to create a central clearance facility that can operate in times of market volume and market stress. We should harmonize margin in different products and inject more capital in the trading floors.

During that October turmoil, I spent a good deal of time observing the trading floor. None of us knew how long the sell-off would last or how far it would drop. Our volume tripled, but the specialists increased their trading on our floor sixfold. I saw them plunge in again and again, struggling to bring some semblance of stability to the marketplace. Those specialists suffered punishing losses. Although they were physically and mentally exhausted, they did keep the market open, which gave stability an opportunity to reassert itself. The auction market system certainly did not work perfectly, but it did work remarkably well under extremely difficult circumstances. I believe that, to some extent, the specialists were the unsung heroes of October 1987. Now, with the new technology we are giving them additional tools to work with.

But beyond all this, another step is needed. About two months ago, I conducted a mini-survey of some 45 individuals who know this industry—heads of firms, institutional investors, specialists, brokers, listed-company CEOs, small investors, large investors, business school deans, and others. I found an astonishing diversity of opinion among this group. There was pessimism, optimism, concern, anger, confusion, and, perhaps most of all, a lot of finger pointing. The only thing I did not find was indifference.

These conversations led me to the proposal I made in April 1988 before the National Press Club in Washington. I recommended that the President, Congress, and industries appoint a special study commission. Now to be sure, there will be much Congressional opposition to that idea. They will say, "Oh, here they go again. Another stall tactic. They want to create a commission to delay anything happening. This is more of those free market ideologues taking over."

Well, I don't believe that. I do believe that the public is largely out, and disenchanted with the market. It will take two things to bring it back. First, the public must believe that the system is fair, which it *doesn't*. Second, it must be persuaded that it can make money in this marketplace, and certainly recent experiences tend to deny that. As to the fairness of the market, the public must believe it has at least as much an opportunity as the institutional investors do, and it *doesn't*. Now, that fact will not change overnight or on the basis of any study—no matter how good, profound, or far-reaching that study may be.

I don't propose that this commission be established instead of, or to evade, the recommendations of the Brady commission, which, as I have said, is the best of the studies that have been issued. I say that in order to re-establish the kind of public confidence that is necessary, in my judgment, to refuel the process of capital re-formation that I think has stumbled badly in recent months. We will need a long-term view of what went on in October; an inventory of the various elements that are involved; specific recommendations as to changes that can and should be made; and, perhaps most importantly, some reassurance to the public that our system really can and will work. The commission should consist of people of unquestioned public acceptance, and it should be headed by someone of the caliber of a Paul Volcker, who probably enjoys the greatest public respect from individuals and business people throughout the United States today. Its recommendations shouldn't differ to any extent from those of the Brady commission. But it can go further. It can take a longer perspective, and its recommendations can be strategic as well as tactical.

This proposal does not absolve our industry from its responsibility of taking those steps *now*. As we do take them, we must focus on a particularly disturbing aspect of our current situation. Those markets—which throughout their history have provided corporate America with stable, long-term investment funds—have become so short-term-oriented that they threaten the capital raising process. This reflects, in part, the preoccupation of our society with short-term gain. Instead of looking beyond the horizon, corporate America is focused on the next quarter. We need to refocus our market, tax, and incentive structures away from quick profits and toward long-term profitability. Short-term trading strategies may contribute to liquidity and may smooth disparities between markets. But there are no substitutes for investing in the future: investing in jobs, in productivity, and in competitiveness.

Among the casualties of the October crash were nearly 50 public offerings, initial public offerings that were ready to come to the American Stock Exchange but were then forced to withdraw. That meant postponement of new plants, new jobs, and expansion into new markets. Since that time, only six of those companies have come back to the marketplace.

Last year, our listings soared nearly 50 percent to 152 companies. Those companies aren't just ticker symbols; they represent America today and tomorrow. Last month, our exchange listed a company from Cambridge, Massachusetts, that is developing techniques for redeveloping new skin and other organs for reconstructive transplant surgery. In December, we listed a company that is a leader in international student exchanges. Over the past year alone, the companies that have joined our ranks, run restaurants, build mobile homes, operate cable systems, develop thermal energy, construct power plants, and publish newspapers. They operate hotels, create greeting cards, run cruise lines, manage banks, and produce fruit and clothing. And they also include competitive industrial companies from—what until recently has been called—the Rust Belt. This is all in just one year's listings.

Study after study proves that mid-size growth companies, like the ones that predominate on our trading floor, are the most dynamic segment of our economy. They tend to be risk takers and innovators. But the qualities of these companies alone are not enough to restore the confidences of individual investors to share in their growth. Our industry must address this issue and restore investor confidence in the system. If we fail to do this, not only our companies will suffer, but, I believe, we as well. Inevitably it will lead to business bashing in general and Wall Street bashing in particular.

We really are in the business of trust. Even before October, investors were disturbed by the insider-trading scandals. They were uneasy by the way the market was being moved around by big institutions. They wondered whether they should be in the market at all. The public either trusts the financial system or it doesn't. Either it believes it can make money and entrusts its funds to a system that is fair and efficient or it doesn't.

We must actively explore and implement measures that will invigorate our industry and reinforce the public trust. These are critical concerns. Consider that for the past several years we have had the most laissez faire administration this country has seen in perhaps 50 years and that we also have had a fairly laissez faire regulatory environment. You have a Congress that is champing at the bit to reregulate, a major ethical crisis in terms of a business scandal, and a major market collapse—and you have the ingredients for the kind of reregulation that I believe none of us look forward to. Hopefully, our industry can organize itself, and the self-regulators and the oversight committees can do what we really don't want the Congress to do for us. We can do a lot to help restore public confidence in the securities industry, but it is clear that we cannot do it alone.

In the next several years, further advances in technology will enable investors to move among global markets with an ease that we can barely imagine today. The challenge is to see that we have the international agreements, systems, products, and investor safeguards that can keep pace with these advances. We have tremendously talented and resourceful people in our industry. If all of us do our share, we can reap the fruits of technology and maintain our industry's traditional role as an engine for world progress. I hope we can engage the industry's continuing support, trust, belief, and—perhaps most of all—some healthy skepticism and some constructive optimism.

CHAPTER 7

THE VIEW FROM THE CHICAGO MERCANTILE EXCHANGE

William J. Brodsky

This paper presents my thoughts on the relationship between market volatility and information technology within the context of the October 1987 stock market crash, and examines some of the changes to market structure that have been recommended so far.

Over the last few months, several government agencies, including the Securities and Exchange Commission, the Commodity Futures Trading Commission, and the General Accounting Office, and a special presidential task force—the Brady Commission—have completed studies about the October 1987 stock market crash. Media reports and other analyses of the crash often erroneously tried to associate market volatility with increased efficiency in information technology. Computers and the infamous program trading were frequently blamed by the press and members of Congress for the rapid drop in stock prices which occurred on October 19.

Following the release of these studies, the president established the Presidential Working Group on Financial Markets. This group comprised Secretary of the Treasury James Baker, Fed Chairman Alan Greenspan, Chairman of the Securities and Exchange Commission David Ruder, and Chairman of the Commodity Futures Trading Commission Wendy Gramm. They were charged with developing agreement within the administration on what changes, if any, needed to be made as a result of the stock market crash. On May 16, the working group presented its report to the president. Although representatives of the futures industry do not fully agree with all the report's findings, we do believe that its findings and recommendations are basically sound.

In recent years, the equity markets have been marked by a tremendous increase in institutionalization. At the same time, the demand for portfolio-hedging strategies is great, and it is satisfied through the use of index futures and index options. During the crash, much media attention centered on program trading and index arbitrage. Many were quick to jump to the conclusion that program trading and index arbitrage caused the 508-point drop in the market on October 19. The evidence, however, points to the contrary. Index arbitrage accounted for much less of the NYSE volume on October 19 than some press reports would have you believe. For example:

> **CFTC Interim Report:** index arbitrage sell programs represented about 9 percent of total volume on the NYSE.
> **Brady Report:** index arbitrage was about 8.5 percent of total NYSE volume.
> **SEC Report:** the overall finding is that index arbitrage was about 6.1 percent of total NYSE volume.
> **NYSE/Katzenbach Report:** total program trading on that day represented 7 percent of total NYSE volume. If you use the same measure as the other studies, you would find index arbitrage was about 14 percent of total volume on that day.

The market has also been heavily influenced by macroeconomic forces. In evaluating the October market decline, too much emphasis has been placed on market structure, while too little attention has been given to macroeconomics. I was particularly pleased that the Presidential Working Group recognized this fact. Although it did not entirely dismiss the role technology played in exacerbating the situation, it emphasized that fundamental economic forces were a major factor leading to the market decline.

The Presidential Working Group accurately noted that, prior to October 19, stock prices had reached excessive levels as compared to the real earnings of the companies. It also stated that the size and speed of the decline initiated a fundamental re-evaluation of stocks. The interaction of technology and the ability of information to be disseminated led to a rapid market correction. As a result, volume overwhelmed the ability to process trades, which impaired the accuracy and timeliness of information. Ripple effects in terms of credit and cash flows ensued, creating uncertainty about the financial viability of the system.

Another important issue concerns what the working group called "de facto and ad hoc market disclosures" and other market disruptions. When, if ever, should a market be halted because of an overall decline in prices? The working group agreed with the conclusion of the Brady Commission that the stock, stock index futures, and stock options markets are closely linked—that they are, indeed, one market. Participants in the futures and options markets have known this for years—the markets are directly and mathematically related. Yet, prior to the issuance of these reports, a large segment of the participants in the securities side of the market was unaware of just how inextricably linked these markets really are.

One of the most important conclusions of the working group relates to circuit breakers—a term coined by the Brady Commission. The CME's Standard & Poor's 500 futures contract has in effect a daily price limit—that is, trading cannot occur above or below a certain limit within one day. The working group noted that if the futures market hits its limit (and therefore stops trading on a particular day), but the stock exchange or options exchange continues to trade, the two markets become disconnected. The working group felt strongly that circuit breakers must be coordinated across markets. This suggestion has caused much debate between the exchanges. Is this a good idea? If so, what should be the level and terms of the circuit breakers?

The CME currently has a circuit breaker, or price limit, in place which equates to approximately 120 Dow points. The NYSE preferred a much larger number; the resolution was that both markets would stop trading at about a 250-point *drop* in the Dow. Under this plan, we have what is called an "asymmetrical circuit breaker" because the public perception is that it is un-American for markets to go down, but all right for them to go up. Thus, the proposed circuit breaker would kick in only when the market moves *down* 250 points in one session.

The CME uses the S&P 500 Stock Price Index, and the NYSE uses the Dow. Therefore, the CME has a mathematical counterpart in its S&P product, which is about 30 S&P index points. It is probable that if the market experienced a precipitous decline, the S&P 500 futures contract would stop trading first because it is one homogeneous product. On the NYSE, we are dealing with approximately 1,500 stocks. Our market would stop trading if the futures contract went down the limit. Our market could bounce off the price limit only until such time as the NYSE halts. If we were to hit the limit first and then there were a rally, trading on the NYSE would not halt unless the NYSE were to hit its 250-point limit. Alternatively stated, both markets will halt trading only if the NYSE hits its 250-point limit and the CME is also at its limit.

We expect that this halt would occur throughout all U.S. stock and derivative markets. Because there is general agreement among the futures, stock, and stock options markets that trading halts are not generally desirable, the 250 limit would only remain in place for about one hour. Following that, there would be a reopening. Although the details are still being worked out, we on the futures side intend to wait for a certain number of NYSE stocks to reopen (to make sure there will really be a reopening). If we reopen and the market continues heading down, we could be at a new limit of 150 more Dow points. We have not yet determined whether there will be a reopening if the market goes down as much as 400 points plus an additional 150 under this scenario.

Another important aspect of the Presidential Working Group report relates to the clearing and settlement systems. We have learned a tremendous amount in terms of the market decline of October about how interrelated all the settlement systems are with the banking system. Much work has been done since the crash to improve these systems. The Fed has been and will continue to be involved in the work we do to perfect and improve these systems. The Fed Wire system and the banks are the glue that holds these markets together from a financial standpoint.

A number of suggestions were made in the report about the need for cross-margining and what is called "futures style options margining." During the crash, we encountered situations with completely hedged positions, but where banks were unwilling to lend money because they did not understand the nature of the hedge. The clearing houses of the various exchanges and the banking community are currently working on ways to minimize the problem of liquidity.

One of the most controversial parts of the report relates to margins and confirms what we in the futures industry have been maintaining all along: margins in the futures market work very well. The level of margins in stock index futures should be based on the guidelines of financial integrity. We raised margins several times during the October period, and we are currently at the highest level we have been at in a long time. Margins on the CME's S&P 500 contract are currently higher (that is, we are at approximately 15 percent of contract value) than typically advocated by economic analysis. The Presidential Working Group concluded that current minimum margins for stocks, stock index futures, and options provide an adequate level of protection for the financial system.

The working group recommended that margins should be prudential and went on to say that prudential margins required for carrying an individual stock should be significantly higher than margins required for a futures contract based on a stock index. To those in economics or finance, this is probably very obvious—a single stock bears not only market risk but firm-specific risk as well, whereas firm-specific risk is diversified away by investing in a basket of stocks.

Another issue of controversy has been the question of jurisdiction. This was the only point of disagreement for the working group. The CFTC believes it currently has sufficient authority over futures margins which it can exercise in emergency situations. The Chairman of the CFTC felt that, given the track record of the futures industry, no further regulatory oversight was necessary. The other members, however, felt that margin oversight authority should be given to the government.

The report of the working group discussed many other ideas. The concepts of contingency planning and intermarket communications will continue to be explored among the exchanges and regulators, and different aspects of capital adequacy are being reviewed. The working group felt there was no need to create another regulatory structure to oversee market issues, although it emphasized the importance of cooperation and coordination among the exchanges.

In closing, it is important to note that none of the reports that have surfaced since the stock market crash have advocated turning the clock back to a time when computers did not play a vital role in trading on exchanges and in upstairs offices. Automation and technology are here to stay!

CHAPTER 8

REACTING TO CURRENT TRENDS

*Richard G. Ketchum**

The last time Congress thought a lot about the markets was in the early to mid-1970s, after the paperwork crisis and the elimination of fixed commissions. What have been the trends in the markets since that time, and how do they relate to the market crash?

The first thing to realize is that those trends did not develop in several months or even in the period that futures have been trading in the United States. Instead, they go back to the start of institutionalization in this country, and to the change in the way institutions began to trade and invest. The change dates from the late 1960s and early 1970s, when institutions gradually became more active in equity securities.

Early developments involved liquidity pressures from large purchases and sales of individual securities. This caused an approach to upstairs trading very different from that which had occurred before the development of block positioning. The equities markets developed in the 1970s as an auction price setting mechanism on the floor of the NYSE and as a price clearing mechanism for blocks. The application of dealer capital along with specialist coordination brought the market together. This change, along with efforts by the NYSE to modernize its markets,

---

*My comments are not intended to reflect the views of the Securities and Exchange Commission, individual commissioners, or any other of my colleagues on the staff.

helped create what is indeed the best example of a modern stock market today.

In the last five or six years, a number of institutions have developed a preference for trading portfolios rather than individual stocks. This trend has come from the increase of passive management, the reduction of commissions on the stock side, and—perhaps most importantly—the development of index futures and options. This preference became possible because of several developments, including (1) increased availability and liquidity of index products on the derivative market side; (2) extremely large and unlimited hedge position limits with relatively low cost; (3) low transaction costs; and (4) the reduction in market risks realized by effecting a single transaction at one time, rather than attempting to accept transactions in 451 stocks. These factors created the possibility and feasibility of substantially greater portfolio trading, both in the stock markets and in the derivative markets.

At the same time, the futures market became significant, and arbitrage opportunities between that futures market and the stock market became greater. The index future, as a single product, is like a PT boat that can turn in a much smaller wake than can a stock market. With 451 or more stocks and thousands of products that can turn, the result is that discounts or premiums develop on prices between futures and stocks. Through the use of arbitrage, one has the ability to lock in gains, and very little money is required to effect those transactions. These trends allow much more effective portfolio trading on the stock markets.

The last important trend involves automation, including the development of automatic execution systems on the regional exchanges. Technology has provided the designated order turnaround system (DOT) on the NYSE, similar systems on the Amex, and automatic execution systems in the OTC market. Technology provides the capability to reduce the time difference in considering 451 stocks at once. Whether it be for arbitrage or portfolio trading purposes, technology has reduced the time to process transactions. Timing differences in transactions increase in a very significant way the opportunity for trading a portfolio.

Putting all these factors together, what did we see in October? Among other things, a substantial number of liquidations occurred on a portfolio basis, both in the futures and stock markets. Portfolio insurance strategies, as well as other trading strategies that depended on liquidating a substantial number of portfolio stocks quickly after the market had already begun to turn down, combined with index arbitrage to create a major movement in the market.

The shift to greater amounts of portfolio trading has had an impact on the floor of the NYSE. In the mid-1970s, systems evolved through the creation of an upstairs block positioning capability to interposition additional capital on the stock exchange floor, and to deal with the greatest imbalances of supply and demand between those systems. But with portfolio trading, instead of seeing single trades with intermediaries of upstairs firms that may choose to liquidate a single trade gradually over a period of time after having positioned it, we now essentially see all that activity in smaller sized orders because they are shifted to 100, 200, or 400 stocks shooting directly down to the specialist post.

For the first time in years, the specialist is again a primary provider of liquidity for institutional trades rather than just public trades. Not only is he a primary provider of that liquidity, he is a primary provider without seeing the entire story. Instead, that entire story is being played out throughout the floor of the NYSE.

The orders coming to the specialist are transparent as to whether they are public orders or orders that come from institutional-type trading strategies. The specialist sees the orders come in rapidly, one after another, down to his post through the DOT system. He can only determine the trading volume by looking at the screen to see what the discount or the premium in the future may be for the stock. He then calculates whether or not what he sees is activity reacting to the futures market.

There is nothing inherently unsound about this process, but it represents a great change in trading and market culture. If one is considering changes in the way systems are designed, one has to understand that the new pressure point in the markets is really the old pressure point of the 1970s. It is the specialist being placed in the midst of all the action.

We also see greater volume on the futures side of the market. Futures traders in periods of extreme pressure are being required to provide liquidity entirely by themselves. The nature of the futures market was exacerbated by the fact that upstairs firms are discouraged from interpositioning in the market because of concerns about the potential view of prearranged trading by both the futures exchanges and the CFTC.

What can we do about today's trading environment? The SEC continues to believe that, at least for an interim period, we ought to slow down volatility. We must also address some of the leverage differences between the markets by increasing margin requirements in the derivative markets. We must also accept the fact that, at least for the near-term, we are going to see periods of greater volatility and a stronger relation between the derivative markets and the stock markets. These trends will require that people have adequate financing capabilities and that markets are sufficiently liquid.

Several recommendations have been made by the Presidential Task Force. One issue is circuit breakers. No one likes circuit breakers; they create a risk of increased panic that one must accept. We will never be enthusiastic about putting circuit breakers on stocks at the level presently found in the derivative market.

Circuit breakers are asynchronous because the world is net long, and there is less potential for panic or fast liquidations as the market moves up. Upward movement provides much more potential for profit taking, thus creating more contraside liquidity than when the market moves down.

There is more reason to be worried about downward than upward price movements in the stock markets. Firms also tend to be net long, and they get into financial problems much more quickly when the market is going down.

Circuit breakers are a response to the fact that market movements can create an environment where concerns about the ability of systems to handle and execute orders efficiently (contraparty risk) are so great that buying simply dries up. It appeared to the Presidential Task Force that whatever the risks of circuit breakers, the risks of having no preplanned circuit breakers were also great if, in fact, the market became unable to cope. The risks of free fall markets due to contraparty concerns are significant enough that at some level, such as 250 points, it makes sense to have circuit breakers.

A second issue involves the commitment of capital for market-making. Capital is not a magic answer to liquidity, and it will not assure that people will step in front of a freight train. If most of the futures market on the floor and most specialists on the NYSE face dropping off a cliff, this represents a different level of liquidity and a different level of risk than if they are just facing substantial losses. The risks of having to put together the markets and of losing the confidence of the banks, suggest that market-maker capital (in the derivative markets, in the OTC, or on the floor) deserves a second look. The exchanges have studied these matters, and I believe there has been much improvement.

Let us now consider the objective of increasing liquidity and confidence in the banking system. One approach is to look at the clearing system itself. On October 19 and 20, one of the major pressures for large firms was the tremendous cash-flow payment obligations generated by the derivative markets and by the variation margin requirements for those markets. It makes sense to try to find ways to reduce those cash flows. Most importantly, we need to share information so that all the clearing corporations can effectively identify the firms they should worry about.

If there is a way to reduce cash flows by a linked market or one market (as the Brady Commission suggests), it makes sense to look at this alternative. The White House working groups talked about cross margining. At the moment, cross margining simply reflects the fact that if you have hedged options and futures positions, and if these positions are held in a single place or in some way through cross liens, you may be able to reduce at least the initial obligation to these positions. The problem with cross-margining is that in the option-style system, one does not have to pass through margin.

On the purchase side of a premium, the options buyer puts up the entire premium and has no risk other than premium purchase. It is theoretically possible to pass through gains in both directions, and then to take that money back through the premium buyer. This approach doubles the number of people or positions that the options clearing corporations have to worry about as a potential loss.

It also provides, though, an ability to recognize hedged positions. Many of the firms that had problems on October 20 had much less risk than they had liquidity problems because of the enormous variation margin charges. If options move to a futures-style margining, it creates that capability—if we can get satisfactory protection of both positions, so that we have the cash flow.

This strategy creates the capability of substantially lower cash flow payments in the derivative markets, and substantially lowers the number of bank financing decisions that have to be made on an overnight or next morning basis. There are many problems and risks with future-style margins, but in the option study the Presidential Task Force thought it was worth further study.

The Brady study discussed the concept of one market and a unified clearing system. However, a unified clearing system is not likely to be useful if stocks remain on five-day settlement. There are many reasons and costs involved in moving stock from the five-day settlement, most particularly related to the institutional settlement side where there may be two, three, four, or even five parties involved in settling any trade.

Notwithstanding this fact, I am not sure the world needed another next-day settlement product on those days after October 19. If you can put it all together and identify how to control hedge positions, stock options, and futures, the savings may justify reducing the settlement period of the stock market to make it effective and sensible. I am not at all sure that it is; but we should nevertheless look at technology, trading capability, and where that technology can be put to use.

There is no reason why we cannot do institutional settlement in a day. An institutional settlement used to take 60 days; today it is done much more quickly by a terminal system. Faster settlement adds additional costs, and the working group suggested it is an area for study.

The working group really did not discuss liquidity. Creating liquidity is not easy, and indeed I am not sure any capabilities will deal with it effectively. It is interesting to note that at the moment we have an increased emphasis on portfolio trading, but we essentially require that portfolios be disaggregated when sent to the NYSE floor. The result is that one has much less information about exactly what is being bought or sold than if one were trading in the cash market at a single post.

This trend is the reason the commission's staff report suggested the concept of trading market baskets—thus providing a capability to liquidate portfolio positions in a single trade rather than requiring disaggregation on the floor of the exchange. Such a change might increase liquidity. Whether such a mechanism will do so is not clear to me; it may just create another vehicle and cause fragmentation of existing order flow.

Finally, the halt in program trading for brokerage firms' own account suggests that there is a more structural problem of liquidity in the institutional market than is directly related to futures trading. At the moment, there are two components of value in effecting a transaction. The first is the relatively insignificant one of commissions and transaction costs; the second component is execution costs. The first part is quantifiable, but the second part is not. The capability to quantify a single part but not the second, combined with the availability of so-called soft dollars, creates an unlevel playing field.

This trend almost inevitably pushes volume and order flow to third party brokers—those non-block positioning brokers who offer low commissions plus soft dollars, in contrast to the major houses that offer block positioning. The major houses are perfectly capable of responding to that competition and have done so: they no longer provide as much liquidity and block positioning.

The conditions I have described may simply be the ways of the market and may be quite acceptable. However, it raises an interesting question: Have we built bias against providing liquidity as opposed to providing low commission rates?

CHAPTER 9

THE INCREASING IMPACT OF COMPUTER TECHNOLOGY

Susan M. Phillips

A conference on electronic trading capabilities for the secondary capital markets today is quite different from what it might have been 10 or 15 years ago. In the 1970s, the discussion about electronic markets centered around the technology questions—could a black box accommodate trading? The advocates of black-box trading urged the concept of one large mainframe where all the orders are entered and lined up by price, time of entry, and perhaps even customer priority. With all this information entered, the perfect Walrasian auction could occur, and there would be no need to pay the proverbial auctioneer, only the electricity cost.

Although a number of attempts to develop the all-encompassing black-box market have been made over the past few decades, this perfect computerized market never quite seemed to get off the ground, for one reason or another. On the futures side, the best contract for electronic trading probably was never tried. Further, an active floor trading population on existing exchanges already had a time-tested means of trading and was not enthusiastic about turning over active, successful contracts for computer experimentation. On the stock side, the participants were different with different traditions, but, again, there was not much incentive to turn a successful stock trading system over to a computer.

In short, the institutions in place handling trading desired to maintain the *status quo*. Thus, in the 1970s the discussions about trading technology contained many conflicting points of view. The technicians and systems design people tended to describe how computerized trading could be done, and the exchange community tended to state why it would not work. They believed liquidity would simply dry up without the market-making functions on the floor (specialist and pit locals).

But, as might have been predicted, technology rolled on, not waiting for the politics at the exchanges to sort out and inevitably produce specifications for an electronic market. A number of separate, perhaps even random, technological developments have occurred in the markets which are bringing us to our present state of analysis. In no particular order of importance, I believe the following not only have had an impact on our present market structure and its regulatory environment, but also provide some clues about future market development.

First is the computerization of back-office operations by brokerage houses and exchanges. These include the proverbial recordkeeping and billing, but also involve certain surveillance functions such as monitoring for insider trading infractions and violations of speculative limit rules or trade practice rules. And computerized audit trails are now state of the art.

A second area somewhat related to the first has been the increased integration of computers with exchange operations, including price display information (computers hung around the posts and pits), limit order books, automatic execution of small orders, theoretical option pricing models, and sophisticated option and futures risk-based margin and capital systems. In short, traders are becoming used to computers and have integrated computers into their daily trading activities.

Third, a number of technology developments away from the exchange systems have moved things along. In a sense, some are serving as competition to the exchanges. Some institutional block trading activities have developed from mini or even complete computerized market systems. Forward markets in interest rates and oil contracts, interest rate options, and swaps are other examples of computerized mini trading systems.* These systems have provided an impetus to the exchanges to develop similar capabilities on exchange floors so that they will not lose their markets to these off-exchange systems.

The fourth change is the integration of the securities and commodi-

---

*Where the CFTC had jurisdiction in domestic markets, these activities have been somewhat inhibited, although not entirely. In contrast, these activities have been generally encouraged in the securities markets. These different approaches are perhaps the source of the regulatory dispute now occurring in the off-exchange area.

ties markets brought about by the development of financial futures and options. I agree with the Brady Commission's conclusion that securities and index futures and options markets are in fact one integrated market. Coming from a commodities perspective, however, I found this conclusion surprising because it seemed so obvious. The fact that the Commission had to make this statement demonstrates the perception that the markets were separate.

A fifth development has also had an important impact. The introduction of the new financial instruments has allowed brokerage and trading houses to institute sophisticated integrated trading techniques and arbitrage techniques utilizing computers. These computers have allowed much faster trading and greatly increased volumes.

All five developments have allowed us to increase technology in the markets. But it has been a rather bifurcated approach. On the one hand, we have had organized exchanges utilizing new technology to enhance and expand operations, but not basically changing trading style. Some of this expansion has even been international. Further, exchanges have developed new products which provided market users with the tools to develop new computerized trading techniques. On the other hand, quite apart from these organized exchange trading activities, we have seen mechanized trading capabilities develop which have provided a major source of competition to exchanges.

The confluence of these developments brought us to October 19, 1987. Late in the 1980s, we now find ourselves looking at the *effects* of technology on the markets. This is a subtle, but real change in the nature of the discussion regarding technology and the markets. We are past the point of arguing the mechanics of the black box—we are now assessing the effect of lots of black boxes on the market. Ironically, many of the proposed solutions to the perceived problems would result in more technology within the market mechanisms, not less.

The effect on the market of technology and those derivative products on which most people seem to concentrate is market volatility. While many people simply do not like downward price movements in stocks (which seem to be initially unexplainable by individual firm operational and financial performance), they rarely criticize upside volatility. Price increases are characterized as recognition by the market of fair intrinsic values. Nevertheless, a lot of folks are spinning their computer disks trying to figure out whether we have more volatility, less volatility, too much, too little, and so on. At the extremes of this analysis, terms like manipulation and artificial pricing also enter the discussion.

Various proposals first surfaced in the Brady Commission report and have been discussed widely in Congress and among regulators. Much of the discussion is now becoming focused on several proposed solutions. Chapters 7 and 8 in this book outline the next agenda for discussing the proposed solutions.

One proposal that has attracted much attention is the circuit breaker concept. Both price limits and circuit breakers would allow information about either new market or firm fundamentals to be fully reflected and digested by traders in all markets. Many economists would not find circuit breakers a particularly salutary solution, however. At the least, these mechanisms must be described in advance, so all know the rules, and they must be brief enough so only adequate information is disseminated. If trading breaks are too long, traders at risk will simply find ways of laying off their risk outside the system or beyond our domestic shores. Personally, I hope these proposals are temporary, until trading and communication systems can be expanded to permit continuous trading with adequate market information fully disseminated.

As we turn from discussing October 19 and start thinking about future trading systems and their technology, I believe we can draw a number of lessons from our recent history. The role of exchanges should be significantly strengthened. Exchanges not only serve as a trading place (which may take a different form in the future), but they also serve as important organizations to enforce contract performance, trading rules, capital requirements, margin rules, and other general credit considerations. Perhaps I am going out on a limb, but I would like to suggest that the exchanges will take a much more active and leading role in developing solutions than they have in the past. In many ways, they have great incentives to do so—they simply do not want to lose their market share.

We are moving toward a more technologically oriented trading system. People who sit down at their terminals to enter a trade will think of the person on the other side of that trade, of their credit ratings, and so on. In this environment, people will discover that an exchange performs a vital function. Not only is it a trading place where one goes to execute an order, but it is also an institution that provides a means by which contract performance can be assured. Trading rules can be assured and capital requirements enforced, so that there will in fact be money on the other end of a transaction. The enforcement of margin rules, capital requirements, and financial integrity is one of the most important functions that exchanges will continue to perform. Thus, I expect that the future arguments about technology and trading systems will also center on who should be in the system, how to monitor their positions, and how to assess their risk position in a portfolio sense.

Risk positions can change rapidly. The entire margining system and questions about margins should not be focused myopically on whether margins are too high or too low. A new generation of margining systems must fully recognize the portfolio impacts of margins. These new systems will probably require more timely payment of commitments so that credit considerations do not end up dominating trading decisions and thereby reducing the price discovery and risk transfer functions of the markets.

I hope that coming out of October 1987 and out of January 1988, we will see traders utilize the tools that are available to them in a more informed and sophisticated manner. The institutional traders must recognize both the abilities and the inabilities of exchanges to provide liquidity, given their size. If a large trader launches into a particular trading program that requires a certain level of liquidity, it is best that he or she make sure that the markets can in fact provide that liquidity when all the elephants decide to go to the door. I expect to see traders revise their use of various portfolio management tools. I have been comforted to see that many of the studies have not advocated eliminating the tools, but rather are trying to make sure that the systems and traders are using them to their potential.

In conclusion, the design for future electronic exchange systems will not center on what kind of computer to use, what the screen should look like, or even the hours of trading. Rather, the focus of the discussion has shifted to who should be in the system, how to monitor their positions, how to assess their complete risk position, and how to keep the money moving. Since risk positions can change so very rapidly, there probably will be a new generation of margin systems assessing aggregate risk and much faster payment of margin deposits. I expect that exchanges will take a leading role in the development of the next technological generation of trading systems. All of this must be done in an international environment recognizing that if U.S. markets do not meet the needs of today's investors and traders, other markets stand ready to do so.

CHAPTER 10

SURVIVAL STRATEGIES FOR EXCHANGES

Robert A. Wood

The rate of change in the structure of capital markets appears to be accelerating. The evolution of four forces is causing change: (1) futures and options markets; (2) computerized trading, which permits professional investors instantly to focus liquidity demands of essentially unlimited size on exchanges; (3) trading strategies, such as portfolio insurance, index arbitrage, "hot money" strategies, etc., which result in immense liquidity demands being placed on exchanges within very short time frames; and (4) upstairs block trades and, more recently, basket trades utilizing the DOT system. These forces have created great stress in capital markets.

Capital formation is the basic economic force that drives exchanges (used here to include any entity where securities are traded). Financial executives and others involved in the business of capital formation should periodically be asking, "Where should a particular stock be traded so as to minimize its firm's cost of capital?" Included in the cost of capital are issue costs, regulatory and reporting costs, and all trading costs including commissions, bid-ask spreads, market impact, trading delays, poorly executed orders, frontrunning costs, liquidity costs, volatility costs, the trading cost implications associated with the ability of market participants to lay off risk, etc.[1] The resolution of questions regarding where to trade secutities will determine the survival of exchanges. The stresses created by the rapidity of the structural changes mentioned above, which were exacerbated by the market break of October 19, 1987, threaten the survival of exchanges as presently constituted.

This paper focuses on three important aspects of the changing nature of capital markets. First is the rapid increase in liquidity demands by market participants and the associated changes in market behavior. Second is recent public attitudes toward futures and options markets and the implication of these attitudes for exchange survival; the paper also discusses potential solutions for these problems. Finally, the paper explores the implications of allegations recently appearing in the press that markets are being manipulated through the use of basket trading.

LIQUIDITY DEMANDS AND MARKET VOLATILITY

The demand for liquidity is increasingly focused within very short time frames as computers look for arbitrage opportunities between, for example, futures prices and spot index prices and arbitrageurs attempt to execute simultaneous sells and buys within seconds in futures and spot markets, or as baskets of stocks are initiated with computer programs to implement portfolio insurance and other strategies. Investment professionals complain that equity markets are becoming more erratic and that these markets are beginning to resemble commodity markets.

In response to these concerns, a number of studies have focused on the volatility of markets. Using fifteen-minute-interval data for the Dow 30 stocks from 1910 to 1985 and daily data for the S&P 500 from 1970 through 1985, Birini and Hanson (1985, 1986) find that the level of volatility has diminished over time, although a slight increase is observed since 1982. Using daily data for the period 1978 through 1986, Harris (1987) finds volatility of the CRSP equally-weighted stock index to be less in each successive three-year period. Over the same interval, the volatility of S&P 500 listed stocks increased relative to that observed for a comparable sample of nonlisted stocks. Harris speculates that the increase may result from futures and options markets for the S&P 500. He notes that the added volatility is only 14 basis points, which may not be economically significant.

The *Report of the Presidential Task Force on Market Mechanisms* (1988) examines both the variance and skewness of the 60-day return distributions for the period January 1928 through October 1987.

The report concludes that volatility has increased since the introduction of futures and options markets and particularly in 1987 prior to October 19, but that the peaks in 1987 did not exceed those of many previous years. The report also examines the number of days with big moves and finds that the number has increased in 1986 and 1987 relative to the recent past, but does not approach that of the 1930s.

Using transactions data, Wood (1987) examines the intra-day movement of a value-weighted index formed from that subset of the S&P 500 that is traded on the NYSE both for the years 1980 through 1986 and for the months of January, March, June, and September in 1987. Wood focuses on the extreme tail of the market return distribution, rather than on the entire distribution, and on short trading intervals. The measure employed is the sum of the absolute value of the minute-by-minute index for all thirty-minute intervals that do not span trading days. This metric is referred to as *path* since it measures the distance traveled by the market over an interval.[2] Either 330 or 360 path measurements are obtained per trading day, depending upon whether the day falls before or after October 3, 1985, when the trading day was lengthened from 361 to 391 minutes.

Figure 10–1 (reprinted from Wood, 1987) shows the 50th through 99th percentiles of the path distribution for each year. Note that the value of path for all percentiles tends to drift up over time, although at the higher percentiles the movement becomes more dramatic. The value of path for the 99th percentile increases particularly rapidly in the last two years. If data for October 1987 had been included in the study, the jump for 1987 would be far larger. Figure 10–1 reveals extreme cases where the market is moving much more rapidly over time. These findings are consistent with the hypothesis of a growing tendency for highly concentrated and massive liquidity demands being placed upon markets within short periods and resultant rapid market movements.

Examination of rapid market movements for the past few years reveals periods when the market melted down and others when it melted up. In both cases disorderly markets result. Of deep concern is the panic that can result during a meltdown, such as was experienced on October 19 and 20.

For the purpose of characterizing the market behavior during extreme periods, traders are defined as *dynamic asset allocators*, such as portfolio insurers who demand instant liquidity, or *tactical asset allocators*, such as value traders or market timers who trade at a much slower

FIGURE 10–1
Path—S&P 500 Subset. Percentiles formed from path distributions for all 30-minute intervals within trading days.

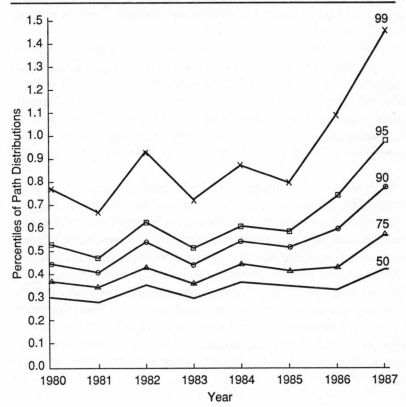

pace. Increasingly, it appears, the tactical asset allocators are sensitized to the behavior of the dynamic asset allocators. Further, two levels of the contra side of the market can be identified. The first level comprises the specialists who are willing to buy (or sell) within limits for (or from) inventory, the limit orders on the book, and those with committed orders. The second level comprises all other traders. When dynamic asset allocators arrive with sufficiently large liquidity demands, the available liquidity at the first level of the contra side can be quickly absorbed. Increasingly, tactical asset allocators who might be in the process of investing funds on the contra side of the dynamic asset allocators have learned to step aside in this situation.[3] If a tactical asset allocator had been willing to buy, for example, a particular stock at $40, perhaps by waiting for the full impact of the liquidity demands of the dynamic asset allocators (price pressure) to be reflected in prices, the stock could be acquired for $38. In this scenario, periods of rapid market movement can result.

On October 19, one portfolio insurer sold $1.7 billion of S&P 500 futures, and three other firms sold over $800 million each. The aggregate net buying of all specialist and futures locals amounted to $700 million. Clearly, the specialist-locals system cannot meet the extreme liquidity demands of modern trading technology. Since the specialist capital must earn an adequate risk adjusted return, requiring much larger capital requirements for specialists will only raise the cost of capital to issuing firms.

As an aside, in identifying portfolio insurers as demanders of enormous liquidity, the Presidential Task Force was not, as I see it, suggesting that they were responsible for the market break. Rather, the market mechanism could not meet their liquidity needs in a reasonable manner. While portfolio insurance was found to be more expensive than had been envisioned, should portfolio insurance be banned if money managers are willing to pay the price? In reflecting upon the nature of equity markets and the fact that closet portfolio insurance has a long historical precedent, banning portfolio insurance does not seem viable. Hence, a survival strategy for exchanges is to re-engineer the market-making mechanism to cope with periods when the dynamic asset allocators overwhelm the contra side.

CIRCUIT BREAKERS

The role of the specialist diminished somewhat as upstairs block trading increased. The specialist provided liquidity to small investors, while large investors negotiated block trades upstairs and reported their trades to the specialist. Imagine the result of all block trades being submitted independently over the DOT system, so that the specialist had to provide liquidity quickly to the block traders. In that event, trading might become chaotic even in the absence of index arbitrage, portfolio insurance, etc. Basket trading using the DOT system is comparable to block trading, except that baskets of stocks are traded instead of large numbers of shares in specific stocks, and with baskets the liquidity demand is instantaneous while blocks are shopped. With the evolution of basket trading, the role of the specialist has once again increased in importance, but the specialist is unlikely to be able to provide sufficient capital to meet the extreme liquidity needs of either block traders or basket traders. How might the market mechanism be redesigned to meet the liquidity needs of basket traders?

While the short time frame given to the Presidential Task Force precluded it making specific recommendations, discussions were held regarding potential circuit breakers. Price limits on individual stocks or on the market in total were not considered sensible. Rather, the task force considered options such as those discussed next. In the event that a computer polling the NYSE order flow sensed a serious order imbalance on either the supply or demand side, exchange officials would have the option of calling a trading halt to be followed by a call auction. This is similar to the process presently followed at the opening of the exchange, but with an important variation—namely, that the supply-demand schedules (the book) would be open to the public as it is developing. The open book is crucial to attract the opposite side of the imbalance. (The Toronto Exchange currently trades 17 stocks at their experimental Post 2 with the book constantly open.) Lack of information adds to fear in a crisis situation. The temporary trading halt gives tactical asset allocators the chance to catch up with dynamic asset allocators, who are demanding quick liquidity, and the open book is essential to allow the tactical asset allocators accurately to assess their strategy.

Cohen and Schwartz (1988) present the outline of all call auction procedure that could coexist along with (that is, would not interrupt) continuous trading. As the auction was developing, traders would have the option of routing their orders either to the continuous market or to the auction. An advantage of this feature is that arbitrage trades in progress when the circuit breaker was tripped would be completed, protecting the arbitrageurs from potentially serious losses from exposed positions in an unstable market. If baskets of stocks were traded, implementation of the auction would be more straightforward.[4]

FUTURES AND OPTIONS

Most, if not all, financial economists agree that equity markets have greater value when there are companion futures and options markets wherein investors may lay off risk. That is, the cost of capital will be lower for those firms whose stock is traded in such markets. Yet increasing criticism has been leveled by some investment professionals against Chicago. Why?

Part of the reason may be sociological. At a conference of investment professionals I attended three years ago, I heard statements such as the following: "I manage $3 billion. I am successful in this business. But when the market goes crazy, my phone rings off the wall with my customers asking me what is happening. I don't know myself, so what am I supposed to tell my customers? I am made to look like a fool with new instruments and trading strategies which I cannot comprehend. Further, the investment and trading strategies I developed which were so successful in the markets I grew up with, no longer work. Chicago and computerized trading are altering the nature of equity markets. The tail is wagging the dog! Let's do all that we can to stop these hated intrusions and return markets to the way they used to be." In my opinion, this sentiment is widespread.

Futures and options are inherently complex. Learning about them, particularly for those without technical training, can be painful and time consuming. With the rapid development of technology, the half-life of knowledge steadily decreases. We fear that which we do not understand. Hence, we have a negative correlation between the age of investment professionals and understanding and acceptance of futures and options markets ("future shock"), and a positive correlation between age and visibility and influence. Some who, by virtue of experience and position, ought to provide wise leadership may be unable to do so as a result of their lack of preparation. So, great pressure is brought to bear on exchange management, the SEC, Congress, and others to curtail, if not eradicate, the derivative markets. A further sociological source of conflict between New York and Chicago is their historical animosity.

Futures and options markets are linked to their underlying markets by arbitrage. In my opinion, index arbitrage is a beneficial trading activity. Price discovery will occur first in the futures markets for several reasons, including low trading costs and quick execution of baskets. Index arbitrage merely transmits the price discovery to the equity market. Since prices adjust more rapidly to new information through this process than would be the case without the futures market, equity prices will be closer to true value. Hence, the equity market's aggregate value ought to be greater, and the cost of capital lower. Closing the DOT system to index arbitrage merely reduces the players from perhaps 50, who through competition share minimal profits, to the handful who are able to print tickets and hand-carry them to the exchange. With the reduced competition, these few firms will reap greater arbitrage profits. Eliminating index arbitrage may actually raise volatility and reduce liquidity. Neither Chicago nor New York will function as well without the arbitrage linkage, and the cost of capital would consequently rise.

As they mature, entities tend to develop internal and external constituencies, which can create barriers to change. If New York is held captive by money managers or others who would just as soon throw sand in the gears of Chicago (such that smoothly and efficiently functioning equity and companion futures and options markets would not be available in the United States), smart money will find or develop such a marketplace elsewhere. Hence, a survival strategy for New York and Chicago leadership is to rise above their constituencies who would prevent cooperation and make their peace.

MARKET MANIPULATION AND BASKET TRADING

Recent news articles have suggested that a process described as *legging* is being used to create market imbalances which could be profitably arbitraged.[5] Legging is also used to describe variants of index arbitrage where, under certain market conditions and depending upon a trader's judgment, one leg of the arbitrage trade is executed slightly before the other for the purpose of generating somewhat higher returns while bearing somewhat greater risk. Note that while this benign form of legging is essentially identical in appearance to the manipulative strategy described in the remainder of this section, the intention is quite different.

Manipulative legging could be implemented in the following manner. Assume a large broker (the only firms with the combination of systems and resources sufficient to implement this strategy) had accumulated a position of $50 million short S&P futures and $50 million long S&P 500 stock during periods when futures were expensive relative to spot prices. Then, at a propitious moment, perhaps when the market anticipates portfolio insurance selling and the customer order flow included such orders, the broker's stock would be sold in one or more baskets over DOT, followed by customer baskets in either the stock and/or futures market. (This strategy would probably be too risky without customer order flow.) If the contra side is overwhelmed with these trades (as described above), cash prices drop rapidly and futures prices, by now sensitized to rapid movements from portfolio insurance trading, etc., drop more rapidly. The broker's naked short futures position gains value as the market drops. If the short position in the futures markets is then covered into the market drop—such that the dollar-weighted average futures buy price is lower than the average stock sell price—the strategy is profitable.

In order for this strategy to make sense, the short-term elasticities (i.e., market impact) for stock and futures, and their short-term cross-elasticities, would have to behave in a manner that would permit profitable execution. Examination of these price responses is an important area for future research.

This manipulative legging strategy, which has the outward appearance of index arbitrage, is purportedly one of many similar strategies that can be utilized to temporarily push markets out of equilibrium for gain. It is reminiscent of the "bear raids" of old. The uptick short-sale rule is avoided. Instead of false rumors being circulated as in the bear raids, signals are sent that simulate, for example, portfolio insurance, or that augment signals sent by customers. Clearly such a strategy, if it is in fact being practiced, is pernicious, in that it destabilizes markets for the purpose of increasing profits of the broker at the expense of uninformed traders who inadvertently get in the path of their strategy. Further, a conflict of interest is created between a broker acting as agent for customer orders and the same broker acting as principal for proprietary trades. In the agent role, the broker has a responsibility to the client to minimize market impact of the trade, and thus minimize trading costs. In the principal role, the broker's incentive is to maximize the market impact of the customer trades so as to maximize the destabilization of markets and thereby increase the strategy's profits. If brokers engage in market destabilization for proprietary trading in addition to agent trading, a conflict of interest leading to such adversarial trading seems inevitable.

If the market imbalance were corrected with the call auction outlined above, with or without a trading halt, the broker's risk would be increased. Hence, this form of circuit breaker might inhibit strategies designed to push markets out of equilibrium.

CONCLUSION

This paper focuses on recent changes in trading practices and the resultant changes in behavior of the market. The mechanisms by which liquidity demands can be focused in enormous quantities and within short time spans were reviewed, along with trading strategies that entail such liquidity demands. Evidence consistent with a hypothesis of more rapid market movements in periods of extreme liquidity demands was presented. The importance of circuit breakers as a modification of the market mechanism, which would alleviate the specialist's inability to provide liquidity to basket traders, was discussed. Popular attitudes toward futures and options markets were reviewed, as well as their implications for the cost of capital. Strategies for intentionally pushing markets out of equilibrium in a manner that would generate trading profits, which have been alluded to in the press recently, were reviewed.

Much more heat than light is being generated in discussions about the relationship between futures and options markets and equity markets, and about program (basket) trading. This paper suggests that the heat may have sociological roots. Yet if brokerage firms are manipulating markets with strategies that are similar to index arbitrage in execution, but with the intention of gaining profits at the expense of uninformed traders who get in their path, then investors on the receiving end of such trading strategies have a legitimate complaint that they are being disadvantaged by program trading. Such pernicious trading strategies would add to volatility, reduce liquidity, and reduce the confidence of investors in equity markets. Further, they would add to the animosity between New York and Chicago. Perhaps the most important step for the survival of exchanges in the United States is the resolution of animosity between New York and Chicago, so that smoothly functioning companion equity, futures, and options markets are available to permit equity investors to lay off risk.

More work is needed to refine sensible circuit breakers. Various auction strategies need to be considered. Experimental economics should be employed to test various alternatives. Further work is needed to define and measure volatility. Additional work is needed to examine the short-term elasticities and cross-elasticities of the demand for stock and futures in order to ascertain the feasibility of pushing markets out of equilibrium in a profitable manner.

NOTES

1. This list of trading costs is not exhaustive, nor are the costs exclusive.
2. The concept of *path* is discussed in Hill and Celebuski (1987).

3. "Program Traders Sway Prices of Many Stocks Even More than Ever," *The Wall Street Journal*, May 2, 1988, p.1.
4. For further discussion of basket trading and a discussion of the literature, see U.S. Securities and Exchange Commission, *The October 1987 Market Break*, (February 1988), pp. 3–18.
5. "Program Trading Becomes More Brutal," *The New York Times*, May 1, 1988, p.1.

REFERENCES

Birini, Laszlo, and H. Nicolas Hanson. "Market Volatility: Perception and Reality." Saloman Brothers (December 1985).
Birini, Laszlo, and H. Nicolas Hanson. "Market Volatility: An Updated Study." Saloman Brothers (December 1986).
Cohen, Kalman, and Robert Schwartz. "Realizing the Potential of an Electronic Trading System." Chapter 2, this volume, 1989.
Harris, Lawrence. "S&P 500 Futures and Cash Stock Price Volatility." Presented at the Q Group Meeting (October 1987).
Hill, Joanne, and Mathew Celebuski. "Path Dependence in Dynamic Trading Strategies: A Risk and Return Analysis." Kidder Peabody (October 1987).
The October 1987 Market Break. U.S. Securities and Exchange Commission, (February 1988).
Report of the Presidential Task Force on Market Mechanisms. U.S. Government Printing Office, Washington, D.C., (January 1988).
Wood, Robert. "The Velocity of the S&P 500." Working paper, The Pennsylvania State University, (November 1987).

CHAPTER 11

DOES TECHNOLOGY MATTER?

Fischer Black

In the United States, we have three of the modern wonders of the world: the New York Stock Exchange, the Chicago Mercantile Exchange, and the Chicago Board Options Exchange. We have amazingly liquid markets with huge trading volumes, unlike, so far as I know, anything anywhere else in the world except Tokyo. NASDAQ is furiously trying to catch up.

The other interesting thing about these three markets is that they are so different. They have different market structure; they have different kinds and degrees of automation. In all of them, some kind of automation is essential, but in none of them is automation the key to the market. None of them, I think, would we describe as automated markets, yet they are all very successful.

I do not know exactly what we are to make of this. I like to think that we can look at these three markets and figure out what they have in common, to learn what it is that makes for a successful market. One thing they have in common is that they are all continuous markets. They do not attempt to have price continuity, but there is trading continuity. When the markets are open, you can usually get a bid price, an asked price, and a last trade price.

One has a specialist system, another has an open outcry system, another has a combination. I believe we could take the structure of any one of these markets and transplant it to the other one. Interchange the structures and they would continue to work well. I just do not think the market structure matters that much. Since they are not greatly automated, it is clear that automation does not matter that much. None of them has the call market feature that people have discussed in this conference. Possible exceptions are the opening on the New York Stock Exchange and some procedures on the options exchanges. The call market does not seem like an essential ingredient for those exchanges. So, while I like to think a lot about technology and advances in how we do things, I would conclude that we can only improve on what we have now incrementally.

CHAPTER 12

IS TECHNOLOGY DRIVING US TOO FAST?

Roger M. Kubarych

The fundamental question is, How does technology, all this ability to trade faster and cheaper, affect markets in a broad economic sense? Does it lead to more orderly markets, or does it lead to more volatile ones?

The ability to trade faster and cheaper does not, in and of itself, mean the public interest is being served. Some fundamental questions have to be asked about whether or not the ability to exploit the dazzling technology is necessarily the best approach. I will give you an example.

I am not a good driver, but an average driver. I assume that most of us are average drivers. Many of us pretend to be excellent drivers, and a few of us even own fancy cars like BMWs. How many average drivers have sat at a four-way stop sign, wondering whether to be the first to venture into an intersection? Often I have ventured out prematurely only to be rescued by my low tech car.

To my mind, a lot of average drivers buy BMWs. They think that owning a BMW equips them to become excellent race car drivers because they have all this horsepower under their feet. My guess is that BMW drivers get into a lot of accidents. This suggests that they really should not be driving BMWs, at least not until they take some lessons.

There is a lot of technology in financial markets, both in terms of hardware and software. Some of that technology is in the hands of people who are not well-trained, who do not know what they are doing. Some people are reacting by making inperfect decisions based on information that is not really information, but data that has been badly interpreted. This creates the potential for high tech fast, cheap, efficient order delivery systems to create more volatility. Eventually this calls for a public policy response.

My former colleague Alan Greenspan and some of his associates in Washington will be deciding what to recommend at the president's behest. Should they put into that BMW a device to make sure it is not driven too quickly through stop signs, at least until the driver knows what he is doing?

There are a variety of ways that one can slow the market down, and people differ stridently and emotionally on what the best way is. One way is to introduce some delay, some slowed response time, and a little thought time into the process. This is known by the rather unfortunate term *circuit breaker*. But circuit breakers, unfortunately, are designed to fight the last war, not the next one. I think they could cause an unwarranted sense of confidence on the part of the general public that something meaningful has been fixed.

Another consideration is the nature of the institutional investors who are capable of generating a 23-percent change in the value of every company in the country in a matter of minutes. The institutions must be made more responsible and more aware of the external impact of quick-fire decisions on the public. Joe Grunfest, an SEC commissioner, has considered the need for additional disclosure for institutional investors who plan to do very large trades. This is a traditional SEC approach, and it makes some sense.

The banking business may suggest other ways. Do we want the institutional investors, who control large pools of funds, to treat stocks as being instantly encashable? In the banking business, every deposit is certainly not instantly encashable. Demand deposits are, but time deposits are not. People who hold time deposits realize a certain yield advantage, and for that yield advantage they accept a restraint—they cannot get out of those time deposits any second they want to.

Why do we do that? Because we recognize that if everyone tries to pull their money out of the bank at the same time, the structure of liabilities will lead—perhaps not to bank collapses—but to much more government involvement, much more regulation, and much more Fed intrusion. And so we try to make the balance sheets of banks more robust to withstand sudden shocks.

This does not mean that some banks do not need help. Even time deposits can be run off, and the selling of a lot of CDs at once can lead to a big cloud over a bank. That is why we use time deposits to slow down the process of responding to information.

I am not going to recommend anything particularly like this. But it is worthwhile to think about what we can do in the equities market for people who hold securities for a long-term. We must give them a sense that they are not all instantly encashable, even though our computer experts and our systems experts are continuously devising ways to make orders flow faster and cheaper and more efficiently. The public policy question is how to structure things so people will not try to leave the market all at once.

Nothing has happened since October 1987 to relieve the sense that volatility in our markets is permanently increased. And so some of the concerns that I am raising are not just of academic interest. They are of great pressing interest because one of these days that volatility may be right back with us.

SECTION 2

ELECTRONIC TRADING

CHAPTER 13

BLACK MONDAY: MARKET STRUCTURE AND MARKET-MAKING

Junius W. Peake
Morris Mendelson
R.T. Williams, Jr.

On October 19, 1987, more than 600 million shares were traded on the New York Stock Exchange (NYSE), while the bellwether Dow Jones Industrial Average declined more than 500 points. The trading volume and magnitude of the market collapse were unparalleled in history. Other equities markets around the world suffered comparable high volumes and steep price declines.

The crisis environment prevailing on October 19 peaked the following day and continued for several weeks. Unease in the world financial market structures continues to exist, and several questions require immediate answers:

• Why didn't the national and international securities markets perform as efficiently as their operators always claimed they would?
• Why weren't the market-making structures of the exchange markets (specialists) and the OTC markets (competing market makers) more effective?
• What structural and/or operational changes should be made to exchange and OTC markets for equities and their derivatives?

The structural and operational weaknesses of equities and related derivative instrument markets were glaringly exposed when the global equity markets experienced extreme stress and volatility during this period and came very close to total collapse.

Foremost among these weaknesses was the inability of the systems employed to provide quick, informed, and effective access by *all* investors to the markets' trading arenas. Securities exchanges give control of trading in the arena to specialists, and over-the-counter (OTC) markets do likewise to registered market-makers. This structure prevents other potential providers of liquidity from effective and equal participation when most needed, and precludes price determination through the free interaction of all market participants. American stock markets have been considered highly liquid, and market-makers have been counted on to keep them that way. Unfortunately, as we have seen recently, liquidity can evaporate almost instantly during periods of market panic. Systems limiting access to the market are inefficient. They do not permit all sources of capital equal access to the trading arena.[1]

Steven Wunsch of Kidder Peabody, an astute commentator on present market structure, suggests this dearth of liquidity that developed during the market break demonstrates the triumph of the use of automation by those who require liquidity (the clients) over the nonautomated processes of the assigned providers of immediacy (specialists and registered market-makers). It is not surprising the existing systems failed. A limited number of market-makers were unreasonably expected to commit their capital in a vain attempt to stop securities prices from collapsing during near-panic conditions across entire national and international equity markets. There was no alternate source of ready capital able to step in quickly.[2]

In the present systems, specialists and OTC market-makers are the nexus of the trading arenas. When they are unwilling or unable to operate, markets cease to operate effectively. To solve this defect, what is needed is a revision of the systems to reduce the dependence for successful market operations on this group of market participants.[3] While the turbulence of the equity market has, at least for the moment, eased somewhat, the strains continue. If there is another period of severe price declines coupled with concurrent extremely high volume, world equities market can collapse and precipitate a global financial crisis.

To date, in response to this lack of liquidity, the exchanges, over-the-counter market regulators, the Brady Commission, and the Securities and Exchange Commission have responded by recommending or implementing steps that effectively reduce the available liquidity or that are merely cosmetic. The market's liquidity is improved neither by halting trading when prices fluctuate intra-day by some newspaper-editor-determined amount, nor by taking away from the market the latest tools of automated order delivery (SuperDot). We are not certain that even raising capital requirements for specialists will help. A smaller amount of loss will quickly drive a formerly secure specialist below required minimums; and transferring specialist books to firms that are accountable (in hindsight) to public shareholders should their losses be deemed excessive may reduce liquidity, since financial controls in these firms are frequently very tight.

We read about proposed circuit breakers. To analogize, in a building circuit breakers are needed only to protect against catastrophe when (1) there is inadequate wiring, or (2) some piece of electrical equipment malfunctions. There has not been a thorough examination of the underlying adequacy of the wiring of the market; certainly some elements broke down during the October debacle, but there has been no trip to the repair shop to see what was really wrong with the market's structural components.

Not only are American financial markets underpowered, but they still operate on the equivalent of direct current, while the rest of the world moves to new standards of excellence. However, if circuit breakers must be used on a temporary basis (the only basis that we believe is rational), they should be implemented across *all* related markets (equities, options, and futures) simultaneously, and implemented only by a *political* decision, such as one taken by the president, rather than on some predetermined basis.

Failure by government, self-regulators, the financial services industry, issuers, and institutional investors rapidly to correct structural deficiencies may have severe, if not catastrophic, economic consequences for global capital markets. A Band-Aid fix is not the solution, nor are rules requiring market-makers and specialists to stand with their backs to the wall even longer, or merely to increase their capital. The solutions to the problems require major structural changes. Anything less will provide but illusory protection. The problems are systemic. Today equity securities and their derivative markets fail to meet many of the objectives stated by their sponsors and, inexcusably, also fail to meet the performance standards mandated in the Securities Reform Act of 1975. (See Appendix C for these Congressionally-mandated characteristics.)

There are now no questions (as there were when we first proposed the PMW system in 1976) that automated execution systems will work efficiently: trading systems of the type we propose are already in place in other markets around the world, and many more are being built and implemented:

• In 1975 the Toronto Stock Exchange started the CATS system, which is similar to the one we propose. This system has now been adopted or replicated at exchanges in France, Japan, Belgium and Spain.

• The Swiss Options and Futures Exchange (SOFEX) commenced commence operations in May of this year.

• Reuters and the Chicago Mercantile Exchange (CME) have agreed jointly to develop an automated trading facility for trading futures contracts globally.

• The London International Futures Exchange (Liffe) has solicited bids for the specifications for an automated trading system.

• The International Futures Exchange Ltd. (Intex) has reached an agreement with Telerate to market the Intex automated trading application developed in 1980 by one of the authors and others.[4]

In addition, many other countries and markets either have or are in the process of developing automated trading systems.

By contrast, the only significant automation that has been applied to U.S. financial markets since October 1987 has been to automate trading halts and to take vital pieces of market trading equipment off-line when prices move by predetermined amounts.

We fear the loss of U.S. capital markets to foreign shores in systems not hamstrung by obsolescent technologies and policies. Capital markets deal in intangibles. There are no factories to move or large facilities to build. Markets will move to any geographic location meeting their requirements. In the 1960s, the United States saw the loss of what are now called the Euromarkets to London when the interest equalization tax was proposed. They moved in a matter of weeks. The loss of existing equity markets will be more gradual; it will, however, be inevitable unless American know-how is unleashed to modernize them to meet the needs of today's markets.

The leaders of the American investment community (dealers, brokers, and bankers) must speak out on behalf of fair and modern systems. Under such leadership, the market's institutions—exchanges and the NASD, together with the Congress and its independent agencies, the SEC and the Commodity Futures Trading Commission—will finally see the establishment of the national market system ordered by the Congress in the Securities Reform Act of 1975. A wise person once said, "You can accomplish almost anything if you don't care who gets the credit." We would like to take this opportunity to call upon everyone who reads or hears us to reflect on our vision of a better market. With wisdom and initiative, America can build an array of financial markets that will once again be the standard—and the envy—of the world.

In the following sections of this paper we will discuss the defects of the present market structures, and proposals for improvements.

THE DEFICIENCIES OF THE PRESENT MARKETS

There are five major deficiencies in the existing market structure for equities and their derivatives:

1. Access to the trading arena by investors—professionals (dealers), institutions, and individuals—is inadequate and inequitable.[5]

2. Information about current prices, levels, and selling interest, as well as bids and offers at and away from current trading levels (and their amounts) in the market arena, is provided unequally to different classes of market participants and in differing time frames.[6]

3. The obligations imposed upon existing market-makers (specialists) on exchanges and dealers in over-the-counter markets do not work well in times of market crisis and are sometimes counterproductive.[7]

4. Unpriced orders (market orders) in the trading arena create added and unnecessary stress on the market structure and on those market-makers whose job is to price them.[8]

5. The differing methods of trading for underlying securities and their derivatives creates asynchronous behavior in related markets, and the cessation of trading in underlying securities results in the inability to value derivatives.

The weaknesses of exchange and OTC market systems during the market crisis were sharply apparent:

• The electronic public order entry and delivery systems of the exchanges did not (and could not) cope with the thousands of orders sent in seconds to the exchange floors. These orders could not be executed promptly by the highly touted, but manual version of exchange auction systems.

• Existing rules prevent specialists from limiting themselves to the role of auctioneer. They were supposed to commit their capital in an environment that would have left them bankrupt if they complied strictly with their obligations to smooth price movements.[9]
• Many OTC market-makers insulated themselves from the flood of sell orders. Since there are no comparable order delivery systems, they shielded themselves from loss by not answering the phones. Those who did take calls found themselves inundated by the flood of orders. The additional capital available to the multiplicity of market-makers in OTC securities did not alleviate the turbulence.[10]

Neither exchange nor OTC market-making systems performed as advertised when they were most needed. In addition, since the markets for the underlying securities failed to perform efficiently, the markets for derivative instruments—options and futures—were unable to operate effectively, if at all.[11]

Efficient markets thrive on information. A major function of price change is to convey rapidly to investors the existence and import of new information. In the turbulence of October 19 and 20 (Black Monday and Terrible Tuesday), the systems failed.[12] Some of the most critical investment information, the actual prices at which securities were trading or could be traded, was unavailable. In many cases specialists could not or would not execute further orders and requested trading halts in their assigned securities.[13]

This information vacuum increased the panic among investors and led to trading halts in most of the derivative markets. Together, these actions increased the loss of confidence by investors of all classes: professional traders, institutional and individual investors, and arbitrageurs. This combination of circumstances produced the near-collapse of the global equities markets.[14]

Computerized trading strategies linking price changes in the interrelated markets had been counted on to keep the relative values of these markets in synchronization. On Black Monday and Terrible Tuesday, the systems for interconnecting the stock, options, and futures market information failed. Without accurate price information for the underlying securities, the pricing mechanisms for their derivatives were emasculated.[15]

When trading in derivatives was halted, investors who wished to hedge their positions or reduce exposure in the cash (securities) markets found themselves unable to do so. Many floor traders on futures exchanges did not have access to the related securities markets. They had previously counted on being able to offset their positions in the futures market either by making a position-closing transaction in the same contract, or by cross-hedging (making a risk-reducing transaction in a different, but similar contract). Traders in these markets, especially traders in the futures markets, had no place to cover their positions.

Adding to the problems, the relative execution speeds of the three markets differ. Before one side of a trading stratagem that required simultaneous executions on more than one market was executed and reported to its initiator, the prices on the other markets had changed from existing quotes, or trading had been halted. On Black Monday and Terrible Tuesday, there were times when investors, including specialists, were unable to determine their actual positions for several hours or, in some cases, days.[16]

Lack of information was a cancer. The fear and panic, small at first, grew rapidly. Careful, intelligent institutional investors and traders alike threw caution to the winds and sent market sell orders to any brokers willing to accept them. These orders were frequently not executable because trading in the issue had been halted, the exchange electronic order delivery systems could not keep up with order volume, or the market-makers refused to answer their telephones or were in the dark about prices. In sum, exchange-based specialist systems, the NASDAQ system, and derivative options and futures systems all failed the acid tests required of proper market structures.

As a consequence of these structural deficiencies, the volatility of both the underlying instruments and their derivatives was exacerbated, much as the water in a bathtub starts to splash more violently from side to side when a small child moves his hand back and forth, slowly at first, and then faster and faster. The child waits excitedly for the water to splash over the side. Securities traders, unlike the small child, however, do not look forward to the waves of excess volatility. Asynchronous price movements in intermarket trading generate fear. Fear, in turn, can lead to panic.[17] In such a scenario, price movements become violent until trading stops entirely, or trades occur at unreasonable prices.[18]

Professional investors usually engage experienced agents with superb information and access to the marketplace. However, on Black Monday and Terrible Tuesday, these agents were also in the dark. Many usually sophisticated traders entered market orders to sell vast amounts of securities. The unexpected use of the market order as an investment tool by professional managers wreaked havoc on both exchange and OTC markets.

Without accurate and timely information, investors of all classes attempted to sell assets or limit losses. Lacking price information, they did the only thing feasible: they sent market orders to their broker. However, under these circumstances, the most advantageous price obtainable was a meaningless reference point. Even the specialist didn't know what the prices were on October 19; orders to sell at the market (that is, at any price) poured in.[19] On Black Monday and Terrible Tuesday there were often no bids in the trading arenas. Under the chaotic market conditions prevailing at the time, this was to be expected. Since investors did not know what the prices should be, it made no sense to enter buy orders.[20]

When trading in major securities is suddenly halted because of panic, cessation itself can increase the panic. If there is a stated policy of continuous trading in a security, it is crucial to continue trading at all times. Otherwise, when panic sets in, order imbalances will inevitably be exacerbated. On the days under discussion, this occurred frequently.[21]

We believe it appropriate, however, to comment on recent public criticism of specialists and OTC market-makers during this period. Their behavior (they are the only recognized sources of liquidity in the present market structure) has been severely and unfairly criticized for failing to live up to their regulators' benighted obligations. Market-makers are not and should not be responsible for providing price insurance for a single issue or an entire market.[22]

When global investment consensus, whether created by a significant event or by panic, is that the market as a whole should decline dramatically, there is no possibility that any set of professional dealers can or should limit that decline. In fact, the speed at which new equilibrium prices are reached is a measure of market efficiency. Market-makers have no economic motivation for bidding (or offering) against such a trend. In addition, the market-makers' usual choices for protective strategies—options and futures—were not available. Indeed, market-makers had every motivation to withdraw from the market. The franchises under which they operate are valuable only because they enable the market-makers to profit from buying and selling with privileged information. If faced with a choice between bankruptcy and commercial embarrassment for withdrawing as a market-maker, the decision is a "no brainer."[23]

"He who fights and runs away, lives to fight another day" is an old saw relevant to specialists who ceased trading and to OTC market-makers who declined to answer their telephones. They were not villains. They were rational capitalists behaving in a prudent manner. The markets would have been much the worse had they gone belly-up trying to stop the unstoppable.

In the face of a market decline in which forced buying threatens bankruptcy, franchises obviously lose their attractiveness. They are valuable only if the market-maker can survive with enough capital for a reasonable expectation of recovery. On Black Monday with the probability of bankruptcy looming, supporting the market would have been economic suicide. When the market as a whole plummets, some players must lose; but there is no reason why the market-makers should suffer disproportionately.

The economic role of a market-maker should be to facilitate quick executions of transactions and facilitate price discovery, not to stabilize prices. There is a difference. Facilitation of trades permits investors to sell (or buy) securities when they wish, without waiting uncertain periods of time for a contra-party to enter an order. Under normal circumstances, market-makers make a small profit from the difference between the price at which they buy securities and the price at which they sell them a few minutes (or hours) later. Market-makers provide search services (finding a contra-party rapidly), as well as dealer services (risking the dealer's own capital temporarily to permit a client to trade immediately). When the market is chaotic, the usual services become extremely costly (since the market risk is much greater) or may not be available at any price.[24] If the equilibrium price falls sharply, the market-maker should not be required to make the fall gradual rather than rapid. A market-maker's function is to provide immediate execution (predictable immediacy in economists' terms) rather than price guarantees.[25]

In panics, dealers will never be Horatio at the bridge, standing fast and supplying liquidity to the entire market, although dealers may well choose to be buyers of the last resort for good clients. That role should be their commercial decision to make. However, so long as market participants are required to enter all bids and offers into an arena whose regulations include price-time priority for bids and offers, even good clients' orders have the potential to be displaced by others arriving first at the same or superior prices.

Specialists and OTC market-makers are also not lemmings. They have no desire to commit economic suicide—nor should they—by using their entire capital in a hopeless attempt to absorb an avalanche of sell orders during periods of market panic.[26] Unfortunately, so long as market-makers are the focal point of trading, the public's access to the market is greatly impaired when market-makers stop making active markets in their assigned or selected securities.[27]

A PROPOSED SOLUTION

Characteristics of an Improved Market

Secondary markets in equities and their derivatives (options and futures) should have the following characteristics:

1. Equal and immediate market data (bids, offers, and transaction information) for all market participants:
- Brokers.
- Dealers.
    Market-makers
    Arbitrageurs
- Investors.
    Institutional
    Individual
- Issuers.
- Regulators.

2. No imposed obligations for market-makers or requirements for them to maintain continuous two-sided markets.

3. Instant execution of bids and offers when like-priced orders meet.

4. The pricing of all orders before their entry into the trading arena.

5. Price-time priority for all bids and offers.

6. Continuous trading during market hours under all market conditions.

7. Complete integration between the trading and clearing systems.

When a market is constructed containing these characteristics, the objectives of the Securities Reform Act of 1975 will have been realized, and many of the existing deficiencies eliminated.

Rationale

We have described the existing structural deficiencies of these markets and the adverse consequences caused by these deficiencies. We now discuss in more detail each characteristic of the new system we propose and the resultant benefits to investors.

1. Equal and Immediate Market Data for All Participants

We have shown that market data are not always available in the present systems. Existing market systems do not take full advantage of available technology. The market system should monitor, in real-time, all bids, offers, and executions in equity securities and their derivatives and display this critical market information to traders and investors. With today's technology, such data can be disseminated through many information providers.

When this level of information is available, information vendors and others will develop innovative systems to facilitate new trading strategies, resulting in the more efficient allocation of market-making capital. By contrast, the existing methods require capital to be committed on the basis of inadequate information, whether needed or not.

The result of better information will be greater profits for those engaging in the market-making function. They should be able to commit capital freely in response to profit-maximizing considerations, and the cost of providing market-making services to the investing public will be reduced. With all market participants able to see buying and selling interests at all times, and having quick and easy access to the markets, panic and fear from blackouts of information will not occur.

2. No Obligations for Market-Makers

All traders and investors should be able to commit capital at any time. Professionals, believing in their acumen and business skills, will devise a variety of commercial strategies to provide potentially profitable market-making services to their clients and the market as a whole.

Free of restrictions, innovation will flourish. With electronic, real-time market information systems available, the power of computers can be redirected to help allocate market-making capital to those issues where it can be employed most productively. Some issues will attract more dealer interest than others. This is appropriate, since some securities are widely held and have a broad market interest, while others are regional and smaller and have wider spreads and lower volumes. Competition will determine prices and spreads.

Investment banking firms will elect to make continuous two-sided markets in equities, as they now do in the securities they underwrite that do not trade on exchanges.

Information vendors will develop better liquidity information about issues traded. Since the time, price, and quantities of all bids, offers, and executions will be available, as well as the number and types of professional market-makers trading in each issue, indices showing historical volatility and depth of each issue could be computed and displayed, providing investors with significant information on which to base decisions.

In a market system without market-maker obligations, regulation will be simpler and more effective. The system itself should time-stamp every bid, offer, and execution and should record the type of initiating participants. Manipulation will be more difficult, and its detection can be greatly speeded and improved.

Since commitments to make two-sided continuous markets are likely to be breached when needed most, franchises and regulatory obligations should be eliminated totally. When the markets are calm, nonfranchised dealers will supply liquidity cheaper without affirmative obligations. When markets are turbulent, mandating unprofitable actions by professionals is costly and futile. Franchise systems cost more since firms are obliged to provide more services than the dictates of their economic self-interest. They will increase the prices of their services to compensate. There is no need for franchisees to supply market liquidity.

3. Instance Execution and Reporting of Bids and Offers
When Bids and Offers Match
When the prices of bids and offers are equal, execution should always occur instantly without manual intervention. If a bid or offer is entered at a price better than the best offer or bid, an execution should occur at the previously resident price. This guarantees eager buyers or sellers an execution if their order is priced through the market.

4. The Pricing of All Orders Before Their Entry into
the Trading Arena
We have noted earlier that market orders contribute to chaos in the market. We propose, therefore, that all orders should be priced prior to entry.

5. Price-time Priority for All Bids and Offers

First-come, first-served is a traditional American measure of fairness. In an effective market, the time of entry into the system of every bid and offer should be recorded. Execution of orders should take place in strict order of arrival within each price, regardless of size. This will guarantee fairness. No order from the public or a dealer should be allowed to displace an order entered earlier at the same price. Investors will thus be assured fair treatment. If there is effective recording and reporting of trades, there is no longer any justification for size priority.[28]

Some of the proposals from others, including the Brady Commission, have suggested circuit breakers such as trading suspensions when markets exceed preset volatility limits. If trading is halted, for example, when an issue (or market) declines (or rises) by some discrete amount or percentage, a number of orders will inevitably remain unexecuted. When trading resumes, an equitable system will assure the status of these orders in the order queue. Otherwise, subsequent orders may be executed first and subject the system to the justifiable criticism of unfairness.[29]

A difficulty with existing systems is their inability to maintain reasonable priority rules when trading is halted. In futures exchanges after daily price limits are reached, this is certainly the case. It is entirely possible for members of the public who had liquidating orders ahead of professionals to have their orders displaced by subsequently placed orders of floor traders. No system without price-time priority can guarantee fair treatment to all participants.

6. Continuous Trading

As we noted above, some of the major problems during Black Monday and Terrible Tuesday were caused by the asynchronous behavior of the cash, options, and futures markets. During periods of delayed openings, trading halts, and market suspensions, traders and clients were unable to determine true values.

Markets should stay open at all times. So long as all potential participants have access to them, securities should trade or not depending on whether appropriately priced bids and offers are entered. If there is a wide disparity between bid and offer, or in the absence of bids and offers, all relevant information should be available simultaneously to all players. Trading in individual securities should never halt for any reason while the market is open. There is no need to prevent market participants form trading with each other if they wish to do so, even while the market awaits a significant announcement. In addition, with many issues now traded globally, halting trading in an individual security (or even in an entire country's market) within one national market does not necessarily stop trading in that issue in other countries.

All investors and market professionals should be able to enter bids or offers in securities, options, or futures contracts when they believe it is appropriate, and likewise they should be able to enter offers at better prices when they are willing to sell more cheaply. Information must be made available to all market participants when there is an unusual event affecting a security. The system can also be designed to provide for automatic cancellation of unexecuted orders when investors wish. Most investors will not trade during such a period. However, if trading does not take place, it will be so because there are no executable buy and sell orders left in the system, rather than because some bureaucrat decides trading should cease. As long as both buyer and seller orders are entered at matching prices, executions should occur. All potential sources of capital should be allowed to seek profit or attempt to reduce loss by continuing to trade, despite the existence of a notice stating important news is pending.

Trading should be allowed to continue except when the markets are regularly closed, and when authorized governmental policy dictates that the entire market should be closed for some period of time. We believe such power should be used only with the most extreme caution. If U.S. markets had been shut down during the October crisis, the results would have been catastrophic.[30]

Under the present systems, there is a great temptation to cry "uncle" when market-making capital is depleted. With the system we propose, funds will always be available to the market, since all investors—dealers, arbitrageurs, institutions, individuals, and issuers—will always have equal and timely information and access to the markets. The potential for a trade will always exist. This will provide more confidence for investors to use the market.

In addition, price movements of securities and/or derivatives should not be limited during a trading session. It is ironic that, while the market was widely faulted for its lack of liquidity during the recent crisis, many proposed reforms and some recent steps taken by exchange regulators would eliminate liquidity entirely for periods of time by halting trading. Such limits do not protect investors. Before such reforms are adopted, a careful analysis of performance in markets in which daily price limits exist is in order.

With continuous markets and no price limits, if there is a surfeit of sell (or buy) orders, there will be no trading. Trading will halt for economic reasons. However, if any buyer is willing to pay the price offered by a seller, regardless of how much lower than the previous transaction, we see no valid reason why a regulator should prevent this trade if all bids and offers are visible to everyone in the market. Unfortunately, in the existing systems, in which information on unexecuted orders is available to only a few market makers, the arguments for arbitrarily halting trading become seductive.

7. Complete Integration Between the Trading and Clearing Systems

The clearing and settlement of financial instruments is an area of major financial risk. Under existing systems, most transactions made in trading arenas (exchanges) or telephone execution systems (OTC) are oral. There is great danger of error in the oral agreements. Written confirmation follows hours or days later. On Black Monday alone, according to reports, there were more than 67,000 so-called QTs (Questioned Trade forms) on the NYSE. These transactions have to be reconciled individually. Each firm has to analyze each of the QTs individually and contact the contraparty. This process takes several days (including a weekend) before all trades are either agreed on or one or both parties to a trade takes remedial action to bring their books into balance. This is often very costly.[31]

In addition to the cost of reconciling QTs, there is the more important risk of the damaging effects of financial failure of one or more of the trading parties between the trade and settlement date. The Options Clearing Corporation (OCC) suffered multi-million-dollar losses as the result of the failure of some of their members after Black Monday. If a major market player had failed, the financial consequences to the financial system would have been disastrous.[32]

We propose locking in each trade automatically. With a locked-in trade (a goal sought since the late 1960s), clearing house and market regulators can keep up-to-the-moment track of the amount and level of financial commitments made by all professional participants (broker-dealers). DKs (Don't Knows) and QTs could not exist, and the settlement process can be completely automated. All these features would offer significant benefits to the market that are impossible in present oral trading environments.

Background to a Solution

In the early 1970s, the United States Congress, responding to a variety of operational, economic, and organizational problems, conducted exhaustive hearings on the U.S. securities industry. These hearings, both investigative and legislative, resulted in the Securities Reform Act of 1975.

Among many other things, this legislation called for the development of a national market system (NMS) for securities trading. The Securities and Exchange Commission (SEC), charged by the Congress with facilitating the development of the NMS through a Congressionally-mandated advisory group (the National Market Advisory Board, or NMAB), sought proposals from the industry and others for plans to implement this legislation. In response to the request for proposals, on April 30, 1976, the authors presented to the NMAB their Peake-Mendelson-Williams national book system (PMW), calling for a fully-electronic secondary trading system for NMS securities. This proposal attracted considerable attention, but was not adopted for a variety of reasons. It would have restructured the U.S. equity exchanges into a single trading arena for eligible securities, and existing market centers argued the present system was working well.

1. Pre-opening through Market Opening
Between the end of one trading session and the beginning of the next session, pre-opening orders would be accepted into the system. Screens would show the uncanceled bids and offers still extant in the market. Trading screens would provide the following information:

- Last trade (with size and time).
- Closing market bids and offers.

Prior to the commencement of trading the system would periodically analyze the orders it contains to determine the clearing (opening) price that would exist if the market opened at that moment. Examples of time duration could be:

- Good until canceled (GTC).
- Good until 15:29:00 New York Time.
- Good until (date and time).

An example of a condition duration could be:

- Execute only at today's opening price or cancel.

During the pre-opening market process, the system would periodically analyze the newly entered orders combined with unexpired orders to determine the clearing (opening) price should the market open at that moment.

TABLE 13–1
Example of the Opening Process Using Unexecuted Orders Resident in the Market

Bids (Size)	Price	Offers (Size)
	$40 \frac{1}{2}$	10,100
	$40 \frac{3}{8}$	
	$40 \frac{1}{4}$	200
500	$40 \frac{1}{8}$	800
6,200	40	
	$39 \frac{7}{8}$	2,200

(All bids and offers at the same price are aggregated.)

If the security were to open for trading with the orders shown, the opening price would be 40. This price would be calculated to result in the clearance of the maximum number of orders. The process would be as follows:

TABLE 13–2
The Opening Process

Bids (Size)	Price	Offers (Size)
	$40 \frac{1}{2}$	10,100
	$40 \frac{3}{8}$	
	$40 \frac{1}{4}$	200
~~500~~	$40 \frac{1}{8}$	800
~~6,200~~ 4,500	40 ←Clearing (Opening) Price	
	$39 \frac{7}{8}$	~~2,200~~

First, the highest bid ($40\frac{1}{8}$ for 500 shares) would be matched with the lowest executable offer (2,200 shares at $39\frac{7}{8}$). Then the remainder of the 2,200 shares (1,700) would be executed against the first 1,700 shares bid for at 40. Since all executable bids and offers would have been accommodated, the clearing (opening) price would be 40. This would leave the market as:

TABLE 13–3
Conditions on the Book Following the Opening

Bids (Size)	Price	Offers (Size)
	$40\frac{1}{2}$	10,100
	$40\frac{3}{8}$	
	$40\frac{1}{4}$	200
	$40\frac{1}{8}$	800
4,500	40	
	$39\frac{7}{8}$	

A total of 2,200 shares would have opened at 40.

Note that bidding at a higher price than the opening price or offering lower than the opening price penalizes neither seller or buyer. Opening price is determined solely by the aggregate amounts of securities executable, and all would be executed at the same opening price.

2. Regular Trading During Market Hours

After the market opens, trading would take place when bids and offers met in price. An order priced through the market on either side (an offer lower than the best existing bid or a bid higher than the best existing offer) would be executed at the resident price.

For example, if the best bid in the system was at $40\frac{1}{2}$ and an offer to sell was entered at $39\frac{7}{8}$, the system would execute all or part of the order at $40\frac{1}{2}$. If not all of the offer were executable at $40\frac{1}{2}$, the remainder of the sell order would be executed at successively lower prices until the order was filled or the balance became the best offer. Any market participant would be able to enter orders at any price. Any person with access to the market through a quotation device or trading terminal would be able to see the entire book for each security, including the total numbers of bids and offers aggregated at each price.

In the event of a pending announcement, the quotation devices and trading terminals could be programmed to display that fact and the type of announcement pending. The system would also be capable of automatically canceling unexecuted orders if the client or dealer wishes to do so in the event of certain types of pending announcements. Should the person placing the order not avail himself of the automatic cancellation, his order would remain active in the system despite announcements. This would permit investors continuous access to the arena. Obviously, if all orders should be canceled during a pending announcement, there would be no trading. However, trading would halt because the investors chose not to trade, rather than because some bureaucrat has decided that trading should cease.

3. Trading During Market Hours

While under the PMW system it would never be necessary to close the market, we recognize the probability that regular daily trading hours will be continued. The system's regulator would be able to halt trading in the entire market instantly in the PMW system. With our system, trading hours could be substantially longer than in a manual system. Participants could be located anywhere in the world.

CONCLUSION

Only one type of system can have all the desired characteristics: a fully electronic system. The secondary markets in equities and their derivatives must be changed to a PMW system as rapidly as possible. Only then will both American (and international) investors have the market technology promised and mandated by the Congress almost 13 years ago.

The system we propose combines the best features of both auction and dealer markets. There would be multiple, competing dealers, whose number would be limited solely by their perceived economic self-interest. All public (and other) bids and offers would be able to interact in a true auction environment.

It is being argued that the operating problem on Black Monday and Terrible Tuesday was not a basic structural weakness of the market, but the fact that the dealers making two-sided markets did not have sufficient capital. It is not clear that if they had had more capital, sane market-makers would have committed more than they did in that environment— and they could hardly be blamed for that. On the contrary, if franchises were not required, and if they had known the extent of the real buying and selling interest or had even known the true levels and sizes of offers, more dealers might have entered on the buy side of the market. Moreover, better information would have brought more investors. Those firms might have brought significant additional support to the market.[33]

In PMW, the economic need for dealers to perform a market-making function will continue and may even grow. However, franchising or restricting their access to the trading arena by regulation would be counterproductive. Dealer services will be provided when they are needed and economic, and will be priced competitively. When issues do not require or warrant dealer services, the interaction of public order flows will permit a true auction environment. The combination of the dealer and auction systems would bring together the strengths of both to form a single, low-cost, efficient electronic secondary trading system.

We can hardly argue that structural defects were the only cause of the problems on Black Monday and Terrible Tuesday, but there is little doubt that these defects exacerbated the difficulties of those two days and the ones immediately following. Some of that volatility was caused by the information blackout, cessation of trading, the inability to access market information or to execute trades, and the resultant price thrashing among the related markets.

To the extent the PMW system relieves these problems, volatility will be reduced. Our system not only improves information flows, it makes the markets fairer and more efficient. These are worthwhile and attainable objectives in themselves. However, volatility created by events cannot and will not be eliminated. No system can guarantee against price volatility.

To be sure, a more efficient system might have brought more sell orders to the market, but would have permitted buy orders as well. However, in so far as the sell orders were responses to the uncertainties generated by the structural deficiencies of the existing market, in an open, real-time trading environment, selling pressure would have been diminished since information and price uncertainties would not have existed.

No system is capable of preventing *all* market turbulence. However, when market turbulence does develop, at least some prices get out of line. During periods of turbulence, so long as the actual price information for all issues is available and orders can be placed efficiently and executed immediately, there are always opportunities for alert traders and investors. To be sure, opportunistic investment involves selling as well as buying; but in a market panic or near panic, buying has a salutary effect. Disasters that strike when selling is pandemic and potential buyers cannot be found *because they do not have access to the marketplace* can and should be eliminated.

We are confident that in any turbulent situation there will be fewer problems in a fully interactive system such as we have advocated for more than a dozen years.[34]

We cannot suggest that systems never fail, particularly when subjected to levels of stress not envisioned by their creators. Reflection suggests we regularly trust our lives and fortunes to computer systems in defense, the space program, electronic funds transfer, and air traffic control, where the potential for disaster far exceeds the worst scenario for the securities markets. Moreover, as we have shown, the systems problems of October 19 and 20 were more accurately the inability for high speed systems to be brought to a near halt in a manual process, and still operate effectively. There is an upper boundary to the capacity of the manual system to operate efficiently under intense pressure and high volume. That volume limit would seem to be somewhere below 600 million shares. With more computers, printers, and bigger floors, the limit may be raised, but it will still exist, and we will exceed it again.

By contrast, if the computers now used in support of the floors and the genius that has linked them together were applied to a system like PMW, we could now handle one-billion-share days, or even greater volumes, with no great trouble and no risk to our financial infrastructure. So long as effective use of our computer resources is not made, we will continue to live in the umbra of catastrophe.

The present market structures are flawed. Whether flawed fatally we do not know at this moment, and hope we never find out. However, failure to fix the existing flaws may certainly mean the demise of the secondary equities markets as we have known them. And it is not an exaggeration to say that it would put the whole global financial system in jeopardy. Time has run out. We cannot risk delay.

STEPS REQUIRED TO IMPLEMENT PMW

One of the most attractive features of PMW is its ease of implementation, at least with respect to equities and options trading. The futures markets may require additional legislation. The appropriate regulators would have to promulgate but one new rule to implement the Congressional mandate and to achieve a superior system. The rule should suggest that:

On and after (December 31, 1990) all trading in designated National Market System securities must take place in a market in which there is absolute price-time priority for all bids and offers; and that

All publicly traded equity securities and exchange traded options on equities and indices are designated as National Market securities under the provisions of the Securities Reform Act of 1975.

There is nothing in this proposed rule that would prohibit or restrict the franchising of market makers by the SEC or exchanges. If a case can be made for such franchises, the regulators would be free to incorporate one or more franchise schemes within a PMW system. There is also no need to require explicitly that the system be electronic. However no system requiring price-time priority can be other than electronic.

With a date certain established for implementation of the rule, the securities industry would be forced to take immediate action. The date we have suggested can be met if the appropriate resources are brought to bear, and the rule is made effective quickly.

At the least, the regulators should propose such a rule to determine the reaction of the industry. The resulting debate would bring forward the best thinking of all participants and should expose the real interests of all parties. If such a rule is not proposed (and implemented), there will be years of debate and inaction. 1988 is a presidential election year. Little controversial legislation is written in such a year. However, the commission, although an instrument of the Congress, is independent. Its members are appointed, not elected. 1988 brings the regulators a unique opportunity to deal with the recent crisis in a decisive manner and to demonstrate their independence from the influences of vested interests.

To do nothing is as much a decision as to do something. The American people will not soon forgive regulators or legislators who, after being warned by an event such as the October financial crisis, do nothing to ameliorate chances of its recurrence.

APPENDIX A: PRESENT SYSTEMS AND THEIR DEFECTS

EXCHANGE MARKETS

On U.S. equities exchanges, specialists—professional dealers given exclusive franchises in certain securities by their exchanges—are both auctioneers and participants in the trading in their assigned securities. Specialists are required under the terms of their monopolistic franchises to

- Supervise trading in all orders entered for execution in their securities; and
- Provide bids and offers for their own accounts when there is an order imbalance to provide price continuity (the phenomenon of forcing trans-actions to take place at the same or close to the same price of the preceding transaction) in a security.

In exchange for these affirmative obligations, specialists are given the exclusive privilege of seeing and managing the book of public orders entered into the trading arena.

The public is denied the right to see this book, even though it contains valuable information that would help investors make decisions. Since exchanges limit that information about existing bids and offers to specialists, when the latter encounter unusual market conditions, they must either:

- Use their discretion as to the prices at which their securities trade (which may be second guessed by exchange officials and other regulators); or
- Request a trading halt from exchange officials.

On Black Monday and Terrible Tuesday specialists took both steps.

Several of those who chose to use their best judgment are undergoing intense scrutiny from regulators who suspect their judgment was unwise or of questionable motivation. Those who stopped trading in their assigned securities did so because they were unsure of what prices to establish and/or were afraid their entire capital might be wiped out.

With 20–20 hindsight it is easy to fault specialists in both cases. Their behavior was rational: Those who continued trading did so without knowing the appropriate prices of their securities. Those who ceased to trade did so to prevent economic suicide. Neither action should be condemned out-of-hand since they acted under the rules of the game.

In the past decade, order delivery systems to exchange floors have become highly automated. On the NYSE, for example, the SuperDOT system delivers priced and market orders directly to the specialist at his trading post. Many member firms have developed highly sophisticated computer and communications systems to transmit orders under the control of proprietary analytical computer programs to effect complex trading strategies, both for their own accounts and for their clients.

During the crisis these order delivery systems, together with others on regional exchanges, were in high gear, delivering thousands of orders within a short space of time. Upon the arrival of these orders at the trading posts, the specialists, who still effect trades manually, were overwhelmed. As a result, exchange officials took the unique step of requesting their members to discontinue the use of these systems. In sum, the disparity between the efficient, modern, automated order delivery systems and the manual execution systems caused the order delivery mechanism to be sacrificed to the antiquated, obsolete telephone and other systems of prior decades. This fact alone demonstrated the structural bankruptcy of the present exchange markets.

To summarize, the exchange market structure is deficient because:

- The specialist as the nexus of the system cannot cope with the speed of the telecommunications system now in use;
- The specialist does not supply liquidity to the market; he offers the twin services of immediacy and price continuity, neither of which is effective during market crises;
- Information about existing bids and offers at and away from current market prices is not always available; and
- The public lacks adequate access to the trading arena.

OTC MARKETS

In the OTC markets, only registered market-makers have access to bids and offers from investors at the current prices, and each market-maker sees only those orders away from the market given to his firm. In addition, since the OTC market does not have a bid and offer book of investor orders, many investors do not enter away-from-the-market bids and offers, and the market is deprived of that support.

A market-maker is a dealer who meets specified criteria set by the National Association of Securities Dealers, Inc. (NASD), regulator of the OTC market. Qualified dealers may register as market-makers in a set of securities selected by them. Registration as a market-maker carries with it the obligation to:

- Make a two-sided continuous market in those securities in which it is registered;

- Execute orders for a limited number of shares at its displayed prices at all times the market is open; and
- Keep its prices competitive.

Failure to make a continuous market will subject the firm to the penalty of being removed as a market-maker in the security for a period of six months; failure to comply with the other requirements subjects it to NASD disciplinary action.

The principal trading system used in the OTC market is the NASDAQ system (National Association of Securities Dealers Automated Quotation System). This system provides registered market-makers with the facility for displaying two-sided markets in their selected securities. These markets are entered through a terminal keyboard (NASDAQ Level III terminal), use of which is controlled by the NASD. The prices entered by a registered market-maker along with the quotes of other registered market-makers are displayed on the NASDAQ Level II and III terminals.

Only the best bid and offer are displayed on NASDAQ Level I terminals and on terminals provided by most quotation vendors (Reuters, Quotron, etc.). Level I terminals are used primarily for the retail brokerage and institutional investment community.

OTC orders are generally executed over the telephone. There is an optional feature on the NASDAQ system permitting registered market-makers to execute smaller orders (up to 1,000 shares) against their quotes electronically. This system is called SOES (small order execution system). At present the use of SOES by market-makers is optional, and during Black Monday and Terrible Tuesday many of them suspended their use of the system or forced its suspension by entering bids and/or offers that created a situation in which the markets were locked or crossed.

A rule change proposed after the recent crisis will make use of SOES by market-makers become mandatory. In the OTC market, aside from the quotes provided by market-makers and reports of execution, there is no confluence of orders at a single point as there is (at least in part) on exchanges. Each market-maker determines on its own the quotations it displays on NASDAQ. Its prices are usually based on:

- Overall market order flow;
- The market-maker's own order flow;
- The market-maker's trading position; and
- The prices posted by competitors.

On Black Monday and Terrible Tuesday when the equities markets collapsed, the informational needs required for rational pricing were not met, and dealers did not know what prices to quote. There was no mechanism by which trading in a single security could be halted, even temporarily. As a result, OTC market-makers, like the specialists, did what they could to protect themselves. The easiest way to do so was to avoid answering their telephone. Without calls, they did not have to execute orders. Since all OTC market-makers have telephone trading turrets with lights displaying the identity of their callers, it was easy to be selective. If a competitor called, they could leave the line ringing. If a client who had recently made a large purchase of a security called and the odds were that a sell order might result, the call was ignored. Lacking bomb shelters, OTC market-makers created their own private fortresses by ignoring calls. They hunkered down and waited out the storm. It is unlikely that many, if any, voluntarily called the NASD and offered to relinquish their market-making registration. They were well aware that their competitors, like themselves, were also not answering the telephone. The NASD was highly unlikely to invoke sanctions against most or all of its market-makers. If it did so, who would make markets?

The latter point is important. The NASD has rule proposals at the Securities and Exchange Commission attempting to strengthen the requirements on their market-makers. At best those rules can provide but illusory protection. Another market crisis will again be met by a defensive response by market-makers. If they are required to execute all trades submitted to them, even those which might bankrupt them, they will abandon market-making in self-defense. Should that occur, the NASD will either have to waive its rules or face the chaos that will result. The former is more likely, just as the SEC suspended rules preventing corporate repurchases of their own stock during the last half hour of trading in an attempt to calm the markets.

At present there is no way a public order to buy a security at a price can meet directly with a public order to sell the same security at the same price in the OTC market. All orders must be directed to market-makers, who will buy or sell the security for their own account. As a result, during the market turbulence, many potential buy orders never reached the marketplace. Without answering their telephone, market-makers simply had no way of determining if they had buy or sell orders. In theory the OTC market has more liquidity than exchange markets because its system of competing market-makers brings with it more capital. It is also structurally unsound because of the inability of the public's orders to interact directly.

DERIVATIVE MARKETS

In the past 15 years, new markets for derivative instruments have developed and flourished. There are two main types of derivative instruments: options and futures. While similar in some respects, the instruments differ greatly.

Options Markets

The options markets trade fungible instruments carrying the right (but not the obligation) of their buyer to receive from (a call option) or deliver to (a put option) the writer (seller) of the option a specified physical quantity of a specified asset, which may be a security or, in the case of an index option contract, a basket of securities, at a predetermined price for a stated period of time. The buyer of an option pays to the option's writer a fee, called a premium, for this right.

Listed, or exchange-traded options, are actually issued by the credit-depository arm of the exchange, OCC. OCC is the guarantor of the option. The writer of an option may liquidate his liability by buying an identical option from another issuer or holder through the same clearing member. The owner of an option may sell his option if it has value. If the option is not exercised on or before its expiration date, it expires; and the writer has no further obligation.

Options on baskets of securities are almost always written on a set of securities making up an index. An example of an index is the Standard and Poor's 500 Industrial Stock Index. Settlement of an exercised index option is made in the form of the cash equivalent of the excess of the settlement price over the exercise price of the underlying basket securities at the time of the option's expiry.

Options are used by speculators, traders, and investors:

* To leverage securities positions;
* For technical trading strategy purposes; or
* To protect profits or minimize losses.

In the United States, exchange trading of options is regulated by the SEC and conducted through "open outcry." A few options exchanges use a specialist system; others use competing market makers.

Futures Markets

A futures contract is a standardized, fungible contract to deliver a specified asset at a predetermined location (delivery point) sometime during a specified future delivery month. A futures contract has no price corresponding to the premium for an option contract. The prices at which futures contracts trade are the prices at which the underlying assets are to be delivered during the delivery month. These prices are agreed upon by auctions in the trading ring. Futures markets are regulated by Commodity Futures Trading Commission (CFTC). They began as markets engaged in servicing agricultural commodities.

In October 1975, trading in futures contracts on financial instruments was introduced. It has since exploded, far surpassing trading in contracts on commodities. Unlike options contracts, both the buyer and the seller are obligated to perform under the contract's terms. There is no expiration date. Rather, there is a date at which trading stops and a delivery month during which the contract must be honored. The only way either the buyer or seller of a futures contract can escape his or her obligation is to offset his or her position by buying (in the case of a seller) or selling (in the case of a buyer) an identical contract prior to the delivery date.

Some financial futures contracts, especially index futures, are settled in the cash value of profit or loss on the underlying financial instruments, rather than by the delivery of the actual securities. Others require the delivery of the actual securities.

The values of derivative instruments, both options and futures, are derived from the prices of their underlying asset. If there are no prices publicly available for the underlying assets that trade in a cash market, it is difficult to establish a true value for the derivatives. Investor buy and sell orders in derivatives can, but do not necessarily, meet directly on options and futures exchange floors. Liquidity in these markets is provided by speculators who are known either as "day," "position," or "local" traders, and who spend their business day buying and selling options or futures contracts, hoping to make a profit from the change in prices of the contracts.

APPENDIX B: COMMENTS ABOUT SYSTEMS PROBLEMS IN AN AUTOMATED MARKET

Some people may criticize the PMW Proposal for an automated system on the grounds that automated systems are more likely to fail than their manual counterparts. In light of the highly publicized difficulties with certain automated exchange systems reported by several of the studies of Black Monday and Terrible Tuesday, particularly the GAO Report, we believe it appropriate to comment on these systems.[35] If computer systems caused part of the problems, does it make sense to entrust the entire market mechanism to computers? There are two parts to our response to these concerns:

1. Computers must be adequately sized to meet peak load problems. If computers are too small, they will be unable to handle the tasks assigned to them.

2. Careful analysis of the systems that failed, and an understanding of how those systems are used, lead to the conclusion that exchange floor environment, and not automation, was the cause of the failure.

ADEQUATE CAPACITY

Computer systems must have sufficient capacity to handle peak transaction loads. The NYSE has stated to the GAO that their planning had anticipated peak volume levels of approximately 400 million shares per day by the end of 1988 and 600 million shares by 1990. Capacity on October 19 and 20 was intended to handle about 300 million shares on a routine basis. Therefore, the system was asked to perform under a load of about twice that which was anticipated. No system can be expected to handle double its maximum design load and survive without problems. Indeed, those people at SIAC and the NYSE should be commended for keeping the systems up as well as they did.

APPROPRIATE USES OF AUTOMATION

The biggest systems problem of October 19 and 20, however, was not the capacity of automation, but the uses to which it was put. When computers were first applied to automating paperwork processing, it was common to see inefficient programs written in which each component of the total system exactly replicated the task of one person in the old manual process. Thus the actual jobs of John or Sam or Mary became briefly enshrined in computer code. System designers quickly learned systems were more efficient if the entire process was rethought with the goal of applying technological assets to do the task required, rather than simply replicating a manual task on a computer. Several tasks or checks could be applied to a single, one-step transaction, instead of passing the transaction through a series of programs in human assembly line fashion.

Systems on the NYSE (and to a lesser extent in the OTC market as well) have been designed to old-fashioned standards of automation in the wrong direction. Instead of enshrining John or Sam or Mary's manual tasks in computer code as they are made redundant, the NYSE has attempted to encapsulate them so their jobs remain forever (specialists and floor traders making hundreds of thousands of dollars per year get better treatment than clerks making $25,000). In so doing, SIAC (Securities Industry Automation Corporation) has created an interwoven skein of systems charged with taking order feeds capable of handling 10 to 50 orders per second per firm and printing those orders out at a rate of perhaps 10 per minute to be addressed by a specialist already inundated from other sources. Once acted upon, the order ticket is then fed back into a system with even slower card readers. Moreover, the nature of order systems is such that printing an order at the specialist's booth does not clear the system of the order. The system must log the order and retain it until notified of the successful execution of the order, cancellation, or some other action to remove the pending order from the queue. Thus on October 19 and 20, orders poured in through highly efficient order systems to be handled by a nineteenth-century clerical process.

A mechanical analog would be to place a quarter-inch piece of household plumbing pipe between two sections of a 60-inch water main. The stress that occurs where the pipe narrows to the smallest part is immense.

According to the GAO, problems occurred with the following systems:

• "Part of the DOT System was halted once on October 16, four times on October 19 and once on October 20."[36]

The failures occurred because the volume of orders caused order counters to overflow. The system, which must log and maintain orders until dispensation can be determined, could efficiently receive and route orders to the specialist post; but because the physical trading process on the floor was too slow, the system clogged with orders while waiting for the specialist to act. In the PMW system, the execution could occur at a pace that would equal the routing of orders, and this would not occur.

• "Part of the Limit Order System stopped processing on three occasions on October 20 because the number of limit orders exceeded the system's capability to store additional transactions."[37]

(The term *transactions* in the report is used in the system designer's sense of any item a system must process and not in the sense of a completed trade.) The limit order system, one of the few useful innovations on the floor in the past ten years, is hamstrung by the requirement that all orders be acted on by the specialist. What will never be known is how many limit orders were lost or ignored that were to be entered in the physical book of those securities that did not have a LOS display book. Ironically, the manual system, which often performs very badly, avoids blame since it lacks an audit trail intrinsic to computer systems. Again, because of the chaos on the floor, executions against limits were missed, and the opportunity to enter bids against attractive offers on the book was not achievable, since would-be bidders could not be certain that specialists would execute their orders fairly and quickly. In the PMW system the book is self-clearing as bids and offers match. In falling markets, prospective bidders can establish resistance levels at prices below the current trading price, and other potential bidders can see these levels develop and enter their orders.

• "On October 19, 20, and 21, the Automated Price Reporting System encountered delays of up to 2 hours in the execution of odd lot orders and the associated delivery of odd lot information to specialists."[38]

The current odd lot system was developed by the exchange in the late 1960s when the market choked on 20 million share days. Little effort has been expended to upgrade this technology because the larger retail houses have developed their own odd lot execution automation. The exchange is now belatedly upgrading these systems, but the problems of October 19 and 20 were purely the result of asking outmoded systems to support volume levels ten times their design levels.

• "The Universal Device Controller experienced significant delays of up to 75 minutes in printing orders on October 19th and 20th."[39]

The universal device controller is a system of software and computers saddled with the uncomfortable task of serving as the technological bridge between late twentieth-century technology and a nineteenth-century manual process. The system must take inputs to the floor from automated systems, route them to the appropriate post, and print them out in a location where the specialist, under siege, is supposed to see and respond to the orders. It must then take the actions of the specialist that are translated onto mark sense cards and route them back to the appropriate output system. That this system works at all is a monument to the ingenuity of its designers. That it failed on October 19 and 20 speaks more to the impossibility of the task than the fault of the computers or software.

• "The Post Support System exceeded its allocated transaction storage capability on October 20 which caused portions of the system to stop operating for several 2 to 3 minute periods."[40]

Again the problem stems from trying to marry a slow manual process with an automated input. If executions had occurred automatically, these processing problems would have disappeared.

• "The NYSE's interface to the ITS experienced delays in delivering orders to the floor of the Exchange on October 19 through 21 because of backups on the card printers."[41]

As noted, when high-speed delivery mechanisms are dependent on electro-mechanical output devices subject to overloads that slow the process and may precipitate mechanical failures, the problems are inevitable. More or faster printers would have resulted in fewer undelivered orders and more unexecuted orders—a questionable improvement.

• "The Consolidated Tape System encountered several failures on October 19 and 20, the longest of which lasted about 5 minutes."[42]

This is the inevitable result of an overloaded system and might occur in any system where design capacities were exceeded. What is not clear from the GAO report is where in the CTA system the problems occurred. The front end of the system is a series of exchange employees hovering near each post listening for executions, marking the price of the execution and the volume on mark sense cards, and inputting those cards into readers at the posts. Finally, information from the exchange is combined with data from other exchanges and sent out to vendors through high speed (9,600 bps) lines. When problems occur, vendors can ask for retransmission of significant portions of data to refresh their own data bases. While the report does not state where the problems occurred, experience with the system shows the back-end interfaces to the vendors tend to be very reliable. We suspect the input part of the system caused the failures.

• "The ticker tape, which displays last sale information from the Market Data System, was delayed for up to 2 hours on October 19 and 20."[43]

As stated in the report, the system is held at about 900 characters per minute, not because of systems deficiencies, but because studies have shown the eye cannot absorb information at a faster pace. All market professionals know the tape is unreliable under fast market conditions and use it only as a barometer of activity, not as a source for accurate prices. Ironically, the 15-minute-delayed information available to investors on cable TV, which is created from the high speed line, may well have run ahead of the tape on October 19 and 20.

• "The As-of-Status Display System, which provides information the next morning on whether a particular limit order has been executed, experienced a software processing problem on October 19."[44]

Once again, we have a problem of a system exceeding its design limits. We suspect excess volume problems may have been exacerbated by the problems in the limit display books.

APPENDIX C

Partial Text of the Securities Reform Act of 1975 [15 U.S.C. 78k Sec. 11A (a)]

Sec. 11A (a)
"(1) The Congress finds that—

> "(A) The securities markets are an important national asset which must be preserved and strengthened.
> "(B) New data processing and communications techniques create the opportunity for more efficient and effective market operation.
> "(C) It is in the public interest and appropriate for the protection of investors and the maintenance of fair and orderly markets to assure—
>> "(i) economically efficient execution of securities transactions;

"(ii) fair competition among brokers and dealers, among exchange markets and markets other than exchange markets;

"(iii) *the availability to brokers, dealers, and investors of information with respect to quotations for and transactions in securities;* [Emphasis added]

"(iv) the practicability of brokers executing investors' orders in the best market; and

"(v) an opportunity, consistent with the provisions of clauses (i) and (iv) of this subparagraph, for investors' orders to be executed *without the participation of a dealer.* [Emphasis added]

"(D) The linking of all markets for qualified securities through communication and data processing facilities will foster efficiency, enhance competition, increase the information available to brokers, dealers, and investors, facilitate the offsetting of investors' orders, and contribute to the best execution of such orders.

"(2) The Commission is directed, therefore, having due regard for the public interest, the protection of investors, and the maintenance of fair and orderly markets, to use its authority under this title to facilitate the establishment of a national market system for securities (which may include subsystems for particular types of securities with unique trading characteristics) in accordance with the findings and to carry out the objectives set forth in paragraph (1) of this subsection. The Commission, by rule, shall designate the securities or classes of securities qualified for trading in the national market system from among securities other than exempted securities. (Securities or classes of securities so designated hereinafter in this section referred to as 'qualified securities'.)

"(3) The Commission is authorized in furtherance of the directive in paragraph (2) of this subsection—

"(A) to create one or more advisory committees pursuant to the Federal Advisory Committee Act (which shall be in addition to the National Market Advisory Board established pursuant to subsection (d) of this section) and to employ one or more outside experts;

"(B) by order, to authorize or require self-regulatory organizations to act jointly with respect to matters as to which they share authority under this title in planning, developing, operating, or regulating a national market system (or a subsystem thereof) or one or more facilities thereof; and

"(C) to conduct studies and make recommendations to the Congress from time to time as to the possible need for modifications of the scheme of self-regulation provided for in this title so as to adapt it to a national market system.

APPENDIX D: GLOSSARY

affirmative obligation An exchange-imposed duty on specialists to make transactions in their specialty stocks during periods of market volatility or order imbalances.

agent A representative of a principal; as used in this paper, an agent executes his clients' orders rather than buying or selling for his own account as principal. (See also **broker**.)

arbitrage As used in this paper, to trade the same financial instrument on more than one market concurrently, or to trade related financial instruments (underlying stocks against a futures or options index contract), with the hope of making a profit from the disparity between the markets.

arbitrageur A person (or firm) who arbitrages financial instruments as a profession.

auction market A market in which both bids and offers for financial instruments are made with bids and offers being executed when they meet.

auctioneer The person (specifically a specialist) who supervises an auction and decides when transactions will occur.

best bid The highest priced buy order in the marketplace at a moment in time.

best offer The lowest priced sell order in the marketplace at a moment in time.

bid An order to buy a financial instrument entered into the marketplace.

Black Monday October 19, 1987

Brady Commission The Presidential Task Force on Market Mechanisms, chaired by Nicholas F. Brady, Chairman of Dillon, Read & Co., Inc.

Brady Report The report issued in January 1988 by the Brady Commission.

broker An agent. (See also **agent**.)

call market A market characterized by periodic, intermittent trading in financial instruments. A call market is contrasted to a continuous market, in which trading in all listed instruments may occur at any time.

call option The right to take delivery of a specified quantity of a financial instrument (or group of instruments) at a specified price during a specified time period.

cash market A market in assets, such as stocks (equity securities), bonds, or commodities, as contrasted to their derivative instruments, such as options and futures.

CFTC Commodity Futures Trading Commission, the Congressional agency charged with supervision of futures exchanges and commodity futures merchants.

circuit breaker   A term used in the Brady Report to suggest that some type of trading cessation be required when markets exceed predetermined volatility parameters.

clearing   The process of delivering and paying for financial instruments, usually one or more days after their trading.

clearing house   An organization providing facilities for the clearing of financial instruments.

clearing system   The method for effecting the clearance of financial instruments.

comparison   The process of agreeing both sides of a securities trade in writing between the two professional parties to a transaction.

continuous trading   The practice of permitting transactions in any financial instrument to occur at any moment when the market is open for business.

cross hedge   Taking an opposite position with an instrument, the price movement of which is similar to those of another instrument which the cross-hedger owns or is short.

crossed markets   A market (especially NASDAQ) in which the best offer is lower than another dealer's bid. Under the present operation of the NASDAQ system, in a crossed or locked market, trading ceases until the market in that security becomes uncrossed.

dealer market   A market in which only bids and offers are entered only by dealers, in contrast with an auction market, which permits bids and offers from nondealers to be entered and displayed.

derivative   A financial instrument whose value is determined from the price at which an underlying security is trading. Options and futures contracts are derivatives.

DK   A term used commonly in the securities industry for transactions made orally that have difficulty being resolved in writing. (See also: **QT** and **out trade**.)

DOT system   See **SuperDOT system.**

efficient market   A market in which information is rapidly reflected in the price of the asset.

equilibrium price   The price at which a financial instrument will trade as the result of the market's absorption of all relevant information.

equity security   A security representing an ownership right of its issuer, especially stocks and convertible bonds.

floor trader   An exchange member whose primary economic function is to trade for his own account on an exchange floor, in either underlying securities or derivatives.

futures contract A financial instrument contracting its seller to deliver a specified quantity of a commodity (or financial instruments) to the buyer on a particular date. Futures contracts are traded on futures exchanges.

hedge A transaction or position in a derivative market which represents a temporary substitute for a subsequent transaction or position in the market for the asset.

immediacy A service provided by specialists and over-the-counter market-makers when they buy or sell securities from an investor who does not choose to wait for the arrival of another investor willing to trade with him at his desired price. The specialist or market-maker "stands in the shoes" of the investor and the order remains unexecuted *in the market*. Immediacy is sometimes confused with liquidity, which is an attribute of a market, not a service to it.

index A mathematical measurement of the price of a group of financial instruments. The best known stock market index is the Dow Jones Industrial Average, an index maintained by Dow Jones & Company on 30 U.S. stocks listed on the NYSE.

institutional investor A corporate or governmental investment organization, managed by professionals, whose *raison d'être* is to attempt to earn income and capital gains by investing pools of capital. Examples of institutional investors are pension funds and mutual funds.

interrelated markets Financial markets trading the same or related financial instruments. A stock exchange trading a specific security and an options exchange trading an option on that security would be interrelated markets.

limit order An order to buy or sell a financial instrument at a stated price.

liquidity The ease with which an asset may be converted to cash at a price close to its last publicly traded transaction. When applied to a market as a whole, it is the capacity of a market to absorb trades without significant price changes *in the absence of new information*.

locked markets Markets (particularly NASDAQ) in which the best bid by a registered market-maker in a financial instrument is equal to another market-maker's best offer price. Under the present rules of NASDAQ, locked markets cease trading until they become unlocked. (See also **crossed markets**.)

market As used in the financial industry, a market is a facility in which transactions in financial instruments take place.

market-maker A dealer in financial instruments who specializes in trading a set of financial products regularly, intending to profit from the timing and the spread between the bids and offers.

market order   An order to execute a transaction at the best possible price upon its arrival in the trading arena.

NASD   The National Association of Securities Dealers, Inc., a self-regulatory organization formed under Section 15A of the Securities Exchange Act of 1934. The NASD is the principal self-regulator of the OTC market and the operator of the NASDAQ system for OTC securities trading in the United States.

NASDAQ   The National Association of Securities Dealers automated quotations system. NASDAQ is an interactive dealer-driven system for advertising quotes in OTC securities in the United States.

negative obligation   As used when referred to specialists, an exchange-imposed obligation not to make transactions in their specialty stocks under certain circumstances. (See also **affirmative obligation**.)

NYSE   The New York Stock Exchange, the United States' largest stock exchange.

offer   The price at which a financial instrument is offered for sale in a trading arena.

opening price   The price at which trading commences in a financial market when the arena opens for business.

option   A financial instrument giving its purchaser the right (but not the obligation) to require the seller (writer) to deliver (or receive) the financial instruments which are the subject of the option at a prespecified price for a specific period of time.

order entry system   A system employed by exchanges and other marketplaces to deliver orders from members to the trading arena.

order imbalance   A condition in a market in which there is a preponderance of orders either to sell or to buy a financial instrument.

OTC   Over-the-counter. An OTC market is one in which the financial instruments are traded, but not an exchange. There are some securities trading simultaneously on both exchange markets and OTC markets.

out trade   The term used in the futures industry for oral transactions made on exchange floors for which later agreement is difficult or impossible to attain. (See also **DK** and **QT**.)

PMW Proposal   The Peake-Mendelson-Williams Proposal. A proposal made originally to the SEC in 1976 by the authors for an electronic trading system employing a price-time priority rule.

portfolio insurance   A trading strategy of altering the equity component of a portfolio in the direction in which the market is moving, reducing the stock component when the market is falling and increasing it when the market is rising, designed to simulate a long position on a put in a portfolio. In practice the futures market is usually used to implement the strategy because the transaction costs are lower there than in the stock market.

price continuity The phenomenon of having successive transactions occur at prices close to the price of the previous transaction. On the NYSE, for example, specialists are supposed to make transactions for their own accounts to smooth price changes when there is an absence of public orders or a temporary order imbalance.

price limit A regulatory device restricting the amount or percentage by which the price of a financial instrument may rise or fall during a trading period. Price limits are used by some futures exchanges, and the NYSE has proposed the implementation of price limits under certain conditions. Proponents of price limits argue that market volatility will be decreased with their use. (See also, **circuit breakers.**)

price matching The condition that exists when a bid and offer for a financial instrument are equal, or when the bid is higher than the offer.

price-time priority A regulatory proposal or rule calling for the execution of transactions in financial instruments in the order of their arrival at the trading arena within each price. Under a price-time priority system, the first bid at a price, would be executed ahead of all later bids at that price.

primary market The market in which new issues of securities are floated.

program trading A computerized strategy under which buying and selling transactions are triggered by algorithms.

put option A right to sell a specified quantity of one or more financial assets at a specified price at any time during the option's life.

QT Questioned trade form. A term used by the NYSE for transactions made on its floor for which there is difficulty in reconciling the reports of the buyer and seller. See also **DK** and **out trade.**

retail investor A retail investor is usually an individual or a small business organization, in contrast to an institutional investor.

SEC The United States Securities and Exchange Commission, the Congressional agency charged with supervision of the U.S. securities industry.

secondary market A market in outstanding securities, as contrasted to **primary market.**

short The condition of having sold a financial instrument without owning it. A short seller hopes to buy the instrument back for a profit between his short sale price and his repurchase, or cover.

short sale A transaction in which a short seller establishes a short position.

size   The quantity or number of shares bid for or offered at a price.

SOES   The small order execution system is an automated execution offered by NASDAQ in which up to 1,000 shares of an eligible security may be executed against a bid or offer of a registered market-maker. The NASD is proposing a change to this system to make its use mandatory.

specialist   A member of a stock exchange with an exclusive franchise from the exchange to act as sole dealer and auctioneer in a set of exchange-traded securities.

stabilization   The process of engaging in transactions (usually purchases) by a specialist or other dealer to slow or eliminate price movements in securities.

SuperDOT   A system developed and used by the NYSE for delivery to the specialist and execution of small orders.

Terrible Tuesday   October 20, 1987

trading floor   The space allocated by a securities, options, or futures exchange for the actual trading of financial instruments.

trading halts   A period of time, usually unscheduled, during which trading in one or more financial instruments is suspended by exchange or governmental regulators. (See also, **price limit** and **circuit breaker**.)

trading strategy   A strategy for buying and selling securities adopted by an investor or trader hoping to make profits by its employment.

underlying security   With respect to an options or futures contract, the stock or group of stocks on which the contracts are based.

writer   The seller of an option.

NOTES

1 *Report of the Presidential Task Force on Market Mechanisms* (The Brady Commission Report). U.S. Government Printing Office, January 1988, pp. 47–48.
2 Ibid., p. 50.
3 Ibid., p. 50.
4 Junius W. Peake was a founder and the first president of Intex.
5 Ibid., pp. 47–48.
6 Ibid., pp. 49–50.
7 Ibid., pp. 47–50.
8 Ibid., pp. 36, 48.
9 Ibid., p. 50.

10 Ibid., p. 50.

11 Ibid., pp. 34, 36, 40.

12 " 'Unsettling signs,' Then a Sweeping Selloff, in October Stock Plunge," *The New York Times*, January 11, 1988, Section D, p. 9.

13 The Brady Report, p. 45.

14 Ibid.

15 Ibid., pp. 40–41.

16 Ibid., p. 30.

17 Robert A. Schwartz, *Equity Markets: Structure, Trading, and Performance*, (New York: Harper & Row, 1988), pp. 467–470.

18 *Market Information*, October 13–23, 1987, Section: Other Markets—Chicago Mercantile Exchange, p. 2.

19 A market order is to be executed at the "most advantageous price obtainable after the order is represented in the Trading Crowd" [NYSE Rule 13].

20 The Brady Report, pp. 47–48.

21 *Financial Times* (London), October 27, 1987.

22 "Study Raises Serious Questions About Performance of Specialists," Steve Swartz, *The Wall Street Journal*, January 11, 1988, p. 20. See also, the Brady Report, p. 50.

23 A "no brainer" is a colloquialism for an easily executable order received by a broker. These orders usually receive the lowest commission rates.

24 The Brady Report, p. 50.

25 Morris Mendelson and Junius W. Peake, "The ABCs of Trading in a National Market System," *Financial Analysts Journal*, September–October 1979.

26 George Anders, "One Plan for Preventing Another Crash," *The Wall Street Journal*, January 11, 1988, p. 20; Randall Smith, Steve Swartz, and George Anders, "Black Monday: What Really Triggered the Market's Plunge on Oct. 19?" *The Wall Street Journal*, December 16, 1987, p. 20.

27 The Brady Report, p. 50.

28 Ibid., pp. 47–48.

29 Ibid.

30 *Financial Times* (London), October 27, 1987.

31 The Brady Report, p. 51.

32 Ibid., p. 52.

33 Norman S. Posner, "Repairing the Big Board," *The New York Times*, December 16, 1987.

34 Price-time priority is discussed at greater length in Junius W. Peake, Morris Mendelson, and R. T. Williams, Jr., "The National Book System," paper submitted to the National Market Advisory Board of the Securities and Exchange Commission (April 30, 1976); and Junius W. Peake, "The National Market System," *Financial Analysts Journal* (July–August

1978). See also Morris Mendelson, Junius W. Peake, and R. T. Williams, Jr., "Toward a Modern Exchange: The Peake-Mendelson-Williams Proposal for an Electronically-Assisted Auction Market," reprinted in Ernest Bloch and Robert A. Schwartz, eds., *Impending Changes for Securities Markets: What Role for the Exchanges?* (Greenwich, Conn.: JAI Press, 1979).

35 United States General Accounting Office, *Financial Markets: Preliminary Observations on the October 1987 Crash* (January 1988) pp. 69–78.

36 Ibid., p. 73.

37 Ibid., p. 74.

38 Ibid.

39 Ibid.

40 Ibid.

41 Ibid.

42 Ibid., p. 75.

43 Ibid.

44 Ibid.

CHAPTER 14

MOVING FROM TODAY'S TO TOMORROW'S TRADING SYSTEM

J. Pearce Bunting

The only constant is change. Those who adapt to change survive, others do not. American and Canadian business leaders say that they accept the idea of change, yet most act as if they do not. The idea that the most important thing managers do during their business day is to change their organizations for the future is not reflected in their actions.

We have a great propensity to wait until the changes in our environment are life threatening. A successful business has a physical and psychological investment in the status quo. Often a less successful business will be among the first to see that a development in the macroenvironment is life threatening, while a stronger, less-clearly threatened business will be among the last. Since the rate of change tends to be exponential, the firm that moves last has the least time to adjust. For the past 20 years, global markets and electronic trading were always coming, but never here. Now they are here, and the changes in the next few years for stock exchanges will be breathtaking.

The business of a stock exchange is turning out widgets called trades and providing information about the making of those trades to whoever is interested. There are two significant technological driving forces in the environment surrounding the business. The first is increasing computer data management, and the second is increasingly cost-insensitive communications.

Trading is, after all, a data management process. Historically, individuals have performed both the decision-making and the data management process. In the data management process, data in the form of an order comes into a trading square; rules about trading dictate how that data will be handled to produce a trade. Historically, the ability to manage the data has been limited by the human memory. Absolute time priority, for instance, was impossible. How could anyone be expected to keep track, in his head, of the flow of orders arriving in a trading crowd? Today, of course, the computer can keep track easily. Thus there are new possibilities for innovative data management and display.

The second driving force is change in the cost of communication. Communication has become more and more distance insensitive. Today one can bounce a signal off a satellite and bring it down on London or Tokyo at almost the same cost as bringing it down on Broadway and Wall.

Clearly, the first exchanges to make effective use of computers and modern communications to improve customer service will gain an innovative advantage. Since 1969, the Toronto Stock Exchange has recognized the significance of these technological driving forces and has struggled to be among the first to make those changes that will provide the customer with the service today's technology makes possible.

I became a member of the Toronto Stock Exchange Board in 1968. In 1969 we were already hearing about the possible effects on stock exchanges of systems like Aerial, Autex, and Instinet. I suggested that the Toronto Stock Exchange should examine the possibility of automated trading. My argument was that if terminal order entry into an electronic committed order file worked, we would not be left behind. The board agreed, and the systems division of Bell Telephone Company of Canada was hired to answer the simple question, "Could computers be used for trading?" After expending $25,000, they told us that computers could, but that it would cost $28 million to build such a system. As you can imagine, the board was less than enamored with that idea.

A year or so later, I went back to the board with a request from two members of the exchanges's systems and trading staff (one is now a consultant on automated trading and the other the president of Instinet Canada), who asked if they could try to build an automated system at a much lower cost—in other words, start a skunkworks. Permission was given, and by 1975, at a cost of less than $5 million, the Toronto

Stock Exchange computer-assisted trading system (CATS) was ready for operation.

While we were developing the system, we had a development committee, of which I was the chairman and on which we were lucky to have Dr. Oman Solandt, who had previously been the chairman of the Canadian Science Council. He kept saying to us: "You are not trying to duplicate the system you have today—you are trying to build the best system you can." In doing so, one of the points we recognized was that if the system was to be effective, all the information that had previously been available only on the floor had to be available to the upstairs trader.

In 1975 we proposed that a CATS test should take place in thirteen member firms. There was an immediate uproar, not because of the automated trading, but because of the informational advantage that other members felt these thirteen firms would have. Dr. Solandt suggested that if the information was that advantageous, we should sell it to the members as a floor trading information system, thereby getting terminals into the member offices that later could be used for automated trading. Thus was born the Toronto Stock Exchange's CANDAT sytsem—Canadian Data. Two years later, there were 200 terminals spread among our 80 members.

In July 1977, I left my own firm to become president of the exchange, and in October we started automated trading with one stock, 200 upstairs terminals, and one market-maker. Gradually we built the system to about 25 stocks, all of which were relatively inactive. A year or so later, because of crowding on our old exchange floor, it was agreed that more inactive stocks would be added to the system and that a number of floor market-makers would switch to automated trading. Perhaps if we had stayed in our old building the pressure of space would have forced more active stocks onto the automated system. However, in 1983 the Toronto Stock Exchange moved to a new, 30,000-foot, electronically-assisted floor. The pressure to put new stocks into CATS was gone. By that time, almost 800 stocks, roughly half the total listings of the Toronto Stock Exchange, were in the system. However, those 800 were only 20 percent of the dollar value of trading.

Since 1983, whenever a suggestion was made that more active stocks should go into CATS, the reaction of the floor traders has been that they have not been given the opportunity to bring their system up to its peak effectiveness. Studies done during this period indicated that CATS would be more effective for active rather than inactive stocks; and it would be more cost effective and possibly make a better market. The studies were statistical and contradicted by other studies. We have been mired for years in a floor-versus-CATS argument. As it turned out, we were all missing the point.

In December 1986, the board of governors decided that some highly active stocks interlisted with New York should be tested on CATS. The immediate effect was the formation of a professional traders association on the floor and the presentation to the board of a plan by the floor traders to dramatically upgrade the floor trading systems. The board decided to accept the traders' proposal and to abandon the immediate test of active stocks on CATS, while clearly stating that this did not mean they would not do so in the future. The consequence is that over the last year or so many changes have been made in general on the Toronto Stock Exchange trading floor and in particular on what we call our experimental post. Floor trading has been taken to a very high level of automation. Nevertheless, when the board was faced with the question of whether the benefits of the experimental post should be made available to the entire floor at a cost that could well exceed $3 million, it decided that it could not make a fully-informed decision without taking a complete look at the costs and benefits of upgrading the floor or switching to automated trading.

McKinsey & Co. was selected to do a study on behalf of the Board and began its work in October 1987. The work is in three stages. The first, which has been completed, is to understand our trading process: what our customers, the upstairs trading desks, thought of it, and what they wanted it to be. What they wanted was greater visibility, greater fairness, easier access, and lower costs.

McKinsey is now in the second phase of the study, working out the rules of a new trading system. They are developing a two-track test of the rules: one of which will be of a minimally changed CATS, and the other of a further automated floor trading system.

The third stage, their final recommendations and plan for implementation, is expected by December 1988 at the latest. In my judgment, the rule changes already adopted and that call for a committed order file, upstairs visibility, and decentralized order entry are the key. I personally will not have a problem with the decision about whether the final system interacts with a floor crowd or runs on upstairs terminals only.

Although it seems fairly obvious in retrospect, the greatest contribution of McKinsey has been to recognize that the fight is not between a floor system or an upstairs terminal system. Our objective is to achieve the best possible trading rules to satisfy our customers' needs. When we know that, we can use whatever systems are necessary to deliver them.

Our new system, which is still not totally defined, will have a committed order file at its heart. In other words, orders must be in the book and fully tradeable. Trading desks everywhere will be able to see all the bids and all the offers. The rules of trading will be imbedded in the system and equal for everyone. It will be possible to execute orders just as easily from London or Kuwait as from the trading floor.

Our test of the new system should be completed by October 1988, and we expect to have a full recommendation from McKinsey by December. I have no doubt that two years from now, when our new system is in place, the Toronto Stock Exchange will be providing its customers with the most visible, the fairest, the most easily accessed, and the most cost-effective trading system possible.

Our struggle to achieve this has been difficult for many reasons, the greatest of which may, in fact, have been that the trading systems we have are doing the job by today's standards. Abandoning a system that works is a difficult decision. We have, however, recognized that the test is not how well we are doing now, but how well we will be doing tomorrow.

CHAPTER 15

THE DISPLAY BOOK: THE NYSE SPECIALISTS' ELECTRONIC WORKSTATION

Anne E. Allen
Lois Zarembo

As a result of the events of October 1987, the New York Stock Exchange is undertaking major upgrades of its automation facilities. In fact, specific planning targets call for the handling of one billion share days by the end of 1989. The display book—the NYSE specialist's electronic workstation—plays the key role in the trading floor automation plan. This status was not achieved overnight, nor was it achieved effortlessly. This paper describes the growth of the display book from a planning concept to a full-blown NYSE production system.

HISTORY

The average daily volume on the NYSE has grown dramatically recently. Table 15–1 illustrates this tremendous growth from 1975 to 1987.

In the mid-1960s when a similar growth in relative volume occurred, the exchange was forced to close during the week and restrict trading. However, what differentiates the present from the past is technology, principally the automation of many manual floor processes,

TABLE 15–1

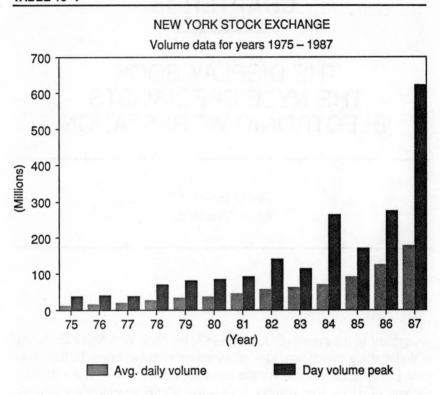

NEW YORK STOCK EXCHANGE
Volume data for years 1975 – 1987

(Year)

☐ Avg. daily volume   ■ Day volume peak

including electronic order routing and execution reporting (SuperDot) and the electronic specialist book. Further automation is critical in helping the exchange prepare to trade one billion shares per day by 1989.

SUPERDOT

In 1976 the exchange introduced SuperDot, its designated order turnaround system. SuperDot enabled NYSE members to electronically route market orders of up to 199 shares directly to the specialist post, bypassing the floor broker's booth. This effectively linked the specialist to the individual brokerage firm offices around the country—small orders could be efficiently and instantly dispatched to the post where the stock was traded. Orders were executed by the specialist, and reports of execution were routed back to the originating firms.

FIGURE 15–1
NYSE orders handled by SuperDot

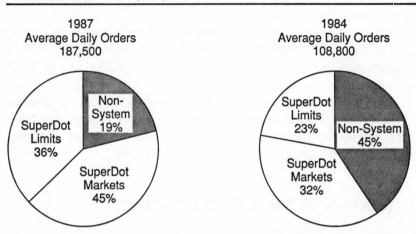

1987
Average Daily Orders
187,500

1984
Average Daily Orders
108,800

Use of the SuperDot system has expanded geometrically since its introduction, as have the capabilities of the system. SuperDot can now handle market orders for up to 30,099 shares each and individual limit orders as large as 99,999 shares. Figure 15–1 illustrates the increase in orders received by the exchange and the larger increase in the portion of those orders handled directly by SuperDot.

THE SPECIALIST BOOK

A primary responsibility of the specialist, acting as agent of the broker, is to hold customer limited price orders (those orders where a customer has specified a specific buy or sell price). The specialist holds these limit orders until such time as the stock price moves to a point where the order can be executed. This inventory of orders makes up the specialist's "book." This book is a looseleaf notebook maintained by each specialist for each stock. These orders are confidential and must be executed in a prescribed manner.

Listed in the book are the prices and shares of individual limit orders entrusted to him by floor brokers. Orders are arranged by price in arrival sequence and are executed on a first-in-first-out basis. Orders can either be limit orders, good for the day, or good until cancelled (GTC). When the specialist is given a new limit order, he enters it into the book at the appropriate price. If a trade from the book is made, the specialist removes the limit order from the book and notifies the originating broker that the order was executed.

After the close of the day's trading, all unexecuted day orders are removed from the book. Unexecuted GTC orders remain and are rewritten onto new looseleaf sheets. For certain stocks, the book of orders could contain several thousand orders.

By the 1980s when trading in some individual stocks exceeded one million shares a day and the numbers of orders being processed in these stocks was in the thousands, the time was ripe to involve the floor community in the automation of the specialist's book.

AUTOMATION OF THE SPECIALIST'S BOOK

Successful implementation of an automated specialist book required the participation and cooperation of a major specialist firm and the selection of a pilot stock.

In 1982, the specialist firm of Wagner, Stott and Company volunteered to help develop and to be the first to trade a stock using an electronic specialist book. Wagner Stott specialists and support staff devoted many hours to the design of screen and keyboard formats as well as to addressing operational concerns and clearing implementation hurdles. This effort was critical in launching the pilot specialist book.

It was determined that the stock selected should have a low price per share (under $10), trade in a narrow range of prices, and have a large book. These criteria were selected to protect against large monetary risk in the event of operational or system errors. A large book was important to insure a true test of the system in active trading. Pan Am, meeting these criteria, was selected as the pilot stock.

It was also determined that the manual processes associated with the specialist book be automated. Automation freed the specialist from error-prone manual record keeping and calculations and allowed more effective utilization of time. Additionally, it was determined that the new automated specialist system should interface directly to the Super-Dot order processing system, which would provide the brokerage firms with a mechanism to electronically route limit orders to the specialist's book. Similarly, automation of the book allowed execution reports to be electronically routed back instantly.

The equipment used at the post for the electronic display book included a nine-inch monochrome screen and a customized keyboard. The equipment, placed on top of the counter for the specialist and his clerk, was connected to a microcomputer remote to a computer control room 800 feet from the trading floor. The microcomputer was connected to the existing host SuperDot order delivery and reporting systems that service the floor. However, because SuperDot was only designed to electronically route retail-size limit orders to the post, an on-floor order entry mechanism was required. This terminal, a personal computer located at the center of the trading post, was also connected directly to the SuperDot host system. It allowed the specialist to maintain the correct sequence of all limit orders, whether routed through SuperDot or hand delivered to him by a floor broker. Additionally, this order entry terminal served as the fallback device in the event of a display book hardware or software failure.

The main screen of the electronic book displayed the cumulative total of all limit orders in the system within a full point range. Since stocks generally trade and are quoted in eighths, the best eight prices were continuously displayed with buy volume displayed on the left and sell volume on the right. Prices appeared in the center column highlighting the best bid and offer. Execution reports were entered in group fashion rather than on an order-by-order basis—that is, if there was a summary bid for 10,000 shares consisting of 100 orders of 100 shares each, and an order came in to sell 10,000 shares, one report entry of 10,000 shares was made, and the display book system formatted the reports for the 100 individual orders.

Additionally, the specialist could access a "page of book" display to view by price the order-by-order listing of limit orders in correct sequence. All displays, functions, and data entry techniques were designed to be user friendly in anticipation of heavy use. Equally important, they were designed to mimic the functions as performed in the paper environment in order to minimize the psychological hurdles.

The electronic display book was introduced in June 1983. As fate would have it, on its first day, news was released regarding Pan Am, which created an influx of activity in the stock. As a result of the news, Pan Am was the most actively traded stock on the floor, trading over one million shares, more than triple its average daily volume before the news. As expected, on that first day, limit execution reports were transmitted to customers within seconds. Late in the day, however, the electronic book failed. But because of the fallback procedures, not only was trading not interrupted, but most brokers in the trading crowd were unaware of a failure. Within a few days, the problem was corrected, and the book was brought back on-line.

Within days of continuous operation, the pilot was deemed an overwhelming success by those who were close to the project. However, full floor acceptance did not come easily, and the electronic book was not completely embraced until later that year.

AT&T DIVESTITURE

In 1983, the Judge Green decision caused the divestiture of the seven operating companies from AT&T. Immediately, the exchange began planning for what would be a dramatic feat of operational logistics— the simultaneous listing of the seven Baby Bell stocks. A total of nearly two billion shares would be listed and opened for trading simultaneously. The interest in these issues was unclear, but it was necessary to prepare for a tremendous influx of retail size traffic.

It was determined that utilizing the electronic display books in these stocks would add order and efficiency to the opening of these new listings. On November 21, 1983, these stocks began trading on a "when issued" basis. The Baby Bells and the old AT&T were moderately active, trading 780,000 shares on average that day. The when issued AT&T traded eight million shares. Thousands of orders were processed through the book, and even the most diehard skeptics had to acknowledge the significance and performance of the electronic display book in this application. The AT&T-Baby Bell installation demonstrated that the technology worked, and immediate demand for the electronic display book developed floorwide.

EXPANSION AND ENHANCEMENT EFFORTS

During 1984 and 1985, installation of the display books on the floor was slowed, while behind-the-scenes planning and development efforts were in high gear and the infrastructure of the Floor was being modified to accept a display book at every specialist position. By the end of 1985, the 24 display books on the floor were being used daily in very active stocks or "breakout" situations, such as news or mergers. If necessary, a display book could be installed overnight at the post where the active or breakout stock was trading. Windowing techniques were introduced to increase the amount of information that could be displayed on the specialist's screen. Color monitors were used to highlight selected information. SuperDot market orders were integrated into the book for execution, and formats were created that allowed multiple stocks to be traded from one display book. The display book was now a comprehensive specialist workstation, accepting market, limit, and special orders for multiple stocks.

In 1986 a data distribution network was implemented, which, for the first time, allowed the intra-day recovery of the display books in the event of a hardware failure. New equipment could be installed and the files downloaded with service interruptions of no more than several minutes in most cases. Prior to the introduction of the data distribution network, the fallback scenario was to revert to the paper book if an electronic display book experienced a hardware failure.

The data distribution network also allowed the specialist to electronically "pass the book." In the old environment, if a single specialist was handling a number of stocks and one of those stocks were to become excessively active, that specialist could physically pass the paper books to an adjacent partner with no disruption in service. The network permits the electronic transfer of files at high speeds so that the books for stocks in one system could be quickly passed to an adjacent workstation with little disruption in activity.

These enhancements to the display book expanded its possibilities. By the end of 1986, there were 100 display books active. By year end 1987, there were 256 books with over 600 stocks automated. At the end of the first quarter of 1988, 361 workstations with 1,100 stocks were automated. Each specialist position on the floor now has a display book workstation. Significantly, 250 most-active stocks, all S&P 100 stocks, and most of the S&P 500 stocks listed on the NYSE are on the display book. Approximately 80 percent of the orders flowing through the SuperDot systems are processed through the display books.

IMPACT OF SUPERDOT AND DISPLAY BOOKS

The impact of the display books on the floor and on the upstairs members firm community has been simple, but dramatic in terms of service and cost.

The service impact can be seen in the processing of market orders and through the measurement of turnaround time, that is, the time it takes a specialist to execute and then report a market order. In 1985 the average turnaround time for a market order was 90 seconds; in the first quarter of 1988, it was 36 seconds—a decrease of almost two-thirds. The impact on the servicing of limit orders is far more significant. Under the old system, limit orders were manually reported one at a time and subject to clerical workload constraints. By design, the display book processes limit orders sequentially and reports groups of orders at a single time so that all execution reports are issued on a timely basis. Automated edit checks and the reduction in manual processing have reduced error rates significantly.

Proliferation of display books has resulted in a dramatic reduction in the number of "as of" reports issued. (An "as of" report is any report issued after the actual trade date.) The number of "as of" reports has plummeted from several thousand a day in 1985 to 200 a day in 1988—the overwhelming majority of which are now for nonsystematized orders. Customers can now receive prompt notification of execution reports. Industry estimates indicate that each "as of" report results in an incremental processing cost of $75 to $80.

The most dramatic cost savings to the firms are realized in the post-trade comparison process and in clerical staffing. All trades executed through SuperDot are directly submitted to the post-trade process as fully compared and are subsequently charged only a trade recording fee. This fee is approximately 33 percent less than the normal comparison charge. The efficiency of display book processing has caused a tremendous growth in the percentage of systematized orders, thus extending that cost savings further. This system penetration has also been largely responsible for the significant decrease in the uncompared rate from 2.6 percent in 1984 to under 1 percent for 1988. (The uncompared rate is a measure of those trades that do not match by price or broker discrepancies or failure by a party to submit.) This translates into very real savings in back-office operations processing because fewer uncompared trades mean fewer questioned trades with less exposure to market risk.

Clerical staffing on the trading floor has remained constant over the past 5 years despite a tripling of average daily volume. The SuperDot system and most notably the display book provided the floor with tools to process more volume not only faster but less expensively.

FUTURE PLANS

The display book works. It works in breakout stocks, and it works when the whole market is busy—which is why it is featured so heavily in planning for the one-billion-share day. The wide acceptance of the display book, as well as the network designs, has made it possible for us to plan that *all* stocks can be traded in automated fashion and that the NYSE can realistically plan on trading one billion shares in the existing facility.

Future plans include the development of features such as a specialist principal inventory management system, multiple access terminals including hand held technology, and a series of user-driven algorithms to improve the efficiency of quotation reporting. The display book and its features position the floor of the NYSE well for the 1990s and beyond.

CHAPTER 16

NASDAQ: EXPERIENCE WITH PIONEERING AN ELECTRONIC MARKET

Robert N. Riess

This paper discusses electronic markets in both a broad sense and a narrow sense. In a broad sense there is more to electronic markets than automatic execution. One must consider order processing (getting orders to the point of execution), market-making (keeping the prices up-to-date in a fast-changing and increasingly automated market) and post-execution processing (getting trades matched for clearance and settlement). Then, in a narrow sense, this paper will focus on automated trading in a particular electronic market, NASDAQ.

BACKGROUND

A few facts and figures help locate NASDAQ in the worldwide securities industry. In 1987, NASDAQ's share volume reached 38 billion shares, for a total trading value of $500 billion. To achieve this volume, 545 market-making firms traded 5,500 issues, representing the shares of 4,700 companies, over an electronic network linking their 3,300 interactive terminals to a central database. An additional network of computer-to-computer linkages connects the in-house systems of NASD's larger members to the central NASDAQ system for trade and volume reporting and order entry. Service bureaus offer a similar service to many smaller firms. To provide information to retail brokers and the investing public, NASDAQ inside market prices and last sale details for its top tier of issues are displayed on 185,000 market data vendor terminals around the world. With 97 ADRs and over 200 foreign listings, NASDAQ is clearly the international market of choice for world-class issuers. NASDAQ is further expanding its international presence through additional linkages with other markets and the extension of its network to NASD members and others abroad. In short, a growing number of commentators conclude that NASDAQ is the U.S. node of the international market of the future.

Looking back over recent automated enhancements to the market, and into the future at initiatives either planned or in development, the basic quotation system of about 1971 seems modest indeed. By the end of its eighteenth year, NASDAQ should have the facilities in place to execute (either automatically or with trader intervention) or compare and lock in nearly 100 percent of transactions in NASDAQ issues. Through a linkage with AIBD's TRAX and ISE's SEQUAL and SAEF systems, similar facilities will be made available internationally. Altogether, the existing and planned services make up perhaps the most complete equity market system in the world, one that is ideally suited to worldwide, continuous trading.

SERVICES

The basic NASDAQ system in 1971 allowed for trader input of quotations and end-of-day volume reports. Competing market-makers' quotes were then available in reply to inquiries from NASDAQ level 2 and level 3 terminals; representative bid and offer quotations were released to vendors for distribution to retail brokers (level 1 service); and end-of-day level 1 quotes and reported volume were released to newspapers. Today, this basic service has grown to include immediate trade reports (last sale service) on 3,000 NMS issues and an inside (or best bid and offer) quotation for all NASDAQ issues. In addition, dealers in the third market now submit their quotes and reports of trades in listed issues to NASDAQ for distribution through consolidated tape facilities.

A major additional service area affecting users is the capability to enter trade reports, volume reports, and orders via computer interface and to receive execution reports back via computer interface. Twenty firms now use this capability; on a typical day they enter over 3,000 small orders, about 4,500 end-of-day volume reports, and over 30,000 trade reports.

Another major addition to NASDAQ was the consolidated quote system, which allowed third market dealers in exchange-listed issues to see their quotes on a NASDAQ-like level 2 or 3 screen, together with all exchange quotes. In support of third market trading, an automated execution service, CAE, was also built. CAE allows users to enter orders either through NASDAQ level 2 or 3 terminals or via computer interfaces for automatic execution in the third market. CAE trades are then automatically reported to the consolidated tape and, at the end of the day, to the national clearing corporation. Exchanges may access the third market through an intermarket trading interface and receive automated executions, and NASDAQ also provides automated means for third market dealers to access exchange markets.

Very efficient execution of trades in NASDAQ issues is provided by a small order execution system (SOES). Through this system, firms with orders may enter them through NASDAQ terminals or through a direct link from their in-house computers to NASDAQ market makers at the inside market price. These orders receive immediate electronic confirmation and are also automatically reported to NASDAQ's last sale tape and, at the end of the day, to the clearing corporation as locked-in trades. Typically, executions can be confirmed by brokers to their customers within seconds of entry. Orders up to 1,000 shares in size may be executed in NMS issues (3,000 of NASDAQ's 5,500 listed issues) and up to 500 shares in the balance. On Black Monday, for example, this system executed 21,555 orders.

Because many NASDAQ trades are still negotiated over the telephone and comparisons are received two days after an order slip is filled out, a relatively high rate of trouble trades (5 to 6 percent after the first run) must be resolved. To solve this problem, NASDAQ built TARS, an automated system for accessing compared and uncompared trades and for correcting entries. In this way, firms using NASDAQ terminals installed in their back offices can efficiently manage the reconciliation process and, in fact, receive immediate notice from the contraparty of entries affecting them. During the clearing crunch in the seven days following Black Monday, this system processed over 110,000 correcting entries. This system was a major reason the NASDAQ market did not experience the problems with questionable trades that plagued other U.S. markets last fall.

Since early 1986, NASDAQ has been displaying quotes on approximately 300 U.K. and international issues traded in the SEAQ and SEAQ international systems. The ISE in turn displays quotes on a similar number of NASDAQ issues. Last year we added individual SEAQ market-maker quotes and last sale trade reports to this display, and added 50 issues to the linkage. This linkage is to be followed in 1989 by a trading and comparison linkage to be described below.

Supplementing the central NASDAQ facilities, but nevertheless an integral part of the market, are trading systems operating by securities firms and vendors. Through these facilities, and utilizing information released by the central NASDAQ system (including inside market prices, last sale data, and market maker quotes), securities firms are able to execute their small order flow automatically at the best price in NASDAQ. In fact, between the facilities of NASDAQ's automated execution systems and these internal systems, over one-half of the order flow in NASDAQ issues is executed automatically today.

Finally, to complete the description of the current NASDAQ system services, a new PC-based trader workstation, which functions with a distributed data base maintained by a sophisticated broadcast capability, has been recently introduced. Using this workstation, traders can not only perform all the NASDAQ level 2 or 3 functions (including trade and volume reporting, quote updating, and order entry) in a more efficient manner, but they can also monitor on a continuous, real time basis trade and quote activity in up to 300 NASDAQ issues at each station. Though less than a year old, the workstation's distribution data base has already become a key strategy in NASDAQ's plans for the electronic marketplace.

ENHANCEMENTS TO NASDAQ

These capabilities constitute the current NASDAQ system and have been successfully used to process as many as 165,000 reported NMS trades and 288 million shares on a given day. However, based on the experiences of Black Monday and subsequent days, the NASD has determined that certain additions are needed to provide a more complete trading market. These enhancements, most of which will be completed in 1988, will provide the most complete and efficient automated marketplace anywhere.

In the NASDAQ market at present, many trades are negotiated over the phone. And traffic problems can occur. A market-maker's phone lines can become saturated, and another firm wishing to trade with the market-making firm may be unable to reach the firm on the phone. Alternatively, the trader might be too busy with other phone lines to answer one that is ringing. Automatic execution systems are a way of getting around this problem. However at present, SOES and similar proprietary systems are programmed to suspend executions in securities in which a locked or crossed market exists, that is, when one dealer's bid price equals or exceeds other dealers' ask prices, or vice versa. Thus, small orders that might be executed in the automatic system must be negotiated over the telephone. During the week of October 19, locked and crossed markets were a significant problem.* As a result, in order to make the market more efficient, the NASD board has determined that, starting in June 1988, all market makers in NMS securities must participate in the small order system, and that executions will continue to occur even if the market in an issue is locked or crossed. In this way, small orders will continue to execute in the automatic system, and market-makers responsible for the locked and crossed markets will have an economic incentive to change their quotations rapidly, thus eliminating the lock or cross.

Because participation will become mandatory, market-makers will be provided a safety valve. This will function when a market-maker has received executions totaling 5,000 shares (in most issues) and has not responded by either changing his quote or re-entering his exposure limit. At this point, the market-maker will be suspended from execution and quotation for five minutes. If at the end of that time, he has not responded by re-entering a price or size, he will be removed as a market-maker in that issue and not be permitted to return for one month. This penalty may be waived if the market-maker can demonstrate that his nonresponse was due to circumstances beyond his control, such as equipment malfunction. To accommodate the varying liquidity of different issues, stocks subject

---

*It is important to note that there is a fundamental difference between order-driven and quote-driven markets. Order-driven markets under uncertain conditions, such as on October 19, reach a stage of order imbalance and call a formal trading halt until trades can be passed. Quote-driven markets continue to function but with fast, frequent, and large changes in quotes that result in locked or crossed markets, and, in some cases, bring the market to at least a partial, informal trading halt. The NASDAQ market is based on the principle that markets should function continuously and that competitive market-making should determine market prices.

to mandatory SOES trading will have varying execution size limits, initially tiered at 200, 500 and 1,000 shares. Another planned SOES enhancement with important implications for the small investor at the heart of the NASDAQ market is the addition of a limit order file to SOES. When this capability is implemented, limit orders left with SOES will be automatically executed on a first-in-first-out basis when the inside market reaches the appropriate limit price.

A capability already implemented that capitalizes on the automation available in the NASDAQ market and that relieves the strain on the telephone communications system is the order confirmation transaction, or OCT. If a member wishes to trade with another market-maker but cannot reach that firm by phone, he can enter an order into his NASDAQ terminal using a preformatted message layout. The message includes the security ID, price, number of shares, and ID of the designated market-maker. The order is immediately received by that market-maker as an unsolicited message on the appropriate trader's NASDAQ screen. That trader can then accept or reject the order by entering the unique order number assigned by the system and pressing one key. The entering firm then receives the acceptance or rejection on its NASDAQ screen as a forced reply message. Orders not responded to within two minutes (or some other time interval to be determined) are treated as rejects. Resulting transactions are automatically reported to the NASDAQ tape and are locked in for clearing.

Recent OCT enhancements offer additional negotiation capability, again with a preferred market-maker. Now, an order entry firm will be able to specify whether or not a partial execution is acceptable, or if the order must be filled all or none. The market-maker may accept the OCT in whole or partially, if allowed, or make a counteroffer. The counteroffer may vary the price or size, consistent with the type of OCT. The counteroffer is presented to the trader at the entering firm immediately, where it may be accepted or declined. Later enhancements will provide the capability to offer orders to multiple market-makers simultaneously and to carry on more complex negotiations.

One of the major advantages of SOES, OCT, and CAE is that trades are locked in for clearing purposes; uncompared trades do not occur in this environment. At the end of the day, all locked-in trades are passed on to clearing as compared trades. In order to provide this feature for telephone trades, a new capability is being designed to lock in trades done over the telephone. This capability, called an automated confirmation transaction (ACT), allows both for one-sided input and confirmation by the other side, or for two-sided input and matching. Since market-makers must report all NMS trades to NASDAQ within 90 seconds today, both the reporting mechanism in the firms and the collection mechanism in NASDAQ already exist. Contraside information must be added, and trades in NASDAQ regular, non-NMS issues must be reported. Using this capability, for example, a firm will enter trade inputs on all issues in which it is the reporting market-maker. Only one entry is required for last sale reporting and comparison purposes. The other side, which is usually also a reporting market-maker, may elect either to query a file containing trades against it and accept or reject the trades, or to enter all trades in which it takes part instead of just those it must report for last sale purposes. In most large firms, these trades are captured as they occur and will probably be immediately entered into ACT. In that event, NASDAQ will perform a match. At the end of the day, as with SOES and OCT, all compared trades will be reported to clearing as locked-in. Any trades not explicitly rejected on trade date will be carried over to trade date plus one as "demand inputs," that is, if they are not rejected that day they will become two-sided locked-in trades. Reconciliation of any trades remaining uncompared will be handled by the TARS systems described above.

Participation in ACT will be mandatory for market-makers. For smaller retail firms, once a certain threshold of NASDAQ trading is reached, clearing memberships or arrangements and ACT participation will become mandatory. In light of mandatory participation, a risk management facility is being designed to allow clearing firms to monitor their correspondents' activity on a real-time basis. They will also be automatically notified when a correspondent's activity exceeds a specified threshold. In that case, they may cease to act as clearing broker for the correspondent. Brokers without clearing arrangements will not be permitted to be NASDAQ market-makers nor to use automated execution facilities.

ACES is the NASD's advanced computerized execution system, now in final testing, offering sophisticated market-making support to specifically authorized subscribers. ACES permits a subscribing market-maker to designate a list of order entry firms from which orders in allowable securities, up to specified sizes, variable under the trader's control, will be automatically executed at the prevailing NASDAQ inside market price. Limit orders not immediately executable are held in an open order file pending a change in the inside market price. ACES satisfies all trade reporting requirements on the market-maker's behalf, reports all executions to the national clearing system as locked-in trades, and maintains position accounting records for its subscribers, including mark to the market and P&L accounting.

Using all the above capabilities, a firm will be able to execute and clear trades of all sizes quickly and efficiently. Small orders will be executed and locked in within seconds. Larger orders can be executed and locked in within minutes using either the ACT or OCT. At the end of the day, almost all trades are compared, and the few left uncompared are known and can be handled through automated reconciliation. Periods of high market activity or rapid price change can be accommodated because of the degree of automation. A secondary benefit is that an electronically time-stamped record of all accepted and rejected trades is a byproduct of the process. This entire trading structure operates under the umbrella of market surveillance, with extensive on-line monitoring facilities, serving to guarantee fair and uniform practice and a level playing field for investors and market professionals alike. What now remains is to consider how this market may be utilized in a worldwide framework.

AN INTERNATIONAL SYSTEM

NASDAQ by its very nature closely matches the commonly stated requirements for worldwide trading. It is a geographically decentralized, highly-automated system tying together competing markets or market-makers in a highly-visible and efficient way. What is needed is to expand its hours of service and to develop more extensive overseas linkages. Today, NASDAQ operates between the hours of 7:30 A.M. and 6:30 P.M. New York time. Although the NASDAQ market formally is open from 9:30 A.M. to 4:00 P.M., expansion of system hours is easily accomplished. Of course, expansion of market hours also requires changes on the part of market-making firms. One, though, can envision a time when a subset of NASDAQ issues of international interest will be traded in NASDAQ for substantially longer hours than the remainder of the issues of domestic interest only, and this "submarket" of NASDAQ will be linked to other trading markets to provide continuous, 24-hour trading. The system structure is already in place to provide this type of market.

One capability currently under design is a system with functions similar to ACT and TARS for the Eurobond market. This trade accounting and reconciliation system (TRAX) is being built by the AIBD with NASDAQ assistance. NASDAQ is designing a common communications front end that will enable a firm anywhere in the world using TRAX to enter a NASDAQ trade for comparison as well as a Eurobond trade, and a firm using NASDAQ can enter a Eurobond trade for comparison as well as a NASDAQ trade. As AIBD builds other capabilities, and they will, similar linkages will be available with NASDAQ through the common communications switch.

NASDAQ's linkage with the International Stock Exchange has already been mentioned. As currently planned, that linkage will expand to include automated confirmation and execution systems shortly after such systems are available in London. SAEF, a SOES-type system, is expected to be available in late 1988, and SEQUAL, a system for matching trades in international issues, is scheduled for early 1989. Using these linkages, a London firm will be able to enter orders there for execution or comparison in SOES or ACT, and a U.S. firm will likewise be able to enter orders in the United States for execution or comparison in SEAQ. Compatible clearing linkages, for example the arrangement in place between ISCC in the United States and the Talisman system in London, will help insure smooth settlement.

One specialized area in which the NASDAQ foundation will be used to provide a total market facility is the private placement of securities to institutional investors. A new rule 144A being developed by the SEC, expected to provide guidance for the primary placement and secondary trading of unregistered securities by sophisticated U.S. investors, will enable the huge capital pools of U.S. institutions to participate directly in overseas equities markets through a domestic facility. We have begun development of a system for that market called PORTAL, private offerings, resales, and trading through automated linkages. The dealer market is the natural environment for these transactions, and PORTAL will have the familiar features of NASDAQ, linked with foreign settlement and custody facilities. We believe that this will assure the required level of control while keeping transaction costs down.

FUTURE INITIATIVES

Two subjects not specifically treated by any of these enhancements are order processing and quotation entry. The computer linkages for order entry, described above, by which 30 major firms—some processing orders for others—are connected to NASDAQ through a central location at the main data center in Connecticut. However, since markets are driven by order flow, NASDAQ will soon go out to the source— first by allowing linkages at NASDAQ's seven communications nodes in the United States and, perhaps by then, at international locations; later, access will be through a central routing switch that will provide a common point to direct order flow to NASDAQ as well as to other markets.

In a market with fast, automated executions, equally fast quote change capabilities must be available. In the future, NASDAQ will provide the ability to update markets in related issues simultaneously with one entry; suggest price updates via computer analysis based on previously defined criteria; and, in certain circumstances, automatically generate price entries based on the operation of complex analytical algorithms.

When these enhancements are complete, NASDAQ will be a totally automated market—not in the sense of taking human judgment out of the process, but in the sense of fully integrating automation with human judgment in the total order routing, market-making, and clearing processes. It will be a most effective equity trading market.

CHAPTER 17

QUALITY OF MARKETS:
THE LONDON EXPERIENCE

Michael F. Newman

Much as been written about London's Big Bang—the popular name for the events associated with the major restructuring of the International Stock Exchange's membership facilities and way of trading in the United Kingdom. The high season for articles on Big Bang ran from mid-1985 to October 1987, after which the Big Crash naturally became the new focus of attention. For most of the 1970s and through the early 1980s until September 1983, the role of the London exchange had been seen to become increasingly less relevant to the individual investor, whose participation in U.K. markets as a whole had been in steady decline for years.

HISTORY

The Thatcher Government began a process known as "popular capitalism," which had two major thrusts. These were (1) the sale of state-owned council homes to their rent-paying occupants, and (2) the sale of the state-owned organizations to the private sector with particular emphasis on attracting the individual investor into the process. The effect of the privatization program has been to increase the number of private investors in Britain from under three million in 1979 to an estimated nine million now.

During this period, the government and the stock exchange reached a historic agreement in 1983 for the stock exchange to dismantle fixed commissions and for the government to cease case proceedings of the Office of Fair Trading, the agency concerned with unfair trading practices.

It is a matter of public knowledge that London took the opportunity of the aftermath of the 1983 agreement with the government to reconsider its market mechanisms. After much deliberation, it chose the NASD model. Our early expectations were that if we followed that model closely, our market quantifiers and quality aspects would turn out to be similar.

The extent to which the Big Bang events at the stock exchange had become a media event was reinforced by the clear link between Big Bang and the way the privatization program was promoted. In other words, the public now had a real interest in what was happening at the stock exchange.

Being judged by popular journalism alone was not something the exchange was enthusiastic about. Whether or not Big Bang was a success should be judged not as a media event but on certain market fundamentals. This incentive or threat arose in the build-up to Big Bang. We asked ourselves how can we prove that the new market structure offers a better marketplace than the old jobbing system that was being replaced; thus emerged the Quality of Markets Committee.

The committee was set up to identify ways of analyzing market quality and to make recommendations that might improve the quality. Suggestions could take the form of new or changed facilities or modifications to the market rules or supervision procedures. In other words, the committee and its staff were not to provide just a passive statistical analysis, but were to be the custodian of market quality.

My paper will cover first the significant aspects of market quality and then mention briefly the impact of the new technology on our U.K. market mechanisms.

QUALITY OF MARKETS

The main findings of the quality of markets report regarding the crash were as follows:

• The market crash in the week of October 19 saw a fall of 22 percent in the FTSE 100 Index. It ushered in a period of far greater price volatility than had existed previously.

• Volumes in the week of the crash reached unprecedented levels. Customer transactions peaked at over 100,000 bargains per day on October 21 and 22. Customer value exceeded £3.5 billion on October 20.

• Intra-market turnover was proportionately lower during the three-week period from October 19 to November 6. However, equity IDBs gained and have retained a considerably higher proportion of intra-market business.

• The pattern of customer business during this three-week period suggests that individual investors were substantial net buyers.

• Market-makers performed a valuable stabilizing function on October 19 when they were net purchasers of U.K. equities in the amount of £250 million. In subsequent days, market-makers were able substantially to reduce their positions.

• Market depth was stable on October 19 but fell sharply at the opening on the twentieth. Market-makers' spreads widened sharply at the same time.

Despite the declaration of fast markets for limited periods and the difficulties of keeping pace in a rapidly moving market, strong evidence shows that customer business was generally executed at close to SEAQ screen quotes. No evidence suggests that market-maker's screen prices were significantly away from the market for anything but short periods.

Fears that the high level of visibility of the market may have caused panic among market-makers and thus precipitated price cuts appear to have been unfounded. Results show that price falls were associated with selling pressure.

We are left with an open verdict on the impact of foreign selling of U.K. stocks. Evidence from depositories of ADRs (American depository receipts) suggests that U.S. investors were not disproportionately heavy sellers of U.K. stocks. It is not possible, however, to reach firm conclusions on actions by investors from other countries.

The weeks since the crash have seen a gradual but steady recovery in market quality. Market-makers's spreads are generally narrowing, and the depth of the market is generally increasing. However, continued volatility makes the market more risky than before; and until this volatility declines, market quality will remain lower than before the crash.

Let us look further at some of the key aspects.

Market Price Movements

Over the one-week period, Wednesday October 14 to Tuesday October 20, the FTSE 100 Index fell 22 percent, the Dow Jones dropped 24 percent and the Nikkei Dow 18 percent. As well as the decline in prices, extreme volatility became a feature of the market. On Terrible Tuesday, the FTSE saw a high of 1985.1 and a low of 1748.2, a movement of 237 points, although the net change on the day was 65 points. Since the crash, one-day movements are still frequently larger than on even the most volatile days before the crash.

Structure of the Trading Activity

During the weeks following October 19, significant changes in trading patterns occurred. Three features stand out: the massive volume of trading, the significant increase in the proportion of customer purchase orders to customer sales orders, and the changing pattern of intra-market trading.

The "fast market" indicator is used when the volume of market activity is such that market-makers are unable to keep their quotes up-to-date. When the fast market indicator appears on the screens, all prices shown on SEAQ are indicative and must be confirmed at the point of dealing with market-makers.

It is widely felt that during highly volatile periods, declaring a fast market actually improves the quality of market, since this is considered the only realistic option. In fact, during the fast market period, the bulk of customer business has been done at prices very close to the market best quotations as displayed on the screen. Without the fast market safety valve in such circumstances, the market-maker would have three options, any of which would be more detrimental to the market.

These detrimental options are:

- to reduce his quotation size to avoid large hits
- to ensure his bid quote was below the current market bid quote
- to cease dealing; an extreme decision, since reregistration has a three-month registration delay

Fast markets were declared at the following times:

Monday	October 19	9:10–9:23 11:00–12:00	23 minutes 60 minutes
Tuesday	October 20	9:00–11:00 2:32–4:00	120 minutes 88 minutes
Wednesday	October 21	9:00–9:30	30 minutes
Thursday	October 22	9:08–10:00 11:47–12:40	52 minutes 53 minutes

This represents a total of just over 7 hours out of 40 hours that week, that is, about 18 percent of trading time. Even on the worst day, Tuesday, the fast market represented about 43 percent of the Mandatory Quote Period.

Resilience of the Market-Maker System

Net customer sales on October 19 were a very substantial amount—over £250 million—representing additional inventing for market-makers who were generally long of stocks. On subsequent days, the net positions were much smaller until the week ending November 6, when substantial customer buying re-emerged. There is little doubt that the ability of market-makers to hold substantial long positions is a reflection of their valuable stabilizing role in absorbing the weight of selling pressure. Commentators have argued that without the capital restructuring of Big Bang, market-makers may not have been able to weather the storm as well as they did.

Obviously, most, if not all, lost money. Market-maker positions were monitored extremely closely by the surveillance division. Despite the extreme trading conditions, there were no doubts about the ability to meet obligations, and no market-maker left the market during this period.

Market Depth

A key test of the effectiveness of a market is how well liquidity is maintained under pressure. We have looked at depth from three aspects: How did the usual measures of liquidity behave? To what extent were the quotations prices a fair reflection of actual dealing prices? and To what extent did liquidity in less-active stocks suffer?

1. Market-makers generally maintained their order sizes and spreads into Monday afternoon or even Tuesday morning, after which liquidity began to deteriorate quite rapidly. To take one major example: for Shell the spread increased from 5p to 20p, the touch (the difference between the best bid and the best offer) from 2 or 3p to about 10p, and the size from 800,000 shares to around 400,000.

2. The FTSE 100, which is a quote-constructed index, was analyzed against a specifically constructed FTSE using actual transactions. The analysis showed a very high degree of correlation, implying that screen quote prices were, on the whole, a fair reflection of dealing prices.

Impact of Visibility and Internationalism

Our results indicate that there is no significant evidence that volatility has been stimulated by visibility. Nor do they indicate that a domino-like collapse of prices occurred—prices fell as selling pressure developed. These observations suggest that enhanced visibility has meant that the more quickly information is relayed to the market, the more effective the market is—the stock exchange is the messenger not the message.

IMPACT OF NEW TECHNOLOGIES ON MARKET SYSTEMS

Much has been written about the role of technical systems in supporting, or perhaps not properly supporting, the associated markets. At the International Stock Exchange, the service management maintains meticulous records on various aspects of service provision. Internal reports are produced for briefing the management team about what is really going on; reports are not produced for external consumption or whitewash. The November report about the October crash concluded:

> The heavy trading brought with it associated pressures on the trading systems. The central systems were working at 100 percent capacity on many occasions, and there were delays on various network links. Fast market was invoked to assist the equities market in periods of high activity, and SEAQ international prices were declared indicative during several periods of lengthy delays in price updating.
>
> The SEAQ system coped well with the excessive workload during the week of October 19, with 100 percent availability. Response times increased during the peak periods, but generally were not excessive throughout the day. The first failure in four months occurred on SEAQ

on Monday October 26. However, the failure was after the close of the mandatory quote period. The cause of the failure is under investigation.

On October 5, the biggest system change since Big Bang, the installation of SEAQ C, EPIC G, and CRS 7 software went live. Only two minor problems resulted from this change. SEAQ international stocks were intermittently lost, caused by interest flags in EPIC being improperly set by the database handler. A fix was successfully implemented that week.

The SEAQ international system suffered a variety of failures, both of hardware and software. There were also excessive delays in response times at peak periods.

CRS output tasks were consuming 100 percent of CPU capacity. These tasks have now been spread over two CRS machines, and the balance between the input and output tasks improved. A review of the CRS systems and architecture has been instigated.

These were the principal comments. Nothing of a crisis or hysterical reaction can be found in them. With regard to the rather bland statement about delays in SEAQ international stocks, it was known that a major performance boost was due for this system, which has subsequently gone live and doubled the performance capability.

CONCLUSION

In general, results indicate that given record increases in activity and the extent of price movements, trading systems coped remarkably well. As a postscript, it is significant to note that the systems experienced an even greater minute-by-minute throughput on April 14 following adverse U.S. trade figures. For a few minutes the system processed transactions at a rate of 140 percent of the October rate. But regarding the crash, the resulting decline in market quality is only to be expected given the extraordinary circumstances. While that involves increased cost of dealing, the cost of closing or halting trading would be far greater. London did not close, nor did it intend to, nor did any of its major stocks effectively stop trading.

The issue of accessibility to market-makers essentially rests with issues relating to market capacity. The widely reported problems of dealers not answering their phones seemed to relate to their ability to do so, rather than their unwillingness. The widespread use of technology in support of the markets in the United Kingdom was only one year old. Much is still to come. The introduction late in 1988 of the SEAQ automatic execution facility should release considerable resources in the firms to handle much greater volume. Trades under 1,000 shares will be eligible for automatic execution, and all market-makers must participate. At the end of 1989, TAURUS will be introduced, which will begin to halt the paper certificate process, which had proved to be a major hindrance to the functioning of active markets from Big Bang up to the crash.

The systems themselves emerged with their reputations, if anything, improved. One year earlier, on Big Bang day, the image of computers was badly tarnished. Much had been done in the interim to improve the systems, and much was learned in the October week about extreme behavior. The systems could now cope with another October week better than they did last year. I am not sure, however, that people could.

CHAPTER 18

THE EFFICIENCY OF COMPUTER SYSTEMS UNDER STRESS: A VIEW FROM AN INSTITUTIONAL TRADING DESK

James French

Because of the size of the assets under our management, trading activity at Wellington Management Company is substantial and strongly dependent on the aid of computer systems. We depend not only on our own devices, such as our online trading system and developing electronic trading system, but of course on industry developments such as the NYSE's DOT system, the ITS system, the various clearing systems, and, most importantly, the NASDAQ system. I stress the NASDAQ system because today more than one-third of our activity is in this market, compared to only about 4 percent at the beginning of this decade, and it is likely this trend will continue.

I should also point out our growing use and dependence on trading information systems—the quotron system allows us to monitor the market, the AutEx system electronically helps us identify buyers and sellers, and, more importantly than ever, the Bridge Data and PC Quote systems allow us to track the futures and spreads, which recently has become such an important factor. Also of growing use on our desk is the Instinet system, which so far is our only means of pure electronic trading. Because of its efficiency and low cost, this system is capturing an increasing amount of our business. Another electronic approach, called a crossing network, is not yet much of a factor; but it and electronic trading in general could very well play an important role in the future, as more efficient and effective trading systems are developed.

Broadly speaking, these various computer and electronic trading systems have proved quite effective over the long run. Without them we could not have increased our trading volumes more than sixfold over this decade, or with the fewer people we now have dealt with the complexities of the past five year's explosive growth. However, in evaluating their usefulness and effectiveness under stress—and in our trading room I would characterize it as *real* stress—I would have to say that modern technology did not serve us all that well in the trading process and that in some areas it either hindered or hurt us.

In fact, what served us best over the three busiest days in our history—which we refer to as Ominous Friday, Black Monday, and Terrible Tuesday—was the old-fashioned but tried-and-true method of having floor brokers, not computers, work on our behalf as agents on the floor of the NYSE. Because of our emphasis on this basic approach and on trying to avoid the DOT system (where the delays and lack of market information were rampant), we were effectively able to deal with a huge increase in listed order flow from our managers. Over the three-day period, our listed volume rose over 500 percent, and on Terrible Tuesday alone, it rose over 800 percent! Trading at this volume was quite an accomplishment under the old-fashioned methods in use— helped, thankfully, by the fact that we were substantially on the buy side.

The NASDAQ System held us back and, to a degree, hurt us. The electronically linked, multiple markets were changing so fast that, to a large extent, they were either locked, crossed, ineffective, or nonexistent. Over the three-day period, our NASDAQ volume rose only about 55 percent as compared to listed's 500 percent, but I am sure it would have been substantially higher had the system permitted it. Our appetite was there, but it was prevented from being fulfilled by a system that did not work well. While it is a well-known fact that all markets had their share of problems during this stressful period, it is interesting to note that between the competitive or singular market-making systems, it was the singular (or specialist) system that served us best.

In the neutral corner were the trading information systems; they functioned as well as they could, given the delayed openings and the trading halts, but nonetheless caused much confusion. However, aside from tracking last sales (which were fairly up-to-date) and eyeballing the futures and the spreads, these systems provided little assistance. Time was the major problem. For example, rather than electronically probing the market through the AutEx System, the name of the game was to get down where the action was before we missed a trade. We do note, however, that trading information systems would have played a much more significant role if more information had been available on transactions and market conditions in the derivative markets.

Electronic trading through the Instinet system slowed down significantly, primarily due to the ineffectiveness of the ITS system where multiple market-makers on the system play an important role. No thought was given to the crossing networks where for a period of time there is substantial uncertainty about whether you traded or not. We do appreciate more than ever our in-house on-line trading system. We could not have handled the paper flow without the use of a computer. On that point, I am amazed and thankful for the ability of the clearing systems to handle such a massive order flow with what, in our case, turned out to be a low margin of fails or questioned trades. All and all, the paper flow went fairly smoothly, and the nightmare of problems never materialized. It is in this area, not in the trading process, where we feel that the computer system served us quite well.

In summary, we must give mixed reviews to how well systems served us under the severe stress of those never-to-be-forgotten days. That is not to say, however, that the reviews will not be better in the future, given the improvements that are being made, the dependence that we are all placing on automation, and the more efficient forms of electronic trading. At Wellington Management, we are getting ready for the future through the development of a completely electronic trading system, and I am happy to report that our pilot program is working well. On both the NYSE and NASDAQ, improvements are being made. Electronic trading systems are taking on increasing importance as traders such as ourselves begin to realize the efficiencies and opportunities of electronic trading. Information technology has come a long way and hopefully will be significantly aided by more effective intermarket trading information, which is so important in today's environment. These developing systems have served us well over the years. They stumbled somewhat last October, but will no doubt be our salvation in the future.

CHAPTER 19

THE SYSTEMS: A USER'S VIEW OF THE IMPACT OF THE EVENTS OF OCTOBER

Peter B. Madoff

The business of my firm, Bernard L. Madoff Investment Securities, is trading, and we are registered specialists and market-makers in over 140 listed securities—including all the Dow Jones Industrial issues, all components of the Major Market Index, and most of the S&P 100 securities represented in the OEX Index Contract. We are also market-makers in many of the most active NASDAQ securities in the OTC marketplace.

Our business takes place in a unique environment. We trade in several marketplaces simultaneously. Our quotations are disseminated both here and abroad by computer interfaces to many diverse systems. We also receive order flow from broker-dealers, banks, and financial institutions through computer interfaces to our Stratus Computers. These delivery systems are our lifelines. Our internal system generates quotations, executions, order status, inventory status, and hedging possibilities on-line (instantaneously and in dynamic sequence) to our broker-dealer customers and traders.

Through the use of computers and communications systems, our firm has grown. We have been involved in the evolution and development of NASDAQ in the OTC environment, the Cincinnati Stock Exchange, and the Intermarket Trading System (ITS), which is a communications linkage for all marketplaces trading listed securities.

Today's marketplace is global and interactive. Liquidity and volatility have increased substantially. Traders must have the ability to assess their exposure instantly and to be able to access different markets at once. Each of our trader's workstations is a Compaq 386 PC tied to an IBM plasma screen that provides multiple displays using one keyboard. The PCs feed our Stratus Fault Tolerant Computers, which are the central processor for all incoming and outgoing data. The workstations give our traders their edge: *information* and *access*.

There are three vulnerable points in any system—hardware, software, and vendor data.

Our hardware performed extremely well during the October crash. Our Stratus computers operated continuously without any problem. The heavy volume of the week of October 19 did not impair our Stratus processors, our PC workstations, or our communication capabilities.

Software systems presented problems. Design limitations became evident—not only with our own internal systems, but with NASDAQ and ITS. Our system was designed so that trade execution is simultaneously reported to the Consolidated Tape Association. Trade reports had price validity software to prevent inaccurate entries. During the week of October 19, this software rejected valid trade reports because the software found the reports were out of sequence or too far away in price from previous reports.

Software was also written to automatically price market orders on the best consolidated inside quote. Programs were coded to halt pricing and confirm manually any price that was obtained from a quotation with a locked or crossed market. On October 19, this logic resulted in a situation where all orders were being handled manually. These delays, in conjunction with heavy volume, made a difficult situation worse.

Software to handle commitment messages through ITS limits the time that orders sent to another marketplace are valid (one or two minutes). Because most of the exchanges do not have automated execution interfaces (NASDAQ and Cincinnati do have this feature), the acceptance of most commitments from one exchange to another through ITS is manual. If not responded to in a timely manner, the order expires even if the receiving marketplace wants to accept it. This feature caused many marketplaces to ignore better markets that existed elsewhere, resulting in many exchanges trading through other market centers and disseminating quotations which added to the confusion already prevalent in the marketplace. It also shut down most of the automated pricing systems in the marketplace.

The NASD has similar problems with quotations of NASDAQ market-makers. Brokers and dealers could not get through to each other due to the heavy volume on the telephones and private wire networks. Many markets were crossed or locked, resulting in a shutdown of NASDAQ's small order executions system (SOES), which has software written to prevent pricing and execution in that environment. These software restraints all added to the confusion and uncertainty of a marketplace that came to depend on systems.

Vendor services which delivered information and order flow all suffered greatly during these periods. All systems depend on these services to provide interactive data. Routing systems experienced extensive backlogs and delays in transmission times to its customers. In many instances, orders were lost or routed incorrectly. Systems that sent sequenced orders often waited for responses that never came, causing systems backlogs that were not cleared until later in the evening of October 19.

Most of the problems that surfaced were the result of design flaws that had their origins in protecting the user. No one foresaw the extent of the volume and volatility that existed that week. Is it fair to say it should have been anticipated? All systems are a result of experience. No one had these experiences until October. I hope what we learned will provide us with the ability to build better systems for tomorrow.

CHAPTER 20

THE NASDAQ EXPERIENCE

Frank T. Coyle

My discussion is based on NASDAQ's experiences during October 1987. The first important point relates to systems capacity and our experiences in January through March of 1987. Our story beings at the NASDAQ Trumble, Connecticut, facility, a 50,000-square-foot data processing center. Our population of users is spread across the United States and is connected through basic computer networks. We have remote concentrator sites in Chicago, San Francisco, Dallas, New York, Fort Lee, New Jersey, and Rockville, Maryland. Rockville is also the disaster recovery center. We are, in fact, the only market in the world that has such a recovery capability today.

I want to begin in 1985, 1986, and early 1987. The main processors in Trumble, Connecticut, at that time were Sperry-Univac 1184s. We can process 200 million shares a day with this configuration. Since I have been associated with it, the market has traded in plateaus of about 20 to 25 million shares and has moved in a step function. Peak trading in 1982 hit 65 million shares, and in 1986 156 million shares.

We projected that the new plateau for 1987 would be in the range of 120 to 130 million shares a day with a 20-million swing. This forecast gave us a new estimated peak in the range of 175 to 180 million shares a day. We felt the Sperry-Univac 1183 had the capacity to support 1987, and that a Sperry-Univac 1184 was there in reserve to take us up to 260 million shares a day.

In early January 1987, we experienced trading days in excess of the 1986 peak. With a 1986 peak of 156 million shares, on January 8 we did 157 million shares and on January 14, 172 million shares; on January 15, 189 million shares; and on January 23, over 200 million shares. What we saw next was a trading range of 133 to 195 million shares for February and a trading range of a 120 to 172 million shares in March.

The volatility in this market was unprecedented and led us to believe that our projection for peak traffic in calendar year 1987 was too low. We might be looking at a severe capacity problem in the near future.

We have found that peak traffic is typically about 1.6 to 2.1 times our annual average daily volume. Because during the first three months of 1987 we had a 160 million-share average, we projected a new peak somewhere between 260 to 300 million shares. Based on the activity and the volatility of the market, we could not wait for the next NASDAQ board of directors meeting; we called the executive committee of that board together on April 2 in our Rockville computer facility and asked them for the funding for support of additional computer capacity in Trumble and in Rockville.

The board approved $8.6 million for a Unisys 1194 for Trumble and an 1192 for Rockville. The equipment was ordered and installed in August 1987. To the operations staff in Trumble, Connecticut, October 1987 was rather a nonevent. NASDAQ processed 223 million shares on the 19th; the 21st was the most difficult day at 288 million shares. The total weekly volume was 1.2 billion shares. Computer systems hardware uptime was 100 percent. We believe that from an operations point of view we have the capacity today to operate somewhere in the neighborhood of 750 to 800 million shares a day.

CHAPTER 21

HOW SIAC
SURVIVED

Robert A. Van Kirk

"TRADING VOLUME EXPLODES"
"TICKER LATE"
"EXCHANGES TO CLOSE EARLY"
"GRAVE CONCERNS IN WASHINGTON"

During October 1987, headlines like these became commonplace to everyone in the securities industry and to millions of investors who read the daily business news. And yet, if we add "BACK OFFICE PAPER CRUNCH" and "WEDNESDAY CLOSINGS" to the list, the same headlines could describe 1966 when NYSE trading volume skyrocketed to 21 million shares. While some people blame technology for what happened to the market that October, it clearly was the *lack* of technology that nearly devastated this industry in the late 1960s. It was against that background that Securities Industry Automation Corporation (SIAC) was created in 1972 by the New York and American Stock Exchanges.

Since our inception, SIAC has focused on two basic objectives. First and foremost is to provide data processing and communications technology to our two owners, NYSE and Amex. This includes technical planning, and systems development and operations to support trading and market data functions, as well as market surveillance and regulation of member firms. Our second objective is to function as an industry resource, where our technical skills and central position can serve to meet common needs. In that regard, we are the facilities manager for the National Securities Clearing Corporation (NSCC), including its international and government clearing subsidiaries, the Consolidated Tape Association (CTA), the Options Price Reporting Authority (OPRA), and the Intermarket Trading System (ITS).

OCTOBER IN PERSPECTIVE

One of SIAC's most important activities is the continuous process of capacity planning. Together with NYSE statisticians who track market trends, our people analyze the potential impact of changes in trading on each of our systems. We consider not only the total traffic we might experience, but the mix of different types of orders and, most importantly, the peak traffic that might occur during the busiest minutes of the day.

In retrospect, many people are asking why the planning model did not predict 600 million shares. As a matter of fact, it did, but not until the end of 1989. In forecasting volume, one must keep in perspective both the past and the future, which are summarized here:

Previous Record Breakers	
August 3, 1984	287 million shares
Steptember 12, 1986	240
December 19, 1986	244
January 23, 1987	302
Our Capacity Targets	
December, 1987	450 million shares
December, 1989	600

Given that history, many in the industry thought the NYSE was overreaching when it set such aggressive goals. Even the 450 million target was two and one-half times average daily volume. Despite the criticism, the exchange told us to continue preparations, and the rest is history.

When the volume hit, sooner than expected, the systems held up.

Yes, there were problems, but they must be put in perspective. As John Phelan said in testimony to a Senate subcommittee, the market in October can be compared to a skyscraper standing erect in the midst of a hurricane with winds of 150 miles per hour. As long as the building withstands that kind of strain, most people are gratified even if the lights do flicker.

We cannot minimize the problems that occurred in October; but they deserve close attention. Nevertheless, let us not lose sight of the fact that the markets stayed open despite fantastic assaults on their processing infrastructure. NYSE volume on October 19 was more than triple the daily average for the year. On the 20th, it was even higher, and three more days of extraordinary volume followed. The number of orders in 1987 averaged 6 per second before October. On the 19th, the average jumped to 20 per second; and on the 20th, 25 per second, four times the previous average. In the options market, we hit the peak on the previous Friday, October 16, as we reached the expiration date of an options cycle. Trading on the Amex shot up from an average of 296,000 contracts to a record-breaking 653,000. In the clearing area, the total traffic for all markets we clear for NSCC jumped from 864,000 to 2,738,000 sides a day on the 20th.

WHY THE PROCESS WORKED WELL

Despite the overwhelming magnitude of these numbers, most of our processing was unimpeded—for the most important reason that we were doing the right things all along. Ongoing capacity planning, hardware expansion, software upgrades, and system rewrites actually gave us more capacity than we realized. Strategic tools, such as the NYSE display book (an electronic version of the specialist limit order book), played a major role in tackling order flow efficiently. The post-trade network was another important tool in expediting the transmission of clearing data. Putting emergency plans into action and mobilizing our people were the glue that held it all together. In short, all the preparations paid off when we needed it.

Another important area was vendor relationships. Support people from Tandem stayed very close to our trading operations throughout the period. We are the largest single Tandem installation in the world, and they are quite sensitive to the impact that our performance could have on their reputation. IBM was just as good in our post-trade operation. For example, when printing jumped from 20 million to 40 million lines a day, IBM flew two laser printers from California and had them installed in 48 hours.

We also have to give some of the credit to luck. We had just finished reprogramming a major system that handles all the after hours work from the trading area. It went into production just one week before October 19, avoiding significant difficulty. Another example is the Amex display system, which had given us problems on the options floor since the summer. We had been making a series of modifications, the last and most important of which was installed on the morning of October 19.

In the clearing area, we got very lucky with brokers submitting input data on time. In clearing, we are dependent less on what we can process through computers than on timely input from hundreds of firms, service bureaus, exchanges trading systems, the NASD, regional clearing corporations, DTC, and half a dozen vendors. Once we got past the initial comparison cycle, concerns about the rest of the clearing and depository systems disappeared. The power of netting was never more dramatic than for trades of October 19, when the continuous net settlement system reduced 1,300,000 sales records to 85,000 net deliveries, a netting factor of 93 percent. Those net obligations were then settled by automatic book-entry delivery through DTC with barely a noticeable increase in the level of open fails. This clearly is a world different than 1968.

WHERE WE HAD PROBLEMS

While we are proud of our performance under very difficult circumstances, we recognize that we had problems, some of which had a significant impact. System problems fell into three categories.

The first was with physical hardware, primarily electromechanical devices on the NYSE trading floor. Our single biggest frustration was the queuing of orders to floor printers. Printers simply could not print orders fast enough, a condition most noticeable in the Intermarket Trading System. ITS orders were automatically expiring before they could be printed due to their time out feature. This situation has been addressed since October, and more capability has been added.

The second type of problem was with design limitations. The NYSE odd lot system, for example, in very old software that we acquired form Carlisle DeCoppet in 1976 and that runs on antiquated, customized hardware. The system was never intended to cope with anything close to October's volume, and it simply could not keep up. Design limitations also existed in the dissemination of option prices through OPRA. In October, prices exceeded 100, but the industry standard limited the whole dollar amount to two digits. It would have been easy to change our OPRA system, but each of the options markets, as well as the quote vendors and pricing services, needed to change as well. As a result of this limitation in the industry standard, there were widespread pricing problems. For example, option positions were being priced at $1\frac{1}{2}$ when the correct price was $101\frac{1}{2}$.

The third problem occurred with the actual trading dynamics caused by such a volatile market. We have validation routines that prevent the entry of quotes or ticker prints that are too far away from the last entry. Because the market was moving so fast, a lot of valid data was being rejected. Our only choice was to disable those validation schemes, which, of course, then allowed errors to pass through the system. The result was a fair amount of confusion.

PREPARING FOR NEXT TIME

Each of these areas has been examined in detail, not only to correct systems that did not function well, but to insure that the entire complex will work better the next time we encounter high volume. The first step was to set new volume targets. The immediate target was 600 million. We handled that much in October, but there were bumps in the process. By June 1988, we will be able to handle a day like October 19 as smoothly as if it were 200 million. By October 1988, we will be able to smoothly process *any* 600-million day, even with severe peaking of traffic.

The longer-range goal is the billion-share day, targeted for the end of 1989. This is not just an NYSE or SIAC objective, but a horizon that must be shared by the entire industry. Let me remind anyone who thinks a billion shares is reaching too far of 1980, when Mr. Phelan told us to get ready for 100 million. At the time, such volume seemed inconceivable. But he was right then, and he has always been right since then. Even with the financial realities of today's market, capacity planning simply cannot be ignored.

At SIAC, we are devoted to achieving that objective, and much has been done since October. More equipment has been added to our three data centers to support trading, market data, and clearing operations. The old odd lot system has been replaced by modern technology, and the entire NYSE membership converted. A major effort was devoted to extending trading floors themselves, as well as the technologies that support them; within the last three months, the NYSE moved into its Expanded Blue Room and the Amex inaugurated their new Red Room. Display books are being deployed across the entire NYSE floor, and the Amex pilot for an electronic book is moving forward. In the support areas that process end-of-the-day exchange data and all the clearing functions provided for NSCC, the post-trade network is being expanded aggressively so that our interface with member firms becomes totally automated.

Together with NSCC and the two exchanges, we are in the process of designing a new trade comparison system for listed equities. Its primary feature will be to accelerate today's process by 24 hours, comparing trades on the night they are executed. We also are working with the NYSE to develop a screen-based, interactive correction facility to replace today's manual process. Ultimately, all corrections will be made through P&S and floor terminals on the morning after the trade, thereby limiting the tremendous exposure to error costs faced by traders in today's markets. The two systems, linking timely comparison with on-line corrections, will eliminate the monumental task we faced last October of getting trades corrected on little pieces of pink paper called QTs.

LONGER RANGE

A little farther out on the planning horizon is the long-range automation plan we are developing with NYSE. The ability to handle megavolume and still process efficiently will rely a good deal more on better techniques than on faster systems and more hardware. We will be moving toward a new systems architecture with integrated applications and a consolidated database. Advanced technology, heavily dependent on an integrated communications approach, will be the vehicle through which these goals are achieved.

Another major initiative, although not directly related to October 1987, is our preparation for dual site operations. This is extremely important to insure that our exchange and clearing systems remain operational even in the face of a major disaster. In approximately two years, SIAC will be moving most of its people and half of its computers across the Brooklyn Bridge to a place called MetroTech. With hot sites for each major segment of our business operational in both Brooklyn and Manhattan, we will be able to maintain all basic systems even if one location were to become totally inoperative. This is a monumental technical challenge, but one that we think is strategically critical.

Finally, there are some open questions as to what the industry will decide to do in a post-October world, including what structural changes may evolve. These decisions could easily affect our planning for future systems, as could the actions of regulators and the Congress. Our objective is to design systems to meet the demands of the future and, to the extent possible, to anticipate the unknown.

CHAPTER 22

HOW THE AMEX
PROCESSED
THE LOAD

Paul Stevens

I would like to review the impact of October 1987 on the American Stock Exchange (Amex) and offer some observations about what we as an industry have done right, and about what we may be contemplating that is very dangerous.

The American Stock Exchange is unique among self-regulatory organizations; it is the only exchange in this country that is both the primary equity auction marketplace and also a principal market place for listed options. We take both roles very seriously. In October, we were proud and lucky to have remained opened and kept all our systems operating, partly because we did not do 600 million shares. Even though our volume more than tripled to 45 million shares and 650,000 option contracts at those peak volume levels, our on-line systems stayed up. I am referring here to our switching and order-routing execution systems, our market data systems, and, of course, our comparison processing systems.

Several years ago, we embarked on a technology strategy designed to produce a flexible architecture that would allow us to move quickly into the markets and to service our existing markets. We are probably half-way to that goal, and there is much work ahead of us. Last summer we did implement our market data system for options on a Stratus computer, and we are quite pleased so far with the system's performance. We expect to transfer our equity market data onto a Stratus later in this year.

We will begin testing a GTC file, which will be added to our PER/AMOS capacity function later this summer, and that, too, will be evolving onto a Stratus. In October, we had no halts and we had no disruption in trading; the market remained open and our systems continued to function. We did have individual stock halts, perhaps more than we would have liked. I think we are tightening up procedures to avoid, if possible, halting a stock except under the most extreme conditions. There is, however, a legitimate market function served by a trading halt in an individual stock. In the case of a significant imbalance, we also halt the index option and, possibly, the major market index option (primarily because of a rule that requires us to halt it). We have to stop trading when 20 percent of the components of the underlying stocks have halted. Other than that and individual underlying stocks and stock options being halted, which triggers halting of the options, we did not halt trading in any options.

I mentioned the upgrading of our market data systems. One of the last pieces that improved the capacity of our display system was put in on the morning of October 19. We have continued to improve our quote and sale service. We have also been expanding Quick Quote, which we started some years ago. Quick Quote is a touch-screen quote updating system that was initially used for options; it is now being employed for stocks and options. We are also reporting sales over the touch-screen system for both stock and options, and we expect over the course of 1988 to expand the system floorwide, all but eliminating the use of mark sense cards for updating quotes and sales.

We found that the red room, which is handling over 25 percent of our total volume, is functioning very well in this environment of total touch-screen quote and sale service. In addition to Quick Quote, we are implementing on-line Rapid Quote, which enables us to update multiple quotes with just a few touches. Rapid Quote has been a cost saver in terms of personnel time, and it appears that it may be saving us some computer workload effort as well.

Regarding order routing, I referred earlier to PER and AMOS. PER is post execution reporting; and AMOS is Amex option switch, our version of the DOT system. It allows firms to transmit directly to us through the common message switch and to interface another firm's system with our system. This system began in the late 1970s, printing orders at the post. Early in the 1980s, we began going to a terminal that we called AutoPER and then AutoAMOS so that market orders coming over that system and execution limits do not print as hard copy, but rather show up on a screen. That screen allows the specialist, with several touches, to execute the proper contraside, pricing the order properly and causing it to be transmitted back to the office of the member firm that sent the order in. This system is fully available in every stock and option on our floor and has been for some time.

Following October, we expanded this system, which was at 1,000 shares and 10 contracts; it is now up to 2,000 shares in stocks and 20 contracts in options. We are looking forward to bringing the GTC orders into this environment, as well as the day-orders that it currently handles. These next steps are critical because capturing system order flow from the member firms enables one not only to automate the execution process, but to effectively eliminate DKs or questionable trades. We have seen that both market data, order execution, and post-trade comparison systems are coming together, and I think that this will be the hub of our architecture of the future since all these systems will be talking to each other. Ultimately we expect them to be communicating within the same hardware.

Let me now turn from operational performance and discuss some market structure issues. Previously, Arthur Levitt said that we at the Amex generally concur in the observations and conclusions of the Brady Commission. We certainly put some concept of integrated clearing near the top of our list. I think my son will be retired before we convince all the futures, options, and securities exchanges and all the SROs in this country to clear through one organization. Integrated clearance does not mean one clearing organization. The problems of October, in my view, were largely liquidity problems, which, in many cases, could have been avoided by giving proper recognition to truly hedged positions, albeit in different markets. The Options Clearing Corporation has had a filing before the CFTC that would enable them to offer cross margining to participants and participant exchanges to those who choose to take advantage of it. We need to discuss this idea with other exchanges. The commodities exchanges and securities exchanges are having those discussions, and I hope they will be fruitful.

The other phrase coined by the Brady Commission was circuit breakers. The problem in October was quality of information, or lack of quality information, on the options floor and in the index pit. We did not know in some cases which stocks were open and which were not. I am sure this problem occurred for other derivative product areas both in the futures and the options side. The NYSE is taking steps to tighten up the dissemination of information, to coordinate that information better, and to avoid trading halts. I strongly believe that circuit breakers ought to be the result of coordination.

We do disagree violently, however, with some suggested circuit breakers. Price limits, such as have been adopted by the futures exchanges in their index futures, are very dangerous. I commend the exchange for taking that step; I know they are not particularly enamored with them, but it is a familiar mechanism. If one picks an arbitrary price and says at that price we are not going to trade anything through, there is a very disruptive impact on related markets. On the other hand, to close all markets is, I think, very dangerous; it sends a terrible signal to the world at large and to investors. At some point, markets are going to close down.

Someone struggling to come up with something that will quell the potential uproar in Washington as well as send a positive signal to investors who have largely abandoned our markets will consider doing something stupid. I just cannot imagine saying we are not going to be down 500 points; we will stop trading at 450, and we will make sure we never close down. The best way to go, quite simply, is to follow the options model.

Since we started trading options in the early and mid-1970s, we have accepted the fact that we are a derivative of securities and that we contribute to the overall pricing mechanism and to capital formation. Equity markets exist for capital formation. We keep our equity markets open; but if we cannot keep them open for good cause in selected stocks, then we should act accordingly in the derivative products. We do halt trading in a stock option when the stock is halted. We halt trading index options when 20 percent of their components are halted and the index is unrepresentative. I do not know if 20 percent is the right number, perhaps it is too large or too small. The point is that when the information in the primary equity market and derivative is of questionable value, derivative markets ought to consider halting trading in a uniform way. If that is a circuit breaker, then call it that. We think a limit to the stock is much more appropriate than an arbitrary price limit such as down 15 points.

SECTION 3

MARKET
LINKAGES

CHAPTER 23

FORMAL LINKS AMONG EXCHANGES

John T. Wall

Two years ago, the NASD and the ISE in London established the London link. Before examining how we see linkages evolving, we need to review NASD's international activities (see Figure 23–1).

NASDAQ is the leading market in the United States for trading American depository receipts (ADRs) and foreign shares; more ADRs and foreign securities are traded on NASDAQ than on all other domestic markets combined. We expect the growth in use of ADRs to continue, if not to accelerate.

ADR and foreign share volume in the NASDAQ market reached nearly 3 billion shares in 1987, a 20 percent increase over the prior year and more than three times that of the exchanges. ADR volume alone was 1.8 billion shares; and it is growing at a much faster rate than the straight foreign issues volume (see Figure 23–2).

Overseas interest in our domestic NASDAQ securities also grew significantly in 1987, as shown by the jump in the number of foreign quotation terminals now receiving NASDAQ data—from 20,000 to nearly 30,000. More importantly, there are now about a dozen NASDAQ level 2 or 3 terminals in NASD member London offices, from which trading can occur directly through the NASDAQ system (see Figure 23–3).

FIGURE 23–1
ADR Issues: NASDAQ, NYSE, and Amex 1982–1987

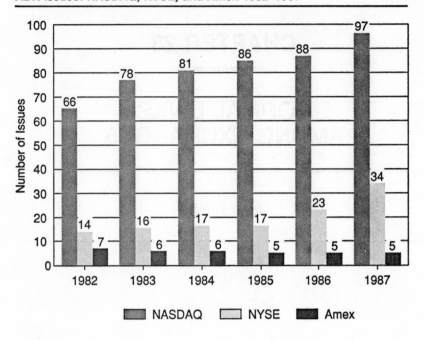

FIGURE 23–2
ADR Volume: NASDQ, NYSE, and Amex 1982–1987

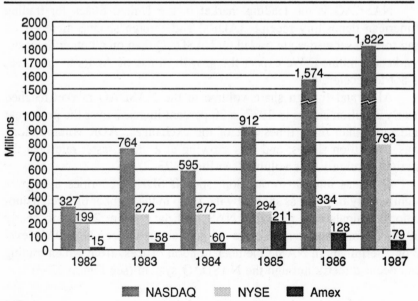

FIGURE 23-3
Growth in NASDAQ Level 1 Quotation Terminals 1982-1987

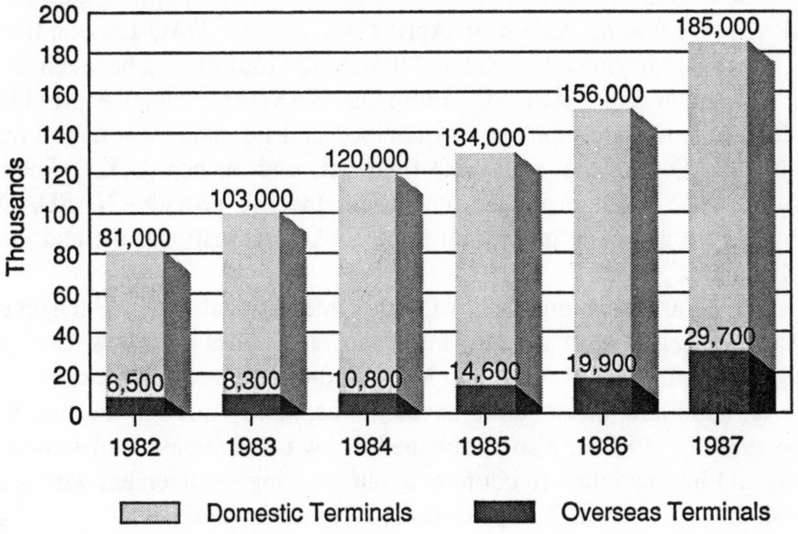

Domestic Terminals   Overseas Terminals

LONDON LINK

In July 1984, the London stock exchange decided to abolish its long-standing methods of doing business and to renew and revitalize itself with a NASDAQ-like computerized communications system, linking competing dealers in diverse geographical locations. Among the reasons cited by the exchange's council for adopting a NASDAQ-like system were

• The efficiencies that computer technology can bring to a dealing environment.
• The advantage of placing all members on an equal basis irrespective of geographical location.
• The lack of reliance of a NASDAQ-like system on the quality and state of mind of one individual for the continuity of the market in any given security.
• The ability of a NASDAQ-like system to lend itself readily to the concept of a 24-hour international market.

As you know, London's International Stock Exchange carried out its restructuring with an automated communications system—SEAQ, for stock exchange automated quotations—and a competitive multiple market-maker trading system. In April 1986, the NASDAQ-London link was initiated, carrying quotation and transaction information between the ISE in London and NASDAQ. From the NASDAQ side, we provide the ISE the complete montage of quotation and last sale information on the NASDAQ-100, the NASDAQ financial, and on non–U.K. ADR's traded in NASDAQ. From the other side, the ISE provides NASDAQ with the montage of information on the SEAQ international list and the FT-100 index stocks.

Our communications link with the International Stock Exchange in London began with slightly less than 600 issues and now carries transaction information on about 700 world-class issues. We expect to offer an automatic transatlantic execution capability through the link in early 1989. In 1987 we also established a new London-based subsidiary, NASDAQ International, to coordinate our growing involvement with the British and continental European investment communities.

SINGAPORE LINKS

On the other side of the globe, the Stock Exchange of Singapore also has gone to a NASDAQ-type system, SESDAQ—for Stock Exchange of Singapore dealer and automated quotations system—and to the competitive, multiple market-maker system. In mid-March, NASDAQ opened a second link, with the Singapore Stock Exchange and its SESDAQ system. In the first transpacific link between stock markets, we initiated a daily exchange of closing quotations and last sale and volume information on 35 NASDAQ stocks.

The NASDAQ transmission is sent at 6 P.M. (EST) and includes quotations from about 25 dealers per security. It arrives in Singapore before the market opens. The Singapore transmission arrives in the United States before the NASDAQ market opens and includes quotations from some five dealers per security.

For NASDAQ companies, our link with Singapore will bring presence for their shares in a new overseas market and opportunity for broadening their international investor base. The 35 NASDAQ securities in the

NASDAQ-Singapore linkage are world-class NASDAQ domestic companies and ADRs (as shown in Table 23–1); but they are also important from the standpoint of Pacific Basin interest.

The two links with London and Singapore will be the basis for an eventual three-way hookup between European markets, NASDAQ, and the Pacific Basin markets. The use of NASDAQ-like screen-based systems has put the 24-hour global equity market within reach.

Just as modern technology enables high-volume automated markets to operate in their own national environments, so it makes possible internationally linked markets. International standardization of communications interfaces and protocols, the extremely low error rates of satellite links, and the processing capacity of even the smallest computers will permit practically any market, regardless of its size or location, to link with practically any other.

TABLE 23–1
NASDAQ Companies and ADRs Included in Singapore Link

ASK Computer Systems, Inc.	LSI Logic Corp.
Adolph Coors Co.	Liz Claiborne, Inc.
Apollo Computer, Inc.	Lotus Development Corp.
Apple Computer, Inc.	MCI Communications Corp.
Beecham Group PLC	Mack Trucks, Inc.
Charming Shoppes, Inc.	Micropolis Corp.
Chi Chi's Inc.	Microsoft Corp.
Cipher Data Products, Inc.	Ogilvy Group, Inc., The
Comprehensive Care Corp.	Rank Organization PLC, The
Convergent, Inc.	Reuters Holdings PLC
Daisy Systems Corp.	Seagate Technology
Dresdner Bank AG	Tandon Corp.
Ericsson (L.M.) Telephone Co.	Volvo (A.B.)
Intel Corp.	Wetterau, Inc.
Intergraph Corp.	Worthington Industries, Inc.
Jaguar PLC	Xidex Corp.
Jerrico, Inc.	Yellow Freight Systems, Inc. of Delaware
KLA Instruments Corp.	

GLOBAL MARKETS

The role of automated systems in building the 24-hour global market-place is tremendously important, in view of the very rapid growth in international trading. In 1985, cross-border trading of equities was esti-mated to account for 10 to 12 percent of the $1.8 trillion traded that year in major world markets. That percentage is likely to double very soon. In 1987, foreign gross transactions in U.S. equities are estimated to amount to $445 billion, some 60 percent more than in 1986, and U.S. investor gross activity in foreign equities probably exceeded $175 billion, 80 percent more than in 1986 (see Figure 23–4).

Not surprisingly, we have received a number of inquiries about the impact of October 1987 on the globalization of markets. On a near-term basis, our best thinking is that it has temporarily slowed—but cer-tainly did not stop—the move toward globalization. In the aftermath of October, it is not surprising that investors are pursuing a more conserva-tive philosophy by investing in issues closer to home and by dealing in markets they understand more fully. This more cautious approach pro-vides a much-needed comfort factor for many individual and institutional investors.

Because the London link is informational and still in its nascent state, the market break did not affect it. There was a slight increase in query traffic in October, but not much. In contrast, as might be expected, the SEC requirement that the NASDAQ service be provided free only to market-makers in dually listed link securities cuts query traffic in half.

On a long-term basis, there is no evidence to suggest that the movement toward a global equity market has ended. To the contrary, a linked world equity market will continue to evolve because it is being driven commercially by three groups: (1) investors who have a *worldwide* hunger for positive performance, as well as a desire to diversify by currency and country; (2) corporate issuers seeking access to a *worldwide* pool of capital; and (3) securities firms searching *worldwide* for new and profitable business opportunities. We think this trend toward globalization will continue.

It should be remembered that the development of linkages heated up four or five years ago when the dollar value of international trading between the United States and other countries was less than one-half of its 1987 level. Thus there is no question regarding the simple commercial feasibility of links between country markets. And in our view, there is no

FIGURE 23–4
Dollar Value of International Equity Trading 1983–1987

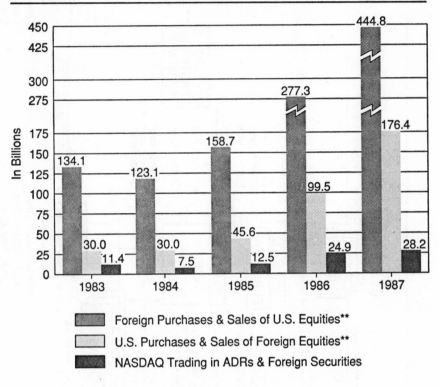

Foreign Purchases & Sales of U.S. Equities**

U.S. Purchases & Sales of Foreign Equities**

NASDAQ Trading in ADRs & Foreign Securities

*1987 data are annualized.
**Source : Securities Industry Association

longer much question about the form that such links will take. The links that grow and flourish will be between screen-based as opposed to floor-based systems. That is true of the NASDAQ-SEAQ and the NASDAQ-SESDAQ links. Also, the linkages require a highly complex interfacing of systems at all phases of the exchange process and among a variety of participants for a variety of needs.

Figure 23–5 illustrates the linkages we see developing between participants and participant facilities. If we can successfully complete the circle of these linkages, then other markets and countries can be added with much less effort and time.

The NASDAQ-London link is operating extremely well, satisfying

FIGURE 23–5
Overview of International Trading

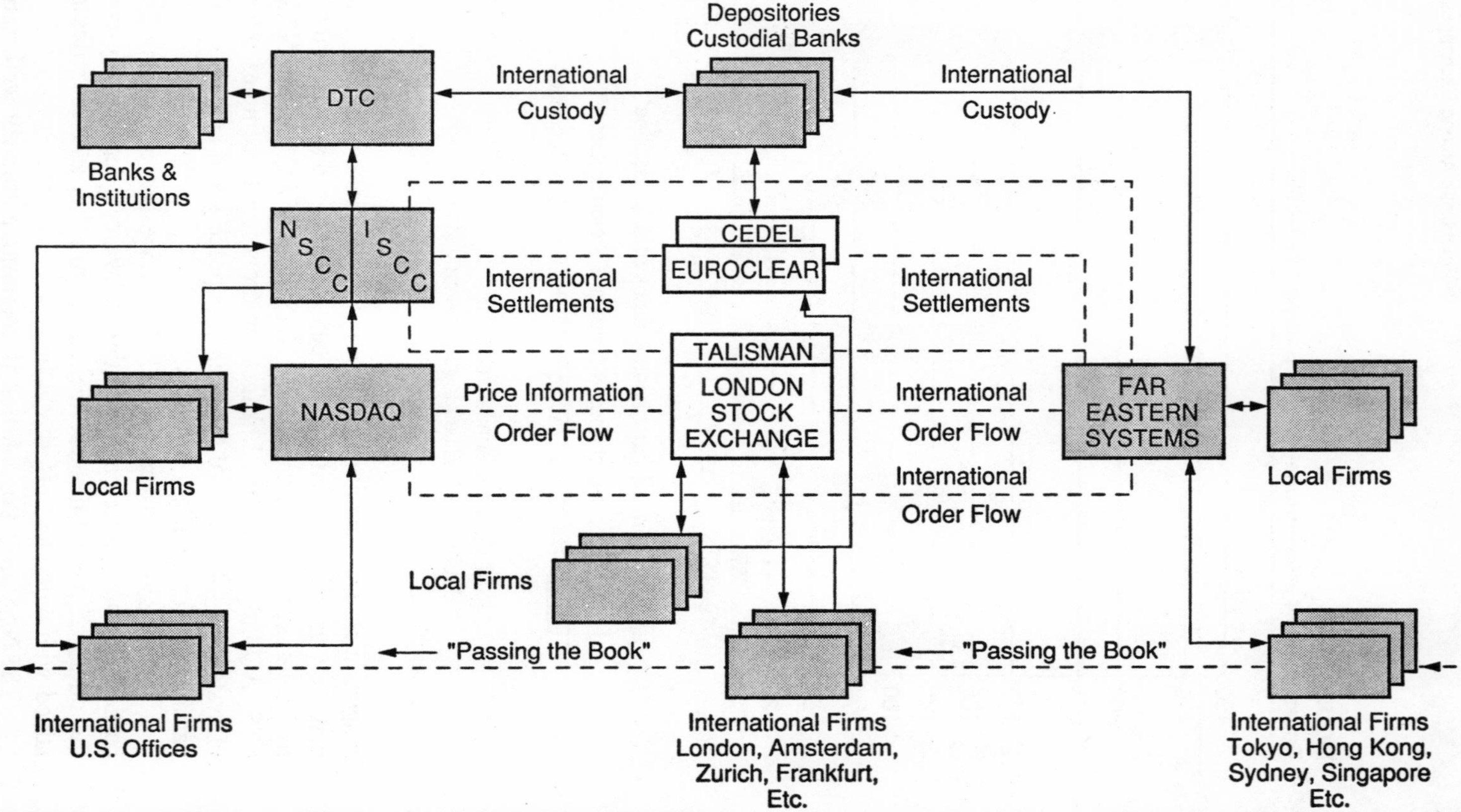

us that the information-quotation exchange part of the linkage is contributing, though modestly, to international market efficiency. Likewise the eastbound clearing and settlement link is operational and is also making a contribution to international market efficiency. Nine large firms are using the eastbound service of ISCC. The westbound clearing and settlement has been awaiting ISE adjustments that are required for firms to enter traffic from the London side.

Quotations, clearing, and settlement linkages are slowly expanding into other markets and other facilities. For example, besides the new NASDAQ quotations linkage with SESDAQ in Singapore, the ISCC is working on linkages with CEDEL, Euroclear, JSCC (Japan), and MAS (Singapore). While progress has been in small steps, we can expect the expansion to accelerate as the loop is completed successfully for the London (ISE) and NASDAQ markets. The completion of the loop, including trade execution and westward clearance, is anticipated over the next two years.

REGULATORY ARRANGEMENTS

Formal linking of exchange market facilities has moved SROs and regulators past the cooperative era and into an era of binding transnational regulatory arrangements. These are not just oral agreements, but rather they are very carefully drawn written documents that commit each market that is a party to assume and meet certain self-regulatory responsibilities.

For example, our agreement with the International Stock Exchange in London provides for:

• Coordination with and communication of relevant information to each other respecting quotation and trading halts, suspensions, resumption of trading, etc.
• Sharing of regulatory information as needed by either party for purposes of their surveillance and investigation responsibilities with respect to the securities included in the linkage.
• The exploration of joint regulatory initiatives such as the development of uniform standards for international transactions in the linked securities.
• Confidentiality protections to assure that the confidentiality of shared data and information is protected—permitting, providing such data

to regulatory authorities or courts, when such production can be legally required.

In addition to the SRO agreements with each other, formal links necessitate formal regulatory lines between SRO and foreign regulatory authorities. For example, to facilitate member access to the London Market and to avoid duplicate regulation and reporting, under a carefully drawn agreement NASD will have overseas securities regulation (OSR) status with the Securities and Investments Board (SIB) of the United Kingdom. NASD will have responsibility for those joint NASD-SIB registrants already designated to NASD under the act for SRO regulatory responsibilities and that have U.K. branches.

CHAPTER 24

ELECTRONIC MARKET LINKAGES AND THE DISTRIBUTION OF ORDER FLOW: THE CASE OF OFF-BOARD TRADING OF NYSE-LISTED STOCKS

James L. Hamilton

Almost everyone's vision of the future of securities trading centers on a network of electronic linkages for transmitting information and orders. In Chapters 3 and 13 of this book, Amihud and Mendelson, and Peake, Mendelson, and Williams have proposed computerized trading systems. In Chapter 14, Bunting has described the CATS that the Toronto Stock Exchange already has in operation. Moreover, the prospect that the new electronic technology soon may interlink all of the securities markets in the world that trade a particular security issue has been discussed by Wall and by Clemons and Adams in Chapters 23 and 25. These technological developments have raised questions about whether such electronic market linkages will redistribute the flow of orders among the linked marketplaces (Amihud, Ho, and Schwartz, 1985b, p. 7). Will traders then spread orders more widely among many marketplaces? If NYSE-listed stocks are traded in several marketplaces around the world, and these marketplaces are all tied together by electronic linkages, will investors then just trade in the the nearest marketplace rather than sending all orders to the United States? Another often heard statement is that order flow attracts order flow. If this is true, then will market linkages open a channel through which all orders will flow to one primary marketplace? Will all orders in NYSE-listed stocks, no matter where in the world they originate, be drawn to the NYSE through the linkages?

For considering how electronic linkages will affect the future of securities markets, one perspective is to look back at the experience with existing electronic market linkages. The intermarket trading system (ITS) is such a linkage. Stocks listed on the New York Stock Exchange (NYSE) also are traded off-board by the regional stock exchanges and by several over-the-counter market-makers. At the same time as the deregulation of NYSE brokerage commission rates on May Day 1975, Congress mandated a national market system (NMS) for stock trading. This mandate anticipated the installation of electronic linkages interconnecting the several U.S. marketplaces that trade NYSE-listed stocks. ITS was the result. It is both a price information link and a linkage for transmitting orders. The first step in the globalization of trading of NYSE-listed stocks probably will be such a linkage connecting existing marketplaces (see Clemons and Adams, Chapter 25). Each marketplace will be self-contained, with electronic linkages transmitting prices and orders among them. My perspective on linkages is to see how ITS has

TABLE 24–1
Market Shares in NYSE-Listed Stocks

Year	Regional Exchanges	Third Market	NYSE
1976	10.1	4.6	85.3
1977	10.4	3.9	85.7
1978	9.2	2.4	88.4
1979	9.8	2.1	88.1
1980	10.1	2.2	87.8
1981	10.9	2.5	86.7
1982	11.6	2.7	85.7
1983	12.2	2.7	85.1
1984	12.9	3.1	84.0
1985	13.5	3.1	83.4

Source: NYSE *Fact Book.*

changed the order flow among the marketplaces that trade NYSE-listed stocks. Commission deregulation and automated executions on regional exchanges are considered as related matters.

Since ITS was installed in 1978, off-board trading has increased. Table 24-1 reports market shares during 1976-85. Using the observed changes in off-board trading during the period 1965 to 81, I have used econometric methods to estimate both the effect of commission rate deregulation and the effect of the market linkages. Since off-board trading has grown since ITS began, does this growth imply that electronic linkages do disperse order flow among marketplaces? In spite of the upward trend in Table 24-1, the econometric analysis suggests that the ITS linkage *per se* has had much less effect on order flow than this trend suggests.

I. LINKAGES, COMPETITION, AND ORDER FLOW

In order to discuss how a linkage such as ITS would affect the distribution of order flow, I must first clarify my use of some terms.

Terminology

Competition. It is essential to be clear about how linkages could increase competition between the NYSE and the off-board marketplaces. In order for the off-board marketplaces to become more competitive with the NYSE, they would have to attract orders that previously would have gone to the NYSE, all other things staying the same. Electronic linkages would increase competition if the off-board marketplaces were able to use the linkages in this way.

Consolidation. A market is said to be consolidated when all of the orders to buy or sell shares of a particular stock are funneled to a single location to be combined into transactions (Mendelson, p. 189). An issue that continues to be debated is whether greater competition among the several marketplaces is harmful because it reduces consolidation (see section IV.)

Integration. The concern about incomplete consolidation is that some orders might not be transacted at the best price available in the market at any moment. A market is said to be perfectly integrated when the time sequence of prices in any one marketplace is indistinguishable from the time sequence in another marketplace (Garbade and Silber, 1979, p. 455; Jorion and Schwartz, p. 603). More intuitively, perfect market integration means that at any moment a stock would trade at the same price in any of the several marketplaces.[1] Obviously, arbitrage among the several marketplaces is what integrates them into a single market (Amihud, Ho, and Schwartz, 1985b, p. 5). Arbitrage requires that some traders have information about prices in more than one marketplace. And providing such information is one role of intramarket linkages. The degree of integration will depend on how closely the time sequences of prices in the several marketplaces are correlated.

When the NYSE has only 85 percent of trading volume, we can say that the market in NYSE-listed stocks is only 85 percent consolidated, but that is not the same thing as being only 85 percent integrated. As Jorion and Schwartz (p. 604) point out, not all traders must be active in all marketplaces: the marginal traders are sufficient to equate prices among the marketplaces. Therefore, even if the market were only 85 percent consolidated, it still could be 90 percent integrated, or 99 percent, or 99.9 percent, depending on the effectiveness of arbitrage. For example, in NASDAQ the order flow still is dispersed among numerous marketmakers. Whatever the measure of consolidation is for the NAS-DAQ markets,[2] the measure of integration surely is much higher.

Fragmentation. My discussion of intramarket linkages and competition will not refer to off-board trading as *fragmentation*. The dictionary says that fragmented means "broken" and that a fragment is "a part broken off" or "a detached or isolated part." This implication of brokenness makes the word excessively pejorative for use in a scientific or policy discussion, because it implicitly prejudges the outcome.[3] Obviously, something that is fragmented can be repaired only by reattaching the part that is broken off. For the stock market, however, whether the optimal arrangement is reattaching off-board trading to the NYSE is the question at issue. Furthermore, the term *fragmentation* does not distinguish clearly between integration and consolidation. An example is Cohen, Conroy, and Maier's analysis of trading when orders are not consolidated in a single place. Their analysis of fragmentation compelled them to raise "the issue of what a fragmented market is." And what they conclude is that "a market with multiple trading arenas is not fragmented if there is full communication between the trading centers" (p. 106). The point they are making is a very important one, which is that consolidation is not a problem for market performance when there is adequate integration. That is, the key issue concerning multiple marketplaces is integration. Since the term fragmentation has no additional meaning, I propose its elimination from analyses of market organization.

Jorion and Schwartz have used the term *segmentation*. While they used it to mean imperfect integration, it seems more apt as a term for a market that is not completely consolidated.

Linkages, Integration, and Competition

Electronic market linkages obviously concern the integration of a market that is not consolidated. If the linkages increased the efficiency of arbitrage, then integration of the several marketplaces would be greater. Since that means that prices in the several marketplaces would be more nearly the same, off-board traders would have less risk of missing the best available price in the market. As traders presumably then would see the several marketplaces as more substitutable, competition for the primary marketplace would increase. The people who proposed the NMS clearly expected the intramarket linkages to make the off-board marketplaces compete more effectively with the NYSE specialists: everything else the same, the division of order flow would shift toward off-board marketplaces, reducing consolidation.

This argument that greater integration makes marketplaces more substitutable seems to contradict the adage that order flow attracts order flow (Amihud, Ho, and Schwartz, 1985b, pp. 2–3). That adage may hold only for markets where integration is low and arbitrage among marketplaces is poor. In such markets, greater consolidation would increase integration. Electronic intramarket linkages are an alternative means of integrating markets.

Prior research clearly demonstrates that linking the marketplaces in an imperfectly consolidated market has the potential for increasing integration. Table 24–2 summarizes five studies that have measured the impact of such linkages. The laying of the Atlantic Cable reduced the communication time between the New York and London markets in U.S. Treasury bonds from 3 weeks to about 1 day. As Table 24–2 reports, the cable reduced the mean price difference between the two markets by over two-thirds. It also reduced the standard deviation of such differences, causing a reduction of 90 percent in the mean square deviation (MSD) of differences from zero (as in perfect integration).[4] Earlier the domes-

TABLE 24-2
Studies of Intramarket Linkage

Linkage (Date) [Prior time lag]	Financial Instrument	Integration Measure	Effect			
			Before	After	Measure	MSD
1. Atlantic Cable (July 1866)[a] New York—London [3 weeks]	U.S. Treasury Bonds	Price Difference: Mean (St. Dev.)	$4.12 ($2.265)	$1.27 ($0.76)	69% (66%)	90%
2. Domestic Telegraph[a]						
A. New York—New Orleans (July 1848) [4–7 days]	Foreign Exchange	Price Difference: Mean (St. Dev.)	5.7¢ (3.4¢)	3.4¢ (2.2¢)	40% (35%)	63%
B. New York—Philadelphia	Pennsylvania State Bonds Reading Railroad Stock	Mean (St. Dev.) Mean (St. Dev.)	55¢ (49¢) 80¢ (62.5¢)	39¢ (29¢) 64¢ (61.9¢)	29% (41%) 20% (1%)	56% 23%
3. NASDAQ (February 1971)[b] [Several minutes]	Unlisted Common Stocks	St. Dev. of Bids on each stock Mean (St. Dev.)	20¢ (11¢)	14¢ (5¢)	22% (57%)	58%
4. Consolidated NYSE Tape[a]	GM, GE, Gulf & Westinghouse Stocks IBM Stock	Price Difference, 2min. after MSE Trade: Mean (St. Dev.) Mean (St. Dev.)	8¢ (9¢) 44¢ (32¢)	7.5¢ (8¢) 23¢ (14¢)	6.5% (13%) 47% (56%)	17% 76%

Sources: [a]Garbade and Silber (1978).
[b]Hamilton (1987a).

tic telegraph had similar effects within the United States. The linkage between New York and New Orleans reduced the communication time from 4 to 7 days to about 1 day. The mean difference in prices of foreign exchange between the two markets was reduced by 40 percent and the MSD was reduced by 63 percent. While the time to communicate prices between the New York and Philadelphia exchanges was only about one day, the telegraph link permitted prices to be communicated between the exchanges while they were still open. For two selected securities, the linkage reduced mean price differences by 20 to 29 percent and the MSDs by 23 to 56 percent. NASDAQ also reduced communication time. While a trader needed several minutes of telephoning to collect current price quotations on an unlisted stock, NASDAQ displayed a comprehensive list of quotations instantly. For any one stock, price differences are measured as the standard deviation among the quoted bids of the market-makers. NASDAQ reduced the price differences by 22 percent on the average and the MSD by 58 percent. Finally, the consolidated transaction tape for NYSE-listed stocks reduced the time for transaction prices on the Midwest Stock Exchange to feed back to the NYSE from 5 to 10 minutes to only 1 to 2 minutes. For four NYSE-listed stocks, the tape reduced the mean price difference between the NYSE-listed stocks, the tape reduced the mean price difference between the NYSE and Midwest by 6.5 percent and the MSD by 17 percent.[5] The message in all of these various cases is clear: the installation of an electronic intramarket linkage to speed communication of prices among the marketplaces did increase integration, as revealed by the smaller price differences among the marketplaces following the linkage.

II. A STUDY OF OFF-BOARD TRADING

For decades, some proportion of the trading in NYSE-listed stocks has been off-board. My study estimated how that proportion changed when commissions were deregulated and the NMS was initiated.

Both commission deregulation and the NMS were expected to redirect the order flow in NYSE-listed stocks. First, off-board trading seemed to demonstrate that the NYSE had set their fixed commission rates well above competitive levels. Commission deregulation was intended to reduce commissions by unleashing NYSE firms to compete for investor orders. Since deregulation of NYSE fixed commissions eliminated that motive to trade off-board, falling commissions were expected to reduce off-board trading. Second, off-board marketplaces were seen as the most immediate opportunity for increasing competition for the NYSE specialists. By providing a more formal and more direct linkage among the several regional exchanges and OTC market-makers, ITS was intended to enable the off-board market-makers to compete more effectively with NYSE specialists.[6] Since better competitiors usually gain market share, the NMS linkages presumably were expected to help off-board traders capture a larger share of trading volume.

Method

The estimates are obtained by analyzing how the changes in the off-board market share during 1965–81 correlated with the changes in commission rates and the installation of the electronic market linkages and other components of the NMS. The period covered by my study ended in 1981 because after that the SEC stopped collecting data on NYSE member commissions.

Since other events during those years also affected the off-board market share, in order to estimate the effects of commission deregulation and the NMS accurately, those other events had to be taken into account. First, block trading by financial institutions promoted off-board trading. Consequently, the growth of block trading during 1965–81 had to be considered. Second, the abolition of give-ups after 1968 and the inclusion of third market trading in NASDAQ both had significant effects on off-board trading and so were included. Third, fluctuations in the aggregate trading volume in NYSE-listed stocks and the fluctuations of their prices were included, because heavier volume and more stable prices promoted off-board trading. As a consequence, the study can estimate how much the changes in off-board trading were due to deregulation and the NMS, and not just to these other factors.

Two commission rate indexes were used. A CR index measures the average commission on one round lot. A CB index measures the average commission on a block trade of 20,000 shares. Two indexes are needed because deregulation of commission rates affected block trades and round lots differently. The two indexes are shown in Figure 24–1.[7]

The NMS has several components: the consolidated transaction tape started in 1975; the Intermarket Trading System (ITS) and the National

FIGURE 24-1
NYSE Brokerage Commission Indexes

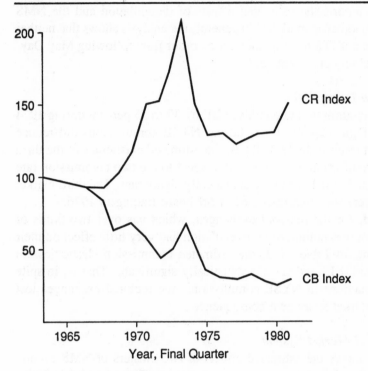

Stock Trading System (NSTS)[8] both started in 1978; and ITS has been embellished in several ways, such as the tie-ins with NSTS and NASD and the automated execution systems on the regional exchanges. The NMS also has entailed some rule changes, especially SEC Rule 19c–3, which liberalized third market trading by NYSE members.

   An econometric time-series model was used to estimate the separate effects of commission rates and the NMS. It related the off-board share of trading volume during 1965–81 to variables representing all of the factors that influenced that market share. Since these factors affected the third market and the regional exchanges differently, two models were estimated. The model estimated the elasticity of the off-board market share with respect to each of the factors considered. Since several of the factors were discrete events, however, their effects were estimated as intercept shift dummy variables.[9]

Results

Table 24–3 reports the estimated effects of deregulation and the NMS from the econometric model.[10] In general, the analysis shows that neither deregulation nor ITS had much effect on order flow following May Day, but some subsequent events did.

Commission Deregulation

The NYSE commission rate indexes fell by 39 to 53 percent during 1974 to 78 (see Figure 24–1). First, falling NYSE commissions did reduce third market trading. In Table 24–3, the estimated elasticities of the third market share of trading volume with respect to the two commission rate indexes are 0.5 and 1.2 and are statistically significant. The third market was, however, less than one-third of off-board trading in 1976.

Second, for the regional exchanges, which has over two-thirds of off-board trading, commission deregulation had very little effect on their market share. In Table 24–3, the estimated commission elasticities are only 0.10 and 0.13 and are not statistically significant. That is, in spite of large reductions in NYSE commissions, the regional exchanges lost very little market share as a consequence.

The National Market System

Table 24–3 shows the estimated effects of two clusters of NMS events. The first is the almost simultaneous initiation of ITS and NSTS in 1978.

TABLE 24–3
Estimated Parameters from Econometric Model

Variables	Third Market	Regional Exchanges
Commission Rates:		
CR (Elasticity)	.47**	.10
CB (Elasticity)	1.22**	.13
ITS/NSTS:		
ITS/NSTS (Dummy)	−.53**	
ITS Stocks (Elasticity)		.00
NMS Embellishments (Dummy)	.21*	.11*

Significance levels: 5 percent (*), 1 percent (**).

Source: Hamilton (1987b), p. 1341

For the third market, a substantial and statistically significant reduction in market share is shown. By contrast, the effect on the regional exchanges was negligible. Table 24-3 shows the estimated elasticity of their market share with respect to the number of stocks traded through ITS. The estimated elasticity is essentially zero.

The second cluster of events centers around 1980 and includes the installation of automated execution systems on some regional exchanges, the linking of NSTS to ITS, and SEC Rule 19c-3. Table 24-3 shows that these events increased off-board trading and that the estimates are statistically significant. In the third market, the estimated effect of this cluster implies that third market trading was 23 percent above what it otherwise would have been in 1981. Similarly, regional exchange trading is estimated to be 10 percent greater in 1981 than it would have been without these events.

Conclusion

Deregulation and the NMS both had somewhat greater effects on order flow to the third market than to the regional exchanges. For the regional exchanges, which have the larger part of off-board trading, deregulation had very little effect, and ITS itself had virtually none. But the regional exchanges did gain some market share from events in 1980–81. A corollary to all of this concerns the NYSE perspective. In spite of its lower commissions and its more direct connection to the off-board marketplaces, the NYSE's large order flow did not attract more order flow to on-board trading.

III. INTERPRETATION

Why have commission deregulation and ITS had such small effects on order flow and the market share of off-board trading? What do these small effects imply about how electronic intramarket linkages affect order flow among interlinked marketplaces? This section explores some possible answers to these questions.

Commission Deregulation

The substantial commission reductions did not eliminate off-board trading. Moreover, when the econometric model is used to take into account all of the other relevant factors, then deregulation hardly reduced regional exchange trading at all. There is an obvious implication: off-board trading has always had other motives than just avoiding the fixed NYSE commissions. This must be particularly true for regional exchange trading. That is, off-board transactions are not homogeneous with transactions on the NYSE. In some instances, and in some ways, investors apparently prefer to transact off-board rather than on the NYSE.[11] If so, then the value of this heterogeneity to investors must be recognized.[12]

ITS and the Regional Exchanges

Although Table 24–2 demonstrates that linkages inherently have the potential to improve integration, in Table 24–3 ITS had virtually no effect on order flow to the regional exchanges. The explanation of this small effect depends on three interrelated factors: the potential that existed for improvement of integration and competition, the extent of transaction heterogeneity, and the NYSE's response.

Potential Improvement
ITS would have had such a small effect if the market already was so well integrated that the potential for improvement was very small. Besides demonstrating that linkages have the potential for increasing integration, Table 24–2 also makes the point that *how much* the linkages can improve integration depends on how well the marketplaces *already* are integrated, before the linkage is installed. In Table 24–2 the studies are arrayed roughly in a descending order, starting with the case with the greatest time delay in communicating between marketplaces prior to the linkage. The measured improvement in integration also declines (generally) in the same order. Thus, the Atlantic Cable integrated two markets that probably were independent previously. It reduced the MSD by 90 percent. U.S. cities were less isolated. The telegraph reduced the MSD by 63 percent between New Orleans and New York and by 23 to 56 percent between Philadelphia and New York. NASDAQ reduced MSD by 58 percent. The market in NYSE-listed stocks was already highly integrated before the consolidated tape, which reduced MSD typically by only 17 percent. Thus, the effect of linkage was smaller in markets that were more integrated already.

The off-board marketplaces always have made a substantial effort to keep the market highly integrated. Anyone who trades off-board takes the risk of missing a better price on the NYSE. In order to minimize this risk, prior to ITS the regional exchanges and the third market paid close attention to the consolidated tape. Since the off-board marketplaces knew the NYSE prices and could submit orders to the NYSE, even without ITS the information flow would have created a very substantial degree of integration. Given the total volume and rapid flow of information and orders through this market, it must have been highly integrated already.

For NYSE-listed stocks, if integration of the market was sufficiently great prior to the installation of ITS, then the off-board marketplaces already were competing with the NYSE about as much as they could. If this was true, then ITS had a small effect on order flow because ITS just had very little to add to integration.

Although the NMS was expected to have a large effect on competition, the view that the potential for ITS to increase integration and competition was small has some supporting evidence. First, Garbade and Silber (1978) estimated that the effect of the consolidated NYSE transaction tape on the difference in prices between marketplaces was small (Table 24–2). Garbade and Silber (1979) also estimated the effect using the time sequence of prices. The effect was sufficiently small that it could not be established as statistically significant. That is, even though the consolidated tape replaced the one-way flow of price information with a more rapid two-way flow, this enhancement of the *linkage* apparently did not enhance *integration* very much.[13]

Second, the SEC (1982) found that ITS had very little effect on the bid-ask spreads of the NYSE specialists. A sample of stocks was divided about equally between stocks traded through ITS and stocks not eligible for ITS. In a standard model of bid-ask spread determinants, no difference was found between spreads in the ITS stocks and those in the non-ITS stocks. Furthermore, the ITS stocks differ in the proportion of total volume that is traded through ITS. No difference was found between spreads in stocks that traded heavily in ITS and those that traded lightly. This negligible effect of the ITS linkage contrasts with how the NASDAQ linkage affected spreads. NASDAQ increased integration a great deal (Table 24–2). And NASDAQ reduced spreads by 14 to 15 percent (Hamilton, 1978). Since ITS had no effect on spreads, it apparently had a small effect on market integration.

While the potential for increasing integration and competition may have been *small*, on the other hand the fact that traders do use ITS seems to imply that ITS *did* increase integration somewhat, even if only a little. The principal reason for a trader in one marketplace to use ITS is to obtain a better price in one of the other marketplaces (Davis, p. 272). Consequently, as traders use ITS they would make prices on the several marketplaces more nearly equal. The Securities and Exchange Commission (1981, p. 33) even discovered that 7 percent of ITS trades were "reach throughs" that found better prices than those actually quoted in ITS.

Transaction Heterogeneity

The experience with commission deregulation showed that off-board transactions may be somewhat different from NYSE transactions. This difference may be a reason why ITS had such a small effect. If transactions on the different marketplaces just are not close substitutes, then interlinking the several marketplaces would not have much effect on how order flow is divided.

NYSE Competitive Response

However much ITS did increase integration, an explanation of its small effect on off-board trading and order flow must also consider the competitive response of the NYSE. The creators of the NMS believed that the NYSE specialists did not behave competitively. If so, then prior to ITS the division of trading volume between the NYSE and the other marketplaces would have depended partly on how noncompetitive the NYSE was. If the linkages *did* increase integration, it would shift the division in favor of off-board trading, *but only if* NYSE behavior stayed the same. The NYSE could, then, have responded in either of two ways.[14] First, since the NYSE is the dominant marketplace, the specialists could have persevered in their noncompetitive behavior simply by accommodating the new competition. If they reacted in this way, the NYSE would have had to accept the new division of order flow and to surrender some market share to the off-board marketplaces. Alternatively, the specialists could have responded by being more competitive. If they reacted in this way, the NYSE would have shifted the division back in its own favor. That is, the NYSE specialists could have responded to ITS exactly as the NMS proponents intended. If this was what happened, then the effect of ITS on order flow was *small* because ITS *worked*.

There is some evidence that the NYSE did respond competitively to ITS. The SEC (1981) shows that in 1979–81 the NYSE received 59 percent of the volume traded through ITS, but originated only 33 percent of that volume. Obviously, ITS was not just siphoning order flow away from the NYSE to the regional exchanges.

Neal (1987) has found a similar competitive phenomenon in the options markets, where the presence of alternative marketplaces has a detectable competitive effect on on the primary marketplace, even though the primary marketplace retains all or nearly all of the trading volume. For off-board trading, as for options, the extreme case of this would be a perfectly contestable market. In such a market, the potential for order flow to be diverted away from a noncompetitive marketplace is sufficiently strong that the primary marketplace would *act* as a perfect competitor even if it *had* a monopoly position.

Conclusion
ITS may have had a small effect on order flow to the off-board marketplaces because the pre-existing potential for increased integration and competition was small, because the several marketplaces just provide different kinds of transactions, because the NYSE responded competitively to neutralize the effect of increased integration, or for all of these reasons.

Marshall and Carlson have commented that ITS has been ineffective because it has failed "to cause a major redistribution of volume" (p. 292). Their judgment is misplaced, however, because they do not recognize that ITS would have been very effective if it prodded the NYSE to respond competitively in order to prevent such a redistribution. During 1981–85 only about 4 percent of trading volume went through ITS. But if the market was perfectly integrated, ITS volume would be zero, because prices would be identical among marketplaces, either by consensus or by quotation matching as implicit arbitrage. Thus, the small volume traded through ITS also seems to imply that the market is highly integrated, not that ITS is ineffective.

The Third Market

The estimated effect of NSTS in Table 24–3 implies that the third market had a 41 percent lower market share in 1981 than it would have had without NSTS. Most of this reduction undoubtedly is due to the fact that Weeden and Co., which was the dominant third market dealer, originated NSTS and withdrew from the third market concurrently with the start of NSTS. But as a consequence, it is impossible to determine how much of the loss of third market order flow (if any) was due to the electronic linkages rather than to Weeden's switch.[15]

The third market was boosted in 1980–81 by SEC Rule 19c–3,

which permitted NYSE members to be third market dealers in newly listed NYSE stocks. In Table 3, the estimated effect of Rule 19c–3 is that the order flow to the third market in 1981 was 23 percent higher as a result. Rule 19c–3 definitely is part of the NMS initiative to increase competition between off-board trading and the NYSE. But the effect of this rule cannot be attributed to electronic intramarket linkages.[16]

Automated Executions on Regional Exchanges

The experience of the regional exchanges with automated executions relates to some of my points about linkages and order flow. After ITS was installed in 1978, some of the regional exchanges gained order flow during 1979–81 (Table 24–1). The estimates in Table 24–3 imply that the market share of the regional exchanges in 1981 was 10 percent above what it would have been due to other factors. This 10 percent effect is attributed primarily to the initiation of automated executions on some of the regional exchanges.[17] Only the execution of small orders was automated. But on those orders, the regional exchanges guarantee that the transaction price will be the best price in the market, in terms of the quotations present in ITS at the moment.

For the period that my study covered (1979–81), the observed increase in off-board trading is explained most directly by product differentiation, *not* by greater market integration from improved linkages. Automated small order execution was a new product. The fact that off-board trading has survived commission deregulation implies that off-board transactions are not homogeneous with NYSE transactions. Automated executions with guaranteed best prices are another way that the regional exchanges have differentiated what they do from what the NYSE does. Marshall and Carlson (pp. 288–89) emphasize that automated executions on regional exchanges reduce costs of brokers. They have less paperwork and spend less time on each transaction. On the Pacific Stock Exchange, automated executions do not have a specialist fee or floor brokerage fee. With guaranteed prices, brokers can get these cost savings without the risk of missing a better price on the NYSE or some other marketplace.

The willingness of the regional exchanges to guarantee the best available price on small orders seems to demonstrate that they consider the market in small orders to be highly integrated. When the regional exchanges guarantee the price, they take a risk of losing money from trading at other than the best price. The regional exchanges that make such guarantees obviously assess their risk to be small. Although the regional exchanges automated trading *after* ITS was installed, their timing may not imply that ITS increased market integration. Automated executions seem to have depended on ITS only as a means for verifying the best price. Integration may already have been high enough.

Since automated executions *do* rely on ITS quotations, the resulting increase in order flow to the regional exchanges could be attributed to the electronic linkage, but it would be a derivative effect, rather than a direct effect. While the linkage may have provided the means for the regional exchanges to develop a new product, it was the new product that increased the order flow. The estimated effect of ITS itself was negligible (above). That is, without the new product, ITS did not redirect order flow just by increasing the level of integration because the NYSE apparently could counteract that competitively. The NYSE apparently could not, however, counteract the competition from the new product. Thus, the new and differentiated mode of executing small orders is the most proximate explanation for the 10 percent increase in regional exchange market share during 1979–81.

Since 1981, the regional exchanges appear to have continued the trend, increasing their share of volume by attracting small orders. Table 24–1 shows that between 1981 and 1985 the regional exchanges increased their market share of volume from 10.9 to 13.5 percent. Because my study did not encompass these post-1981 developments, I cannot say exactly what part of this gain has been due to automated executions. Other factors also influence the extent of off-board trading. In particular, the rapid increase in total trading volume and block trading after 1981 would have encouraged off-board trading (Hamilton, 1987b). Without taking these other factors into account, the impact of automated trading cannot be isolated and estimated accurately.

The growing market share of the regional exchanges cannot be interpreted as evidence that electronic intramarket linkages spread order flow more evenly among the marketplaces, because since 1981 the regional exchanges have continued to have a differentiated product. The NYSE has responded only in a limited way to the automated executions on regional exchanges. SuperDot does facilitate small order handling, but it permits automated executions only for certain stocks when the bid-ask spread is one-eighth. Consequently, product differentiation still is the *prima facie* explanation for the redistribution of small orders. The regional exchanges have not gained market share because the intramarket linkages have increased integration and made the marketplaces closer substitutes. Instead, they have gained market share by differentiating their products to make marketplaces *less* substitutable.

To give some perspective on the problem of distinquishing between the effect of the linkage and of product differentiation, consider the following two questions. First, if ITS was dismantled, could the regional exchanges continue to offer automated small order execution with guaranteed best prices? Second, if the NYSE now began to provide automated executions equivalent to those on the regional exchanges, could these exchanges still retain their share of small order flow?

IV. COMPETITION VERSUS CONSOLIDATION

In the preceding discussion, I have skirted the issue of a tradeoff between market consolidation and competition. Obviously there cannot be multiple marketplaces without some loss of consolidation. The concern that arises about not having a consolidated market is that a trade might occur at other than the best price in the market at the moment. Market consolidation, with all orders channeled to a single marketplace, namely the NYSE, presumably would avoid such occurrences, but it would preclude competition among marketplaces. From the analysis of off-board trading, I have two points to make about this issue.

First, the distinction between consolidation and integration helps. In trading at the best price at any moment, what matters is integration. Cohen, Conroy, and Maier's (1985) point is that consolidation is not a problem if integration is sufficient. Even though a market is, by some measure, only 85 percent consolidated, with sufficient arbitrage this market could be more than 85 percent integrated. In the limit, perhaps 100 percent integration would require 100 percent consolidation. But within some limits, consolidation and integration can be independent. Thus, in a market that is highly integrated (though not 100 percent), forcing an increase in consolidation would not necessarily increase integration at all. And it might blunt the beneficial force of intramarket competition. Similarly, with sufficiently efficient arbitrage, it is possible that increasing competition could reduce consolidation without reducing integration.

Second, the experience with off-board trading may even demonstrate than an increase in competition is possible without reducing consolidation: a tradeoff between competition and consolidation may not necessarily exist. To presume that competition between the off-board marketplaces and the NYSE would be greater only if the market share of off-board trading grew is a view of competition that is too narrow. Although ITS did not increase the market share of the regional exchanges, one possible reason is that it *did* increase competition, not that it failed to do so. If ITS did increase market integration and competition, then the NYSE apparently responded competitively to prevent any loss of market share. If so, the marketplaces became more competitive without reducing consolidation. Neal (1987) also found such a phenomenon in the options trading market. If the market for NYSE-listed stocks is less consolidated since ITS, the apparent reason is that the NYSE has not counteracted the automated small order executions on the regional exchanges.

V. CONCLUSION

In summary, the econometric analysis of off-board trading found that the installation of ITS as an electronic intramarket linkage had virtually no impact on the order flow among the NYSE and the regional exchanges. Nor did commission rate deregulation have much effect. What *did* affect order flow were automated executions. The regional exchanges gained order flow by using ITS to differentiate their product.

Now return to the original question. Do linkages cause a dispersal of order flow among the linked marketplaces? Since the regional exchanges gained their market share by product differentiation, their gain does *not* imply that electronic market linkages will always spread order flow more evenly among marketplaces. My point is that the effect of product differentiation just is a separate phenomenon from the effect of the market linkages themselves.

What does the off-board trading experience imply for order flow, if the first step toward globalized securities trading is a network of electronic market linkages? I confine my speculations to trading of NYSE-listed stocks in different world marketplaces, rather than to relationships among different markets in different securities. Of course, the same issue exists for foreign (non–U.S.) stock issues that are (or could be) traded in several marketplaces in the world. While the global linkages may not be exactly like ITS, my analysis of the off-board trading experience in the United States at least identifies three factors that are likely to influence how global linkages will affect order flow.

First, the impact of a global linkage will depend on how integrated the several marketplaces already are. If they are highly integrated, installing direct electronic linkages may have rather little impact on order flow. But, if they are less well integrated than the U.S. marketplaces were, then global linkages may increase integration more than ITS did.

Second, the competitive response of the NYSE as the primary marketplace will influence how much order flows change. One intention of the NMS was to bring greater competitive pressure to bear on the NYSE specialists. If global linkages have the same effect, then the NYSE may be able to keep its market share just by being even more competitive.

Third, the experience with deregulation of commissions and the automated execution of small orders demonstates that traders do differentiate among modes of execution. They have responded to innovations in the mode of execution. That traders place value on having available different ways to execute orders has three implications for linkages. One is that any electronic network of linkages among marketplaces, or among traders directly, must not impose a single homogeneous mode of execution on all transactions. I think this is a criterion of system design that needs more attention. Another implication is that if traders see differences between executions in different marketplaces, linkages may not redirect order flow. In the global context, and in contrast to the U.S. market, the several marketplaces have different accounting conventions and settlement procedures that may discourage traders in one country from switching to marketplaces elsewhere (Clemons and Adams, Chapter 25). The final implication is that linkages may not affect the division of order flow unless some marketplace uses those linkages to offer executions that are different from what is now available. Just as the regional exchanges have innovated the automated execution of small orders, within a global linkage other marketplaces may offer other innovative products that will attract order flow.

Thus, from my study of off-board trading I suggest that some combination of these three factors will determine how future linkages will affect order flow: increases in market integration, the competitive response of the primary marketplaces, and innovation. And the latter may be the most inportant.

Finally, much of my commentary about electronic market linkages demonstrates that there is a serious deficiency in empirical research on how linkages affect integration, competition, and order flow. The studies of integration in Table 24–2 are insightful; but they are about antique linkages, and they do not even consider order flow. My explanations of the small effect of ITS are hypotheses that could be investigated empirically. More research on the existing market linkages would teach us a great deal about how linkages affect market integration and competition. This new knowledge would be a better basis for predicting how globalized market linkages will affect order flow.

NOTES

1. This definition of integration rests solely on price, since that is the primary trading priority. On such secondary trading priorities as time (first-come-first-served), Cohen, Conroy, and Maier (1985) have noted that an inexpensive means of implementing time priority is to permit more refined price units than eighths; price priority would then almost always implement time priority since bids and asks would rarely be tied on price. In addition, even the desire for best price appears to be compromised sometimes, as in using automated small order executions at ITS quotes rather than always trying to find transaction prices inside the dealer quotations. Finally, as Schwartz (p. 430) notes, secondary priority rules have not aroused much concern among securities traders or regulators.
2. An obvious measure of consolidation is the Herfindahl index, which is $H = \sum s_i^2$, where s_i is the market share of the ith marketplace or market-maker.
3. If the origin of this term were investigated, I expect that the NYSE coined it.
4. The MSD $=$ Variance $+ (\text{Mean})^2$.
5. The experience for IBM was an exception. For IBM the consolidated tape reduced mean price differences by 47 percent and the MSD by 76 percent.
6. In many industries where regulatory structures have been severely pruned or uprooted, the decision to deregulate rested heavily on the existence of a nice example of successful unregulated behavior. In the air passenger transportation industry, the success of the intrastate carriers in California and Texas were the nice examples of unregulated industries functioning quite successfully. In the stock market, I think the two nice examples that strongly influenced the decisions to deregulate and to rely more heavily on competition were the fact of off-board trading and the success of NASDAQ as an electronic linkage among scattered market-makers.
7. Deregulation of blocks actually began in 1969 with volume discounts on large trades. Hamilton (1982) also documents the dramatic decline in commission rates following May Day.
8. Whether the NSTS is part of the NMS is a matter of definition I think. The

official response to the Congressional mandate for a NMS has been ITS. NSTS was initiated outside this official response, although the NSTS is one prototype of a fully computerized trading system. Sometimes the NMS mandate is interpreted to require such a computerized system. At least the NSTS has become part of the official NMS by becoming linked to ITS.

9. The specific details of the study are reported in Hamilton (1987b).

10. The estimated effects of the other factors are not reported. For them, see Hamilton (1987b).

11. Block trading sometimes is facilitated by off-board transactions. Since block trades must be negotiated, often there is no reason to take them to the NYSE floor. Sometimes transactions are faster off-board or can be kept secret for awhile (Hamilton, 1987b, p. 1333).

12. Transaction heterogeneity also needs to be incorporated into the economic analysis of off-board trading and competition. For example, both Mendelson (1987) and Cohen, Maier, Schwartz and Whitcomb (1982) have assumed homogeneous transactions on the several marketplaces in their models.

13. In my study (Hamilton, 1987b), the effect of the consolidated transaction tape on off-board trading could not be disentangled from the effects of commission deregulation because the two essentially coincided in 1975.

14. Of course, if the market already was so highly integrated that there was little potential for ITS to increase integration, then the NYSE would not have needed to respond.

15. NASD connected to ITS in 1982. Since this date is outside the period studies here, I have no estimate of how this connection affected order flow to the third market.

16. While several NYSE members became third market dealers following Rule 19c–3, sometime after 1981 they stopped. Thus, the positive effect of Rule 19c–3 observed during 1980–81 may have been transitory.

17. The Midwest Stock Exchange and the Pacific Stock Exchange pioneered the automation of executions for small orders.

REFERENCES

Amihud, Y., T. S. Y. Ho, and R. A. Schwartz, eds. *Market Making and the Changing Structure of the Securities Industry* (Lexington, KY.: Lexington Books, 1985a).

———. "Overview of the Changing Securities Markets." In Amihud, Ho, and Schwartz (1985b), pp. 1–15.

Amihud, Y., and H. Mendelson. "An Integrated Computerized Trading System." In Amihud, Ho, and Schwartz (1985), pp. 217–236.

———. "Liquidity, Volatility and Exchange Automation." Chapter 3 in this volume.

Bunting, J. P. "Moving From Today's to Tomorrow's Trading System." Chapter 14 in this volume.

Clemons, E. K., and J. T. Adams. "Global Competition in Corporate Capital Markets." Chapter 25 in this volume.

Cohen, K. J., R. M. Conroy, and S. F. Maier. "Order Flow and the Quality of the Market." In Amihud, Ho, and Schwartz (1985), pp. 93–112.

Cohen, K. J., S. Maier, R. A. Schwartz, and D. Whitcomb. "An Analysis of the Economic Justification for Consolidation in a Secondary Security Market." *Journal of Banking and Finance* 6 (1982), pp. 117–36.

Davis, J. L. "The Intermarket Trading System and the Cincinnati Experiment." In Amihud, Ho, and Schwartz (1985), pp. 269–84.

Garbade, K. D., and W. L. Silber. "Dominant and Satellite Markets: A Study of Dually-Traded Securities." *Review of Economics and Statistics* 61 (1979), pp. 455–60.

———. "Technology, Communication and the Performance of Financial Markets: 1840–1975." *Journal of Finance* 33 (1978), pp. 819–32.

Hamilton, J. L. "Deregulation in the Securities Brokerage Industry." In T. Gies and W. Sichel, eds., *Deregulation: Appraisal Before the Fact* (Ann Arbor: University of Michigan, 1982), pp. 75–118.

———. "Market Information and Price Dispersion: Unlisted Stocks and NASDAQ." *Journal of Economics and Business* 39 (1987a), pp. 67–80.

———. "Marketplace Organization and Marketability: NASDAQ, the Stock Exchange, and the National Market System." *Journal of Finance* 33 (May 1978), pp. 487–503.

———. "Off-Board Trading of NYSE-Listed Stocks: The Effects of Deregulation and the National Market System." *Journal of Finance* 42 (1987b), pp. 1331–45.

Jorion, P., and E. Schwartz. "Integration vs. Segmentation in the Canadian Stock Market." *Journal of Finance* 41 (1986), pp. 603–14.

Marshall, R. W., and S. C. Carlson. "Electronic Trading Systems: The User's Point of View." In Amihud, Ho, and Schwartz (1985), pp. 285–95.

Mendelson, H. "Consolidation, Fragmentation, and Market Performance." *Journal of Financial and Quantitative Analysis* 22 (1987), pp. 189–207.

Neal, R. "Potential Competition and Actual Competition in Equity Options." *Journal of Finance* 42 (1987), pp. 511–31.

New York Stock Exchange. *Fact Book* (various years).

Peake, J. W., M. Mendelson, and R. T. Williams, Jr. "Black Monday: Market Structure and Market Making." Chapter 13 in this volume.

Schwartz, R. A. *Equity Markets* (New York: Harper and Row, 1988).

Securities and Exchange Commission, Directorate of Economic and Policy Analysis. "A Monitoring Report on the Operation of the Intermarket Trading System." Mimeographed (February 1981).

Wall, J. T. "Formal Links Among Exchanges." Chapter 23 in this volume.

CHAPTER 25

GLOBAL COMPETITION IN CORPORATE CAPITAL MARKETS

Eric K. Clemons
Jennifer T. Adams

The subject of globalization of the financial markets is of great importance, and after the recent global near-meltdown of October 1987, this is widely recognized. Unfortunately, it is also a very complex subject, not yet well understood by many executives or by much of the public.

Financial markets exist for a wide variety of instruments, and a brief taxonomy is offered below.[1] The extent to which the market for each instrument is global varies. The degree of globalization depends upon, among other things, the demand for a global market in the instrument and the ease with which such a market can be established, given the complexity of the instrument. There are different interpretations of the meaning of the term *global markets*. There is a major difference between linked markets, which exist today to a certain degree, and global markets, which do not exist for most securities. Markets that are linked affect one another, as prices or trading volumes on one exhange affect trading on another. Some exchanges have established a system of formal electronic linkage, whereby there is an exchange of information regarding the activity in each market; this information can pertain to trades that have already taken place or reflect the prices at which market-makers are willing to trade.

A global market can be said to exist when an investor can open a position in one exchange and close it hours or days later on another exchange, easily and without settlement difficulties. The result is that there is a liquid market for the security 24 hours a day; this may entail one market being open all day and night, whether fully staffed or electronically operated, or this may mean that several markets around the world collectively provide the liquidity in an instrument, yielding an uninterrupted trading day.

In this paper we focus principally on corporate securities and on the competition among trading houses and stock exchanges for markets in these instruments. We made this selection for the following reasons:

• Money (i.e., the major currencies) and most commodities trade based more or less on a world price. This is possible because of the fungibility of these instruments and an international understanding of their valuation. Likewise, government-backed securities represent a sovereign risk that is well-analyzed and widely-understood. Therefore, these instruments have a more developed and better understood global market than do corporate securities, particularly equities.

• The potential for global markets in securities will require informed policy decisions. John Shad, in a televised interview as he stepped down as chairman of the SEC, listed globalization and telecommunications as two of the major issues with which his successor would have to contend. These issues have only become more pressing.

• Although the market for corporate securities is also the smallest global market when compared to foreign exchange and other securities,[2] several factors are increasing its importance. In particular, deregulation in London, and to a lesser extent in Tokyo, allows its increase. These regulatory measures are in part a response to the increasing volume of capital flows among countries. The shifting balance of international trade and foreign direct investment, the expansion of multinational corporations, and the economic changes in Europe are among the conditions that have increased the degree of transborder capital flows. Their combination has made a global market for corporate securities more necessary.

In brief, we believe the market in corporate securities will be the most rapidly changing segment of the world's capital markets in the remainder of this century and will pose the most challenges to those making these changes.

We will attempt to address the four following issues in this paper:

• What is the current status of global securities trading? How large is the market? How many issues are traded?

• What are the factors that affect the importance of global securities trading? What have recent events revealed about global corporate securities trading?

• What will be the form of competition among stock exchanges?

• What, ultimately, will be the structure of the global securities market itself?

Unfortunately, it may be too early to make accurate predictions for many of these issues. Although our research included visits with senior officers in most major markets and with officers from the large trading houses in London, the United States, and the Far East, there is very little concrete data available. We believe that we have identified the appropriate issues; we are less confident about some of our answers.

INCREASING IMPORTANCE OF GLOBAL CAPITAL MARKETS

October 19, 1987, demonstrated the true interdependence of the world's capital markets. At all major exchanges the most critical information at the opening bell included what had happened in the other major exchanges the previous night. The increasing ease with which investors can move their funds in and out of markets attests to their global nature.

This globalization has evolved as investors sought ever-higher rates of return from their investment managers, who then turned their attention to foreign markets for higher returns or greater diversification. Because this capability to diversify within a variety of liquid markets has been present to a sufficient degree within U.S. capital markets, Americans have been one of the last major investor groups to internationalize their portfolios.

It was also necessary for overseas exchanges to liberalize membership rules. Some had the character of a club, whose exclusivity inhibited the competition and the cross-border flow of information regarding its securities. Competition on some exchanges has increased. And as companies have shown an interest in having a broad, international distribution of their securities, this information has become available. Dissemination of this information has been more difficult, given language and accounting differences and the required commitment for investment firms to expand their research efforts.

With the recent volatility of its home markets, the United States has begun to recognize the merits of international portfolio diversification, particularly the benefits of multicurrency investments. Additionally, the decline in the value of the U.S. dollar and of U.S. equities has made U.S. securities more attractively priced for foreign investors. Investment firms have responded by globalizing their operations, following and making markets in foreign securities. Although information is better than in the past, more needs to be done to provide the investor with the same level of confidence when investing overseas as at home. This means providing precise knowledge of what he bought, and guaranteeing that he paid a fair price, that he will be informed when circumstances change, and that he can sell it easily at any time he chooses. To highlight the last factor, it is worth noting that recent volume surges in worldwide equity trading have produced settlement bottlenecks in some markets that cause delays in the receipt of proceeds on stock sales; this can be especially discouraging when the delay means missed reinvestment opportunities.[3]

The increased interest in international distribution of securities on the part of the issuer and diversification on the part of the investor has served to broaden the base of security holders. Theoretically, because of this broadened investor base, the price of a security should be subject to less volatility since a more dispersed investor base has more diverse investment criteria; this increases the probability that some will hold when others sell. However, the behavior of the markets more recently seems to contradict this argument.[4] The effect that more extensive geographic distribution of a security has on its price volatility is yet another compelling topic, but one that will be left for later research.

We are certain, however, that this globalization must be demand driven. Although it can be facilitated by deregulation, by information vendors, and by improved technology, 24-hour markets expand with investor demand for foreign issues and with the activities of international arbitrageurs. Also, multicurrency factors and the risks of international investing must be taken into account. A significant impetus in global diversification of portfolios has been currency speculation or hedging. Creating worldwide liquidity in a security does not occur immediately but should come with time, provided the investor's confidence in sending his investible funds overseas is not jeopardized nor his strategy impeded by the actions of governments or exchanges. Unfortunately, predicting demand for future international financial services is extremely difficult, and the timing of their introduction is critical. Massive systems efforts are frequently required for the development of international services, making limited test marketing difficult or impossible.

CURRENT STATUS OF
GLOBAL SECURITIES TRADING

Foreign trading volumes in the relatively deregulated major markets—New York and London—are up dramatically in recent years. In London the increase is particularly striking, from an average daily volume of £290 million in the last quater of 1986 to current volume in 1988 of £1 billion.[5] Although these figures are imprecise, they are quite impressive when measured against the average daily volume in domestic equities, which is only £1.4 billion. No other major exchange has foreign trading activity that is such a significant proportion of domestic volumes.[6] For comparison, it is worth noting that London's foreign government bond volume is ten times higher, and foreign exchange (FX) volumes are again ten times larger.

New York's international trading activity is substantially lower. The SEC's stringent disclosure and reporting requirements limit the number of companies who can or wish to list their stock here. At present, there are 68 foreign issues, including 37 ADRs,[7] traded on the New York Stock Exchange; they account for approximately 4.6 percent of the average dollar volume.[8]

Internationalization has not been an explicit goal of the Tokyo Exchange, and it has not proceeded nearly as far as in London or even New York. Like the New York Stock Exchange, Tokyo trades only a limited number of foreign stocks (approximately 90), and their volume amounts to less than 2 percent of the domestic volume. For their overseas portfolios, Japanese investors prefer government bonds, real estate purchases, and other forms of direct foreign investment over foreign equities.[9]

The efforts of individual trading firms to globalize the market have received much press coverage. Despite all the discussion of the phenomenon known as passing the book, firms do not appear to make a formal 24-hour market in equities.[10] Trading firms maintain 24-hour active management of their foreign exchange and bond positions because the volatility of these instruments over the course of a day is greater than equities. The need for 24-hour liquidity in foreign currencies and government securities is a function of the global dispersion of those holding these investments. Because the Japanese own roughly 30 percent of the U.S. government debt, what they decide to do during their working day affects the New York trading room. More importantly, the value of these instruments is affected by macroeconomic events that can occur at any time and at any place. While the value of a company's stock may be affected by a catastrophic event that can occur at any time, such events do not take place daily. In particular, since factors directly influencing the value of a stock generally occur and are announced during the hours in which its domestic exchange is in operation, the greatest price movements will not take place during the working hours of another continent. Although this may allow a stock's market-makers to rest somewhat easier at night, they can and do make a market in another time zone by executing the trade off any exchange, usually on their own books.

COMPETITION AMONG TRADING FIRMS: NECESSARY STRENGTHS

Firms facing the changing global market environment are responding in different ways. Some are looking for a comfortable and potentially profitable niche; others are seeking to be one of the major, truly global players. The number of global firms there will be depends in part on the characteristics required to be such a player.

If it is necessary for a global player to have the resources to make a market in all major world securities that enjoy a liquid global market, and to do so for most of a day's 24 hours, then there will be only a few such firms. This will be a difficult role to fill, since there are several factors required for the success, if not survival, of a global firm.

Among the success factors listed by the firms we asked were capital, people, information, sales and distribution networks, and information systems. Although this list may appear obvious, it is interesting to note the differences in the priority placed on each factor by different firms. Firms in London tend to list capital and information systems first because these two are factors that many of them sorely lack. In fact, the quest for capital has been a major force driving most of the mergers of trading firms in the city over the last few years.

American firms have put capital high on the list because of the new ways in which they are risking it, namely the re-emergence of merchant banking. Also, their need for information has expanded as they have abandoned their parochial view of the investment world. Likewise, their information and distribution systems, though probably some of the best in the world for their domestic market, must be adapted to allow for the differing standards and customs of other countries.

The Japanese, in particular the Big Four[11] trading houses, state that people come first because as these firms expand into foreign, unfamiliar markets, experienced people and their sources of information are the most scarce and valuable resources. In contrast, capital was not seen as a factor, perhaps because it is available to them in seeming unlimited quantity. Moreover, Japanese firms do not traditionally risk their own capital as a British market-maker or American merchant bank would, and thus these capital requirements do not strain available resources. Although risks may be taken by Japanese firms, they are not publicized; and a great deal of practice precedes these firms' foray into new, more speculative operations.

COMPETITION AMONG EXCHANGES

Competition among exchanges is newly emerging in importance. The potential for global trading reduces natural market barriers enforced by geography, allowing London to compete with Frankfurt, Paris, and even New York for trading volume in those exchanges' domestic issues. "Information systems then take geography entirely out of the account."[12]

London's Big Bang is the most visible example of regulatory action taken to increase the strength of an exchange and the local financial services industry, even if this action had potential to damage local trading firms through increased competition with more powerful foreign investment houses. The exchange no longer views itself as an exclusive club for its members, and SEAQ[13] is run as a business. There are new marketing efforts, a newly formed position of vice president of marketing, and a new quality of markets group that monitors, evaluates, and publicizes the strength and attractiveness of London's International Stock Exchange. The exchange's recent decision to begin trading ADRs in London amounts to a statement that there should be no need to trade British issues anywhere but in Britain, as well as an obvious attempt to regain trading volume that had been allowed to move to New York.

SIMEX's trading volume in Nikkei[14] futures contract is another, more subtle example of competition among exchanges. Current Japanese regulations of trading in futures contracts are quite restrictive; until recently trading these contracts by Japanese was illegal, and futures contracts on the Nikkei index still cannot be traded in Japan. Singapore seized the opportunity created by Tokyo's restrictions and created a vibrant, liquid market in this derivative instrument. No doubt by late 1988, the Nikkei will be traded in Japan. Although SIMEX officials were hopeful that through competitive actions they could keep this market in Singapore (just as much as the futures market in the United States remains centered in Chicago and not in New York), the introduction of the Osaka Index has pulled business in the hedging instrument away from Singapore.

Quality of Markets and Factors Affecting Competition

Numerous factors combine to make a market more or less attractive, and these are used by exchanges as they compete. The most important factors include liquidity, depth, efficiency, fairness, and information.

Liquidity, without a doubt, is most important and most difficult for an exchange to influence. It is a measure of the ability to execute a trade, no matter the size, at any time during a market's hours, and at a fair price. While the market's depth relates to its ability to handle large trades, a liquid market reinforces investor confidence and attracts large and small investors to a market. Since a prudent investor will usually trade in the most liquid market in order to assure that he receives the most accurate price for a stock, liquidity breeds liquidity. After the events of October 19, there is increasing interest in assuring that specialists in New York and market-makers in London have sufficient capital resources to provide adequate liquidity and depth for their markets.

The fairness of a price is a measure of the market's efficiency in assimilating all public information regarding a security and in reflecting that information in the price. The fairness of a market relates to the way it allows all investors access to comparable information at the same time, and the ability to execute transactions based on that information without undue transaction costs.

Underlying all these factors is information; and the access given to it may be the factor most readily influenced by an exchange. Technology allows rapid dissemination of trading volumes, prices, and spreads. How an exchange manages investor access to information affects the other four factors that make a market competitive.

Special Role of Information Systems

Access to information through innovative use of technology is one of the easiest ways for exchanges to compete. As in the case of London's deregulation, information technology gave off-floor investors access to information previously available only to floor-based traders; and it increased the number of market-makers in a market, which, theoretically, makes the market more efficient (since competing market-makers should more rapidly bring prices into line with a security's intrinsic value).

In addition, technology can be used for trading surveillance, thus increasing belief in the market's fairness. And by facilitating the dissemination of information, information systems can augment the pool of interested investors and thus indirectly increase liquidity. Last, but not least, information systems can facilitate after-trade settlement procedures.

The competitive importance of information and information technology can no longer be denied. After Big Bang, London had both its traditional trading floor in the exchange and a screen-based upstairs market. The exchange made a major, multimillion dollar investment in technology to support the trading floor, and firms took three-year leases on trading posts. Yet, within a matter of weeks, the centuries-old tradition of floor-based trading in London was dead; floor-based traders were at a significant disadvantage with respect to upstairs traders, and they soon abandoned the floor for screen-based market-making.

Nature of Competition Among Exchanges Today

Stock exchanges compete today by attempting to influence those key determinants of their market's attractiveness—the critical success factors—that they can modify. Principal among them are information and information systems, the regulatory environment, and, indirectly, liquidity and depth.

While information systems may be the most readily altered aspect of the quality of a market, exchanges differ in their awareness of the importance of systems, their resources available for systems work, and their willingness to use this weapon competitively. Tokyo has been most conservative, automating order matching only for less-actively traded issues. New York has made major investments to facilitate trading and settlement, and systems fared far better than expected on Black Monday; still, New York's investment has also been conservative, focusing on automating the existing manual trading practices of the exchange's specialists and the OTC market-makers. London has been most aggressive in the use of information technology as a competitive weapon:

• The basic trading mechanisms have been replaced by screen-based trading; the increased number of market-makers in major equities has improved the efficiency of the market.
• Dematerialization—the elimination of physical stock certificates—will continue to reduce the cost of settlement.
• Wide dissemination of bid-ask prices and trading volumes increases confidence in the market and the perception of fairness, which increases the number of investors and improves liqidity.
• Information made available to the quality of markets group on the market's activity helps direct the exchange's marketing efforts worldwide.

Deregulation is the second tool that can be used to improve the attractiveness of exchanges. Once again, Tokyo has been the most conservative and least active. Only recently have commissions been reduced; they remain fixed and are higher for retail trades than at other major exchanges. The presence of foreign trading houses is still restricted, with none of the majors making progress comparable to that of Nomura or Daiwa in New York and London. After its May Day deregulation in 1975, New York was already less regulated than Tokyo today, while the deregulation of London in Big Bang was the most comprehensive of any major exchange.

Although liquidity and depth are not readily manipulated, London has succeeded in doing this in many ways. Significant volume of trading has moved from Continental exchanges to London because of the reduced trading costs and ease of settlement London now enjoys. The trading of ADRs in London is bringing volume in U.K. securities back from the United States. And links to other exchanges, such as the evolving linkage between NASDAQ and SEAQ International, may increase the liquidity and depth of both markets.

Fortunately for New York and Tokyo, liquidity remains the single most important determinant of a market's attractiveness; here the dominance of these exchanges appears insurmountable. The almost total lack of response to Cincinnati's major investments in technology indicates the far greater importance investors place on liquidity of the market when choosing a place to trade. However, the almost instantaneous collapse of the London trading floor, as traders abandoned it for the screen-based market, indicates that, all other things being roughly equal, technology can have an enormous impact on traders' behavior. London appears to be the only major exchange that truly understands this; recent improvement in trading volumes, and international volumes in particular, attest to the effectiveness of London's efforts.

FUTURE OF GLOBAL TRADING:
FORM OF THE GLOBAL SECURITIES MARKETS

Several questions must be addressed when assessing the future of global securities trading:

• How large will the market be? How many issues will be traded on a truly international basis?
• How many players will there be? How many firms will participate as truly global traders?
• What will the structure of the market be? What will be the role of trading firms, information vendors, and the exchanges themselves?

Naturally, the answers to all these questions are closely linked: the size of the international market will determine the number of international trading firms, which will in part determine the structure of the market for these issues. Complicating our analysis, the structure of the market will in turn influence demand and, thus, the size of the market.

Demand or need for global securities trading remains fundamental. Demand for an international portfolio of blue chip stocks should grow as countries themselves become more economically interdependent and companies become more multinational in nature. Interest in a foreign stock often begins with overseas recognition of its brands or products. If the company's fundamentals are sound, there is no reason why foreign investment interest should not develop. But providing the means to invest and disinvest easily is necessary before someone will buy foreign stocks. Thus, the structure of the global market, which determines its liquidity, efficiency, and fairness, is a major factor behind the strength and direction of the trend toward a global market.

Prior to the crash of October 1987, investor interest in international corporate securities was growing. Again, interest was driven by investors' need for diversification and desire for the best risk adjusted rate of return, by companies' needs for the largest possible base from which to obtain capital, and by the Japanese need to invest current account surpluses offshore. Despite setbacks related to October's events, we see these trends continuing.

Structure of the Equities Markets

Traditionally, investors have dealt with brokers, who in turn dealt with market-makers on the floor of an exchange. The exchanges principally served local investors and did not seriously compete. Although individual trading houses competed on each exchange, geography and the need for current trading information gave exchanges a near monopoly on the issues each traded.

This simple market structure has been altered by technology. Access to price information provided by third party information vendors such as Reuters and Quotron increased investor awareness in a wider variety of securities. Arbitrageurs then began to use the information to exploit price differences among exchanges, effectively keeping prices consistent for mulitply-listed equities.

Deregulation and changing investor behavior have fueled the changes allowed by information technology. The result of these changes is the multiple roles that the various players in the markets can now fill:

• Information vendors can duplicate at least some of the functions of an exchange, allowing institutional investors to trade among themselves, as Reuters' Instinet[15] illustrates.
• In response to such actions, the exchanges themselves have become information vendors, creating links to investors, perhaps facilitating their bypassing of brokers.[16]
• The large brokers can bypass the exchange and execute transactions for clients without bringing the trade to the floor of the exchange, essentially acting as a market.[17]
• Information systems give foreign brokers access to price information

and trading systems comparable to that of local players. Screen-based market-makers in London can trade U.S. issues as if they were in New York or Chicago.

Thus, instead of a value chain in each country comprising investors, brokers, market-makers, and exchanges, we have four interlocking parties, tied together by information services. Moreover, while the early value chains were separated by geographic boundaries, resulting in de facto near monopolies, the interlocking groups that compose the evolving global market now must either act competitively or find themselves passed by.

Future Structure of Global Corporate Securities Markets

As international markets continue to evolve from being informally linked to being truly global, it is tempting to speculate about their future structure and composition. To do this properly requires understanding the forces at work today and the directions they may take in the coming years.

One means of continuing the linkage of markets is to cross list securities on multiple exchanges. The use of ADRs has grown in popularity, but problems with liquidity for the buyer have surfaced.[18] Because an ADR in a stock is established only at the impetus of a broker or issuer, this seems an ad hoc solution. Even after cross listing, the regulatory and procedural differences between exchanges remain. The fact that settlement procedures, trade suspension policy, and over-the-counter trading practices vary by country can cause trading anomalies. Two investors in the same security should, ideally, not see any price differences between markets.

The formal linking of exchanges has met with mixed results. It is claimed that when these links involve a stronger and a weaker exchange, the weaker usually benefits, unless it is too small even to exploit the larger player; in general, the smaller player contributes little additional liquidity. These linkages to date have entailed an exchange of price information only. The next step would be to allow cross-border execution, initiated by the same system that provides price information. Members of such an exchange need not be in the same country. The link between NASDAQ and SEAQ International is still evolving; ultimately, it is intended to allow market-makers in either market to participate fully in the other.

Perhaps the simplest way to globalize trading is to extend the hours on the home exchange, so that those who are normally awake in another part of the world can get their trades executed by nightowls. Chicago commodities markets seem to be embracing this strategy with evening trading hours. For other markets, a personnel shortage makes this approach impractical. Whether this strategy is economically viable, necessary, or good for the welfare of off-hours market-makers remains to be seen.

Another form of globalization is to set up networks for providing price information and automated order execution. Such networks can be established by an existing stock exchange, by a major brokerage firm, or by a third party information systems vendor. An example of such a system, Instinet, links institutional equity investors, but its usage is comparatively low. Instinet's parent, Reuters, is also planning an electronic post- (pre-) market trade (PMT) system for the Chicago Merc to allow off-hours trading. The main concerns in using a nonexchange network are the liquidity of the market and the efficiency of the prices displayed. This poses a true Catch-22 dilemma: until concerns about liquidity can be satisfactorily addressed, it will be difficult for these systems to generate the volume levels that create the liquidity and efficiency needed to make their prices credible.

Regardless of who provides such a network, we now believe that the most probable form for a global market in corporate equities will be electronically-linked market-makers, an environment much like SEAQ or SEAQ International in London. This appears likely, for the following reasons:

• Most foreign ownership is institutional.
• With the exception of Continental issues traded in London and a few notable exceptions such as Honda or ICI in New York, most exchanges are relatively illiquid in most foreign issues, and most prices therefore remain inefficient or unreliable.
• Institutional investors will use block trading desks for their international trades, much as they currently do for domestic block trades.
• Since most exchanges are shallow and illiquid in most foreign issues, brokerage firms' block trading desks will serve as market-makers, holding inventory until it can be moved to another customer or to another firm.
• A network of electronically-linked market-makers, using market-maker quotes rather than customer order prices, appears to be the most

reasonable way to maintain price information in illiquid markets with sporadic orderflow. This was London's experience.

If firms such as Merrill Lynch or Normura participate as active market-makers in such networks, their liquidity addresses the problem faced by electronic trading systems such as Instinet.

Number of Players

The number of global players will depend in part on the number of issues traded and the liquidity of their markets. If numerous stocks are actively traded and if volume is sufficient to justify the investment in an international infrastructure, many firms can play. Anyone with a telephone and a terminal linked to an information network can broker an agency trade.[19] If markets lack liquidity and if an international player must be prepared to make a market in internationally-traded equities, then only a few large firms will have both the capital and the information needed to take this exposure in an intelligent manner.

The number of global players will also depend on the systems investments required. Should enormous effort on the part of a firm be required to establish an international information network with overseas analysts, traders, sales personnel, and processing staff, the number of players will be small. If, on the other hand, third party information vendors or international settlement processing services are available and liquid markets exist, then with only trading sophistication and a telephone a firm can buy most processing services.

The volume of international trading will determine whether there is a reason for firms to make these investments and for third parties to offer these services. Companies such as Quotron and Reuters are developing products to address the increasingly international character of the information needs of investment firms. Few companies have stepped up to provide back-office processing services to firms not wishing to make their own systems investments. And for the present many trading firms have chosen to stay on their home turf and leave the overseas ventures to others.

Should the volume of global trading rise, despite the new volatility extremes in the markets, many will see the potential profits of joining the globetrotting. If, on the other hand, this volatility translates into a fear of the unknown, investors will pull back to the markets they know—making fewer foreign adventures and perpetuating the current level of global trading.

CONCLUSIONS

International trading in corporate securities, while growing, remains immature, several years behind the markets in government-fixed income instruments. The number of internationally-traded equity issues is small, as are current trading volumes. Still, this activity is expected to increase, due to investor demand, deregulation, and competitive activities by firms and exchanges.

As markets and national economies become more closely linked, trading firms are competing more vigorously in each others' home countries. American firms have a slight edge today, given their aggressive trading practices, trading support and risk management information systems, and capital base. The enormous capitalization of the Big Four Japanese houses, their protected domestic market, their willingness to buy expertise, and their ability to buy market share through lower prices make them destined to be ever more potent competitors.

Greater internationalization has also increased competition among stock exchanges. Information technology and deregulation are the two tools most easily used to vary the attractiveness of a market, and at present London appears to understand best how these tools can be used as competitive weapons.

It is too early to predict the structure of the international securities markets of the next century, or even of the next decade. It is clear, however, that the balance of power among players is shifting. Institutional investors have enormous power, and they can bypass exchanges through third party information vendors and deal directly with each other. Brokerage houses have large established customer bases, technology, and capital; they, too, can potentially bypass exchanges. Technology vendors such as Reuters can subsume many of the functions of markets. And strategic alliances can be forged, as shown by NASDAQ's link with SEAQ or Reuters' partnership with the Chicago Mercantile Exchange. Again, information systems are a very powerful tool in this shifting balance and in forming alliances.

Finally, it is interesting to speculate on the number of truly international trading houses that will survive. Estimates are often quite low, between ten and fifteen.[20] Information vendors, betting that they will be providers of the information and processing services essential to a truly unified global trading economy, often have estimates that are considerably higher.

NOTES

1. Markets exist for selected currencies, commodities, and a spectrum of securities, from equities, to mortgages, to the latest securitized asset. Securities fall into two general groupings: those that are issued by governments (federal, state, local, etc.), and those issued by corporations and other private entities. The corporate capital market is further divided between debt and equity issues. For many of these instruments, markets in derivative securities (i.e., options, futures, and options on futures) have developed.

2. In London, for example, daily volumes are approximately £1 billion in foreign traded equities, £10 billion in Eurobonds, and $90 billion in foreign exchange. Tokyo is perhaps the least international major exchange, with only a few dozen issues actively traded; London is probably the largest, with about 700 active foreign equities.

3. "Bottleneck for Foreign Stocks," *New York Times*, Nov. 7, 1987, p. 37.

4. Recent volatility in Tokyo probably has been slightly increased by foreign investors, who have been net sellers since October. Certainly a major crash on the Tokyo market and retrenchment by Japanese investors, would have a devastating effect on stock prices around the world.

5. These figures, from London's quality of markets group, are unfortunately only approximate. At present, international issues are traded on SEAQ International (the exchange's automated quotation system for non–U.K. issues) both by firms that are members of the International Stock Exchange and by firms that are not yet members; only member firms are required to report their trading volumes, which makes the overall daily figure of £1 billion only an informed estimate. The situation prior to deregulation in October 1986 is even more complex: no firms were required to report foreign trading volumes prior to Big Bang, and thus figures for 1986 are far less reliable.

6. The number of national exchanges in Europe, all operating in similar time zones, and the integration that the European Community allow for more cross-listing and cross-border investing, and contribute to the high

proportion of foreign volume in London. Additionally, the poor quality of many continental exchanges contributed to the loss of significant portions of their trading volume. Most had limited trading systems. Some had settlement delays of six months or more. Others were open for very short trading sessions, or traded with a single daily price fixing for each equity.

7. ADRs are American depository receipts, surrogate shares representing stock in foreign companies. These ADRs are traded in U.S. markets, although the actual equity issue underlying the ADR is not listed nor traded in the United States.

8. The overall dollar volume traded in New York was up by 33 percent from 1986 to 1987. The foreign volume, while still not large, increased by twice that amount, 66 percent. Figures are from the NYSE Listings Department, January 13, 1988.

9. "Japan on Wall Street," *Business Week*, September 7, 1987, pp. 82–90.

10. Passing the book refers to the process of 24 hour monitoring of the firm's position in an instrument. London may be responsible for managing a firm's global investment in gilts (British Government bonds), but at the end of London's trading day, the book can be passed to the firm's New York office, with a description of its position, acceptable trading limits, and instructions to be followed in the event of changes in interest or exchange rates. Similarly, at the end of the New York trading day, the book can be passed to the firm's Tokyo office. However, major shocks, or changes of unanticipated magnitude, generally require contacting a manager in the country of origin of the instrument.

11. The Big Four in Tokyo are Nomura, Daiwa, Nikko, and Yamaichi, which account for better than 55 percent of daily trading volumes.

12. George Hayter, executive director of informations services, International Stock Exchange, London, personal interview October 19, 1987.

13. SEAQ, the stock exchange automated quotations system, is London's alternative to floor-based trading. Like NASDAQ, the system receives market-makers' quotes and displays trading information.

14. The Nikkei is the stock index for the top 225 stocks traded on the Tokyo Exchange. Already the Osaka Index of the top 50 stocks listed on the Osaka Exchange is receiving increasing volumes of futures contracts traded in Japan, despite the cumbersome nature of the index which requires delivery of the index, not cash, at settlement.

15. Instinet, a subsidiary of Reuters, has developed a system that allows institutional investor subscribers to circumvent their brokers when finding a counterparty to a trade.

16. In London, because of SEAQ and its ancillary information products, more than half of institutional trades were self-brokered after Big Bang. Current figures indicate that this trend has been reversed, and that while many

institutional trades are executed net—without broker commission—they are entered through brokers rather than directly with market makers.

17. Large institutional block trades are already handled this way, although they are reported to exchanges. Merrill Lynch in New York and Normura in Tokyo individually handle volumes larger than all but the three largest exchanges in the world; in terms of liquidity, both could function as exchanges if they chose to violate exchange rules.

18. "Scarcity of Sony ADR's Helps Teach Lessons About Certain Intricacies of Global Trading," *Wall Street Journal* September 17, 1987.

19. Bill Lupien, former chairman of Instinet, argues that anyone with a screen and a telephone can be an international broker.

20. "Survey of Wall Street," *The Economist*, July 11, 1987, and Ian Kerr, The Big Bang (London: Euromoney Publications, 1986), both have estimates in this range.

ACKNOWLEDGMENTS

The support provided by a grant from AT&T Bell Labs is gratefully acknowledged.

The assistance of officers at the New York, London, Tokyo, Hong Kong, and Singapore stock exchanges was invaluable, as was assistance from officers at information vendors such as Quotron, Reuters, Quick, and Instinet. Likewise, the time and patience of officers from Merrill Lynch, Shearson Lehman Hutton, Nomura, Daiwa, Mitsubishi Bank, Sumitomo Bank, CitiBank, Bankers Trust, Midland, Casenove & Co, and Hong Kong and Shanghai Bank, and from Booz Allen, McKinsey, and M.A.C. was essential.

Booz Allen in Tokyo, Unisys in Hong Kong, and the National University of Singapore provided essential local logistical support.

Finally, the assistance of Anna Maria and Tricia of Rosenbluth Travel, and of Marge in Decision Sciences in assuring that we arrived when and where we were expected, was extraordinary.